Managing Depressive Disorders

Editor: Katharine J. Palmer

Adis International

Auckland • Buenos Aires • Chester • Hong Kong • Madrid • Milan • Osaka • Paris • Philadelphia • São Paulo • Sydney

Managing Depressive Disorders

Editor: Katharine J. Palmer

Commercial Manager: Gordon Mallarkey
Publication Manager: Lorna Venter-Lewis
Adis International Limited
Copyright © 2000 Adis International Limited ISBN 0-86471-077-1

Earlier versions of some articles in this book were published in Adis International's peer-reviewed medical journals. The editor has collated the articles and worked with the authors to adapt and update the information for this publication.

Although great care has been taken in compiling and checking the information in this book to ensure it is accurate, the authors, the publisher and their servants or agents shall not be held responsible for the continued currency of the information or from any errors, omissions or inaccuracies arising therefrom, whether arising from negligence or otherwise howsoever or for any consequences arising therefrom.

Printed in Hong Kong.

Foreword

This book looks at the many facets of depressive disorders, and reviews how interventions and outcomes may be optimised. It covers areas such as dysthymia, double depression, recurrent brief depression, seasonal affective disorder and psychotic depression. It also looks at depression in the elderly and among children and adolescents, as well as in women post partum and premenstruation.

This is an invaluable collection of current opinion in this difficult-to-treat condition.

Katharine J. Palmer
Editor, *CNS Drugs*

May 2000

CNS Drugs *is a highly-regarded international medical journal. The journal promotes rational pharmacotherapy and disease management within the disciplines of clinical psychiatry and neurology by publishing a regular programme of review articles in the subject area.*

Managing Depressive Disorders

Contents

Depression
Interventions and Their Effectiveness

Lance K. Campbell,[1] Linda M. Robison,[1] Tracy L. Skaer[1,2,3] and David A. Sclar[1,2]

1 Pharmacoeconomics and Pharmacoepidemiology Research Unit, Washington State University, Pullman, Washington, USA
2 Graduate Program in Health Policy and Administration, Washington State University, Pullman, Washington, USA
3 Pullman Memorial Hospital, Pullman, Washington, USA

With the rapidly growing number of medications available for the treatment of depression, as well as nonpharmacological methods, healthcare providers and payers need a comprehensive approach to identify interventions which optimise both patient treatment and budgetary outcomes. This article examines interventions currently employed in the treatment of depression, in terms of tolerability, efficacy and effectiveness.

1. The Epidemiology of Depression

Depression is typically recurrent, and is a severe burden to patients, their families and society.[1-3] It occurs across cultures, throughout life and is about twice as prevalent among women.[4-8] Since World War II, major changes in the epidemiology of depression have included an increase in the overall rates,[5,6,9] and a significant shift toward an earlier age of onset.[9,10] The 1970s and 1980s gave rise to structured psychiatric interview schedules and psychiatric diagnostic criteria such as the Research Diagnostic Criteria,[11] DSM-III,[12] DSM-III-R,[13] and now DSM-IV,[14] which have been credited with greatly advancing our knowledge of the epidemiology of depression.[15]

Depression is one of the most common psychiatric disorders.[16] It has been estimated that 6% of Americans (11 million people) experience a depressive disorder,[17] with a lifetime prevalence rate of 17%.[16] Estimates of the prevalence of depression can vary greatly depending on the method of ascertainment and the study setting.[18] A review of the literature reveals point prevalence rates between 3 to 4%, 1-year rates between 2.6 to 6.2%, and lifetime rates varying widely from 4.4 to 19.5%, with the majority closer to the high-end estimate.[19] Patients with depression, but not meeting all of the criteria for major depression, are at least 2 to 3 times as prevalent as those with major depression.[20]

When correctly diagnosed and aggressively managed, depression is a highly treatable disease.[21] However, major depression remains an underdiagnosed and undertreated condition,[22-25] with only 1 in 3 persons seeking treatment.[26] The persistent social stigma associated with mental illness remains a major reason for its undertreatment.[26] Additionally, concomitant disease states, especially in the elderly, often obscure the diagnosis, consequently leaving large numbers of patients untreated.[22,27] Also, over half of those who do seek treatment in primary care settings are not accurately diagnosed.[28-32] Patients who are prescribed antidepressant pharmacotherapy often receive suboptimal doses and/or do not receive a trial of adequate duration.[33-35]

2. The Cost of Depression

Depressive disorders rank among the top 10 most costly diseases in the US,[1] generating an estimated annual expenditure of $US43.7 billion (1990) in direct and indirect costs.[36,37] Direct costs include the medical, psychiatric and pharmacological care associated with depression and account for 28% ($US12.4 billion) of the total cost. Although more difficult to measure, indirect costs account for the remainder of expenditures and include both mortality costs from depression-related suicides (17%, $US7.5 billion) and morbidity costs associated with depression in the workplace and related productivity losses (55%, $US23.8 billion).

3. Interventions for Depression

The high prevalence of depression and its enormous economic burden clearly indicate the need for accessible and effective interventions. The main therapeutic approaches used to manage depression are: (i) pharmacological therapy; and/or (ii) nonpharmacological techniques, including electroconvulsive therapy (ECT) and psychotherapy.

Table I. Commonly prescribed antidepressants by structural classification, elimination half-life and time to reach steady state[46]

	Elimination half-life (h)	Time to reach steady state (d)
Tricyclic antidepressants		
Amitriptyline	31-46	4-10
Clomipramine	19-37	7-14
Desipramine	12-24	2-11
Doxepin	8-24	2-8
Imipramine	11-25	2-5
Nortriptyline	18-44	4-19
Protriptyline	67-89	14-19
Trimipramine	7-30	2-6
Related tetracyclics		
Amoxapine	8[a]	2-7
Maprotiline	21-25	6-10
Monoamine oxidase inhibitors		
Phenelzine	1.5-4	
Tranylcypromine	2.4-2.8	
Selective serotonin reuptake inhibitors		
Citalopram[47]	33	7-14
Fluoxetine	2-9d[b]	2-4wk
Fluvoxamine	15.6	3-8
Paroxetine	10-24	7-14
Sertraline	1-4d[b]	5-14
Aminoketone		
Amfebutamone (buproprion)	8-24	1.5-5
Phenethylamine bicyclic		
Venlafaxine	5-11[b]	3-4
Triazolopyridine		
Trazodone	4-9	3-7
Phenylpiperazine		
Nefazodone	2-4	4-5
Tetracyclic		
Mirtazapine	20-40	5

a   30 hours for major metabolite 8-hydroxyamoxapine.
b   Parent compound plus active metabolite.
d = days; **h** = hours; **wk** = weeks.

3.1 Pharmacological Interventions

Antidepressants are a first-line option for the treatment of depression.[38] The choice of antidepressant medication is a difficult decision for the clinician. The influx of newer agents in the last decade offers the healthcare provider a multitude of choices for treating the depressed patient. All antidepressants are believed to be equally efficacious for the treatment of depression;[39-43] however, the choice of medication has implications for tolerability and compliance.[44,45] Pharmacotherapeutic options commonly prescribed internationally are listed in table I[46,47] by their structural classification, elimination half-life and time required to reach steady-state.

In the US the number of office-based physician-patient encounters documenting a diagnosis of depression increased 23.2% between 1990 and 1995.[47a] During this time-frame the prescribing of tricyclic antidepressants (TCAs) declined from 42.1% in 1990 to 24.9% in 1995. In contrast, the use of a selective serotonin reuptake inhibitor (SSRI) for the treatment of depression increased from 37.1% of encounters in 1990, to 64.6% in 1995. The rate of office-based encounters documenting the use of antidepressant pharmacotherapy for any purpose increased from 6.7 per 100 US population in 1990, to 10.9 in 1995, a 62.7% increase; documentation of a diagnosis of depression increased from 6.1 per 100 US population in 1990, to 7.1 in 1995, a 16.4% increase; and the recording of a diagnosis of depression in concert with the prescribing or continuation of antidepressant pharmacotherapy increased from 3.2 per 100 US population in 1990, to 4.8 in 1995, a 50% increase.

3.1.1 Tricyclic Antidepressants

TCAs have been available since the mid-1950s and have become the benchmark in tolerability and efficacy by which other agents are measured.[48] The mechanism of action of TCAs is through the inhibition of noradrenaline (norepinephrine) and/or serotonin (5-hydroxytryptamine; 5-HT) reuptake in the CNS.[49] As presented in table I, there are many different TCAs available. In addition, the tetracyclic compound maprotiline and the dibenzoxazepine derivative amoxapine have similar mechanisms of action and adverse effect profiles to the TCAs, and are usually discussed with this class of antidepressants.[49] Neither maprotiline nor amoxapine offer significantly improved tolerability over the tricyclics and are currently considered second-line therapy for depression.[50]

While the efficacy of the individual TCAs is very similar, the rate of adverse effects differs between them (table II). Major adverse effects include:[49,50]

- risks of cardiac arrhythmias
- worsening of myocardial ischaemia
- anticholinergic effects such as dry mouth, constipation, urinary retention, blurred vision, sinus tachycardia and memory dysfunction
- antihistaminic effects including sedation, drowsiness and weight gain
- orthostatic hypotension.

TCAs often require titration and maintenance of an individualised therapeutic dose. Significant clinical improvement of depressive symptoms usually requires from 2 to 5 weeks of treatment with TCAs.[49] Unlike other classes of antidepressants, TCAs can be fatal even in moderate overdose because of their narrow therapeutic index. In spite of their efficacy, many clinicians no longer prescribe TCAs as their first choice for antidepressant pharmacotherapy because of their adverse effect profile and the potential for overdose.[49]

3.1.2 Monoamine Oxidase Inhibitors

Monoamine oxidase inhibitors (MAOIs) have been available for over 20 years and act by reducing neurotransmitter catabolism within the neuron.[50] Specifically, these drugs inhibit the enzyme responsible for metabolising the neurotransmitters dopamine, serotonin and norepinephrine.[48] Patients presenting with atypical depression tend to respond well to MAOIs.[49]

Table II. Comparative adverse effect profile of tricyclic antidepressants[46]

	Sedation	Anticholinergic effect	Orthostatic hypotension
Tricyclic			
Amitriptyline	++++	++++	++
Clomipramine	+++	+++	++
Desipramine	+	+	+
Doxepin	+++	++	++
Imipramine	++	++	+++
Nortriptyline	++	++	+
Protriptyline	+	+++	+
Trimipramine	+++	++	++
Related tetracyclics			
Amoxapine	++	+++	+
Maprotiline	++	++	+

+ = slight; ++ = moderate; +++ = high; ++++ = very high.

Adverse effects associated with the MAOIs include orthostatic hypotension, dizziness, weight gain and sexual dysfunction. Hypertensive crisis may occur when MAOIs are taken with foods containing tyramine (e.g. cheese, soy sauce, fava beans, avocados) and synthetic sympathomimetics, such as over-the-counter cold medications.[51] Deaths from cardiovascular collapse have been reported as a result of combining MAOIs with the narcotic analgesic pethidine (meperidine) and with the selective SSRIs which may induce 'serotonin syndrome': diaphoresis, shivering, tremor, hyperpyrexia, hypertension, seizure and death.[48,52] In general, a minimum 3-week clearance period is required before switching patients from an MAOI to an SSRI.[49] Given the potential risk of these agents, the use of MAOIs is best managed by a specialist able to treat specific disorders such as atypical, refractory and bipolar depression.[52]

3.1.3 Selective Serotonin Reuptake Inhibitors

In spite of their higher procurement cost, SSRIs have achieved a rapid acceptance because of their very favourable tolerability, safety profile and, in general, once a day dosing regimen.[53] As implied by their class name, SSRIs act by inhibiting reuptake of presynaptic serotonin without significantly affecting other neurotransmitter receptor sites.[48] The currently available SSRIs for treating depression include fluoxetine, paroxetine, sertraline, citalopram and fluvoxamine. Fluvoxamine is available for the treatment of depression in approximately 90 countries worldwide, but has only been approved for the treatment of obsessive-compulsive disorder in the US.[50]

Different SSRIs are similarly efficacious.[54] Differences do exist in their elimination half-life. Half-life is an important factor if patients are switched to another antidepressant, or to any agent with the potential to interact with the SSRI, or if severe adverse effects are manifest.[54] The half-life for fluoxetine and its active metabolite, norfluoxetine, is estimated to be between 2 to 9 days, whereas other SSRIs range from 10 hours to 4 days.[54] It is critical that SSRIs are not prescribed with MAOIs since this can result in a serotonin syndrome.[55] When switching from an SSRI to an MAOI, there should be a minimum 1-week washout period for all SSRIs except fluoxetine. For patients receiving fluoxetine, washout should be increased to at least 4 weeks.[49]

Evaluation of the inhibitory effects of antidepressant drugs on hepatic cytochrome P450 isoenzymes can allow clinicians to predict drug interactions occurring via this mechanism *a priori*.[56] There are 5 to 10 important drug-metabolising P450 enzymes in the human liver and their relationship with SSRIs has been studied intensively during the last 5 years. Among the SSRIs, fluvoxamine is a significant inhibitor of cytochrome P4501A2 (CYP1A2). All of the SSRIs inhibit CYP2D6 (sparteine/debrisoquine oxygenase) but fluoxetine and paroxetine are clearly the most potent in this regard. Fluoxetine and fluvoxamine are moderate inhibitors of CYP2C19 (S-mephenytoinhydroxylase), and fluvoxamine might also be a moderate inhibitor of CYP2C9. Thus, although much remains to be learned about SSRIs and CYP, information to date indicates that citalopram and sertraline may exhibit the most favourable profile in relation to drug interactions.[57] The magnitude and clinical relevance of these drug interactions are dependent on many factors including concentration of the isoenzyme inhibitor, contribution of active metabolites with isoenzyme inhibitory activity and toxicity of the concomitant medication.[56]

In general, the SSRIs have a low affinity for histaminic, cholinergic and α_1-adrenergic receptors, which give them a much lower frequency of adverse effects compared with TCAs.[49] The main adverse effects associated with SSRIs are related to their serotonergic actions:[49]

Table III. Comparative adverse effects of selective serotonin reuptake inhibitor (SSRI) antidepressants[46]

Adverse effect	Fluoxetine (%)	Paroxetine (%)	Sertraline (%)	Fluvoxamine (%)
Headache	21	18	20	22
Asthenia	12	15	1	14
Insomnia	20	13	16	21
Somnolence	13	23	13	22
Nervousness	13	5	3	12
Anxiety	13	5	3	5
Decreased libido/sexual dysfunction	4	3	16 (men) 2 (women)	2
Nausea	23	26	26	40
Diarrhoea/loose stools	12	12	18	11

- headache
- nausea
- diarrhoea
- agitation
- insomnia
- daytime somnolence
- sexual dysfunction.

Paroxetine has been shown to have more anticholinergic activity than the other SSRIs, which may account for its seemingly greater association with withdrawal symptoms upon discontinuation.[48] Usually, these adverse effects are mild or can be improved with adjunctive medication.[49] Table III provides a comparison of common adverse effects of fluoxetine, paroxetine, sertraline and fluvoxamine.

3.1.4 Aminoketones

The unicyclic antidepressant has weak effects on noradrenaline, dopamine and serotonin reuptake, but its precise mechanism of action is unknown.[49] It represents a good alternative for patients experiencing sexual dysfunction or excessive sedation from either TCAs or SSRIs, and for patients refractory to primary antidepressant pharmacotherapy.[50] is generally well tolerated, with its main adverse effects being nervousness and insomnia, and a dose-related risk of seizures.[48] Concern over the latter risk dictates the avoidance of in patients with lowered seizure threshold, and upper single and total daily dose limits for this medication.

3.1.5 Phenethylamine Bicyclic Antidepressants

Open-label studies of venlafaxine have demonstrated efficacy in patients with severe depression, and in those found to be refractory to other agents.[58] Venlafaxine is a unique antidepressant that selectively blocks the reuptake of serotonin and noradrenaline, with very little effect on dopamine uptake. It also has no significant effect on muscarinic, α-adrenergic, serotonergic, histaminic and opiate receptors.[59] This results in a adverse effect profile very similar to the SSRIs. The most frequently reported adverse effects include:

- nausea
- anorexia
- insomnia
- headache
- sweating
- increased heart rate
- sexual dysfunction.

Nausea, which is usually the main intolerance issue with venlafaxine, is worse at initiation of treatment and tends to improve with time.[49] Initiation of therapy at a low dose with gradual titration can reduce this discomfort.[49]

The extent of reuptake inhibition of venlafaxine is dose-related. At lower doses the serotonin reuptake inhibition is more pronounced, while at higher doses, the nordrenaline reuptake inhibition is predominant.[48] Unlike the SSRIs, venlafaxine has less effect on inhibition effects on the liver enzyme CYP, resulting in less drug-drug interactions.[60] However, venlafaxine, like the SSRIs, should not be taken concomitantly with MAOIs. Venlafaxine has a short half-life, 2 to 5 hours, and two or more times per day administration is required.[60]

3.1.6 Triazolopyridines

Trazodone has antagonist effects on the serotonin 5-HT$_{2A}$ receptor.[50] Many clinicians do not perceive this agent to be as efficacious as other antidepressants, but its lack of anticholinergic effects and tolerability in overdose make it an important alternative.[49] The main adverse effects of trazodone are sedation and orthostatic hypotension, with a majority of patients experiencing these effects at therapeutic doses. Other problems include headache, nausea, cardiac arrhythmias and priapism, although priapism is relatively rare.[48] The sedating effects of trazodone, while often perceived as a disadvantage, can be useful in combination with other antidepressants which cause insomnia and indeed constitutes a major 'off-label' indication for this medication.[61] Drug-drug interactions with trazodone are rare; however, concomitant use of trazodone and MAOIs is not advised because of the possibility of inducing serotonin syndrome.[49] Multiple daily dosing is recommended.

3.1.7 Phenylpiperazines

Nefazodone is an analogue of trazodone which inhibits the reuptake of both serotonin and noradrenaline while exerting an antagonistic effect on the 5-HT$_{2A}$ receptor.[48] Its efficacy has been established in outpatients with depression, but efficacy data are limited for the treatment of inpatients, the severely depressed and for maintenance treatment.[49]

Like trazodone, nefazodone is associated with sedation and orthostatic hypotension, although these effects are not as severe. Other adverse effects include:[48]

- somnolence
- dry mouth
- nausea
- dizziness
- constipation
- asthenia
- lightheadedness
- blurred or abnormal vision
- confusion.

Unlike trazodone, nefazodone has not been reported to cause priapism.[49] Twice daily administration is required.

3.1.8 Tetracyclic Antidepressants

Unlike other cyclic antidepressants, mirtazapine is a tetracyclic antidepressant that enhances noradrenergic and serotonergic neurotransmission indirectly by acting as an antagonist to presynaptic α$_2$-receptors, and 5-HT$_{2A}$ and 5-HT$_3$ receptors. It has no significant effect on the synaptic reuptake of catecholamines.[49] As with nefazodone, the efficacy of mirtazapine has been demonstrated in adult outpatients with depression, but inpatient efficacy has not been adequately studied.[49] Sedation is a primary adverse effect, which decreases over time. Other adverse effects include weight gain, increased appetite and dizziness.[48] Lower doses should be used in the elderly, or in patients with renal/hepatic impairment because of reduced clearance.[49] Mirtazapine should not be used in combination with MAOIs.

3.1.9 Summary of Pharmacological Interventions

There is no perfect pharmacological antidepressant. All of the agents described above have advantages and disadvantages. Clinicians must consider the type of depression being treated, the desired onset of action, the adverse effect profile and the preferred dosing regimen. Safety from drug overdose should be a paramount consideration given the increased risk of suicide in patients with depression.

3.2 Nonpharmacological Interventions

3.2.1 Electroconvulsive Therapy

ECT has been used for the treatment of depression for over 50 years.[62,63] Although there is still a social stigma attached to this treatment modality, it is currently considered to be well tolerated and effective,[64,65] with an 80 to 90% rate of response.[64,66,67] It is hypothesised that ECT works by creating a generalised seizure, and is used most frequently to treat medication-resistant depression.[68,69] It has been suggested, however, that studies demonstrating high response rates to ECT contained large numbers of patients who were not truly refractory to medication treatment but had inadequate dosage administration.[70]

ECT is highly effective in patients with delusional depression,[66] but there is controversy regarding its other uses.[71] ECT has been suggested as the most effective treatment for severe depression, especially when suicidal or psychotic symptoms are present.[72,73] Concomitant physical illness and severe depression constitute another significant indication for ECT, given the potential somatic risks (e.g. cardiotoxicity) of older antidepressants and the still unclear efficacy of newer medications in this comorbidly ill population.[74] Practice guidelines developed by the American Psychiatric Association suggest that clinicians should base their decision to refer a patient for ECT on the following:[75]

- symptomological severity
- urgency of the presentation
- the extent to which treatment alternatives have either been ineffective or poorly tolerated
- patient preferences.

3.2.2 Psychotherapy

Psychotherapy is often used as an adjunct to pharmacotherapy. Depression guidelines from the Agency for Healthcare Policy and Research[76] and the American Psychiatric Association[77] concur that patients with moderate to severe major depression are to be appropriately treated with medication, whether or not psychotherapy is recommended. Patients with milder forms of major depression who prefer psychotherapy alone as the initial acute treatment choice may be treated with this option.[78]

Treatment modalities including cognitive therapy, interpersonal therapy and behavioural and psychotherapy have been studied in randomised clinical trials.[76,77,79,80] Some have reported psychotherapy for depression to be as efficacious as pharmacotherapy.[81-86] However, most of the studies were conducted over short time periods of typically 6 to 8 weeks in highly controlled environments, at times using suboptimal medication regimens.[87] There is little information available to evaluate long term outcomes[88] or comparative data on the effectiveness of medication versus nonmedication treatment of depression.[87] Further research is needed to elucidate the indications for combining psychotherapy with pharmacotherapy.[3,89]

4. Outcomes of Pharmacotherapy Interventions

Randomised clinical trials are designed to determine the efficacy and tolerability of new medications, with efficacy being defined as some predetermined degree of treatment response superior to a placebo.[90] Clinical trials have established that antidepressants provide significant initial clinical improvements in approximately 60 to 70% of patients with depression; 70 to 80% of patients experience clinical improvement with persistent treatment; and the efficacy of the different types of antidepressants is approximately equivalent.[39-43] However, efficacy and effectiveness are not synonymous terms. Effectiveness is the measure of what really happens in the naturalistic setting, or 'real world' environment of the clinical practice.[39-41,90] Because clinical trials are conducted in very controlled, artificial settings, often remunerating patients for participation, efficacy results may overstate the actual effectiveness of the treatment.[90]

McCombs et al.[34] were the first investigators to compare the efficacy of antidepressants with their effectiveness in the naturalistic environment and to show that these two measures do not equate. In an effort to determine the economic costs of antidepressant treatment failure, they reviewed the paid claims data of 2344 patients treated with TCAs for major depressive disorder in a Medicaid programme in California, US. They found that only 3.5% of patients displayed antidepressant use patterns consistent with successful treatment of major depressive disorder. Cost analyses discerned that compared with treatment success (i.e. a use pattern consistent with successful treatment of major depressive disorder), treatment failure (e.g. subtherapeutic dosing; noncompliance) resulted in increased health service expenditures of approximately $US1043 per patient in the first year post-diagnosis.

Using decision analysis, Sturm and Wells[91] found that because of the primary care physicians' tendency to treat depressed patients with subtherapeutic doses of antidepressants, patients presented with high rates of antidepressant discontinuation, decreased functional status and increased health service expenditures. Findings suggest that the costs of treatment failure are high, and that treatment failure results primarily from treatment discontinuation, because of either poor therapeutic response, or because of unacceptable adverse effects.[92]

Mitchell et al.[93] described four components of effectiveness that may influence the successful use of antidepressant medication in the naturalistic setting.

- Noncompliance: the Agency for Healthcare Policy and Research[76] recommends a minimum of 4 to 9 months of treatment for the first depressive episode to prevent relapse. Compliance is optimised when patients take their medication at the prescribed dosage and intervals, and do not discontinue or 'drop out' of treatment prematurely. Complexity of the dosing regimen and adverse effects can influence the level of compliance.
- Titration: this is the increase in medication dosage required to achieve an optimal and individualised response.[49] Titration may necessitate increased use of physician services and an increased probability of discontinuation of a prescribed regimen because of lack of early response.
- Switching antidepressants: a change in pharmacotherapy may necessitate additional physician visits and delay response time.
- Concomitant medication usage: adverse effects from antidepressants include anxiety and insomnia.[94] The subsequent need for concomitant medications such as anxiolytics or sedative hypnotics may delay response time, increase the probability of discontinuation and add to the cost of treatment.[92]

The development of the newer antidepressants such as the SSRIs has been an important advancement in the treatment of depression. These agents provide comparable efficacy to the TCAs with a more favourable adverse effect profile.[45,55,95] However, the significantly higher cost of the SSRIs has often resulted in restricted patient access based on cost alone. In search of quality healthcare for the lowest cost, managed care organisations often select antidepressants for inclusion on their formularies based on the premise of equal efficacy. As a result, the product with the lowest acquisition cost is assumed to be the prudent choice. SSRIs can be 10 to 30 times more expensive than generic TCAs.[90] However, basing prescribing decisions solely on medication cost ignores the components of effectiveness described above, and may have profound effects on clinical and economic outcomes.[87]

4.1 Noncompliance

In both the psychiatric care setting, as well as the primary care setting, a significant proportion of patients 'drop out', or discontinue antidepressant pharmacotherapy prematurely.[96] Katon and Schulberg[20] found that as many as 60% of patients treated in the primary care setting discontinued their medication before a recommended 6-month period. In a health maintenance organisation (HMO), Lin et al.[96] reported that 28% of patients discontinued antidepressant regimens within 1 month of diagnosis and 44% discontinued by month 3.

A meta-analysis by Montgomery et al.[97] examined 42 published randomised controlled studies comparing SSRIs with TCAs and discerned a pooled discontinuation rate caused by adverse effects of 14.9% for patients receiving an SSRI, and 19% among individuals receiving a TCA (p ≤ 0.01). In the seven placebo-controlled studies examined, the pooled discontinuation rate caused by adverse effects for SSRIs was 19.0%, and 27.0% for patients receiving a TCA (p ≤ 0.01). The authors found no significant difference in discontinuation rates because of insufficient efficacy in either analysis. It was concluded that the risk-benefit calculation favours the SSRIs since there were similar levels of efficacy, but significantly higher rates of discontinuation because of adverse effects with the TCAs.

LePen et al.[98] reviewed 27 studies comparing fluoxetine and TCAs for efficacy and discontinuation rates. While both groups had equal efficacy, patients were more likely to drop out of treatment with TCAs than with fluoxetine (38.9% versus 30.3%; p < 0.001). The drop-out rate due to adverse effects for TCAs was 23.6% compared with 12.7% for fluoxetine. Decision analysis estimated the differences in drop-out rates to be worth nearly $US3000 in favour of fluoxetine by potentially reducing suicide rates and medical utilisation.

In a meta-analysis of 65 randomised, controlled studies Anderson and Tomenson[99] reported a 25% lower drop-out rate with SSRIs compared with TCAs. Song et al.[40] compared the efficacy and acceptability of SSRIs with TCAs in a meta-analysis of 63 randomised controlled trials. Again, no difference was found in the efficacy between the SSRIs and TCAs. The drop-out rate for patients receiving SSRIs was lower than for those receiving TCA, although it was statistically insignificant. Slightly more patients in the TCA group cited adverse effects as the reason for discontinuation (18.8% for TCAs versus 15.4% for SSRIs). The authors concluded that routine use of SSRIs as first-line treatment of depressive illness may greatly increase cost with only questionable benefit. However, no cost analysis was conducted to support their position and only the cost of the medication was considered. Compared with SSRIs, these studies all consistently reported higher rates of discontinuation with TCAs, primarily as a result of adverse effects.

Preskorn[45] compared the tolerability of seven antidepressants: amfebutamone (bupropion), fluoxetine, imipramine, nefazodone, paroxetine, sertraline and venlafaxine. The discontinuation rates for fluoxetine and nefazodone were significantly lower than the other medications. Overall, imipramine had the highest incidence of adverse effects, including:

- dry mouth
- constipation
- somnolence
- sweating
- blurred vision
- urinary retention
- postural hypotension
- dizziness.

4.2 Titration

SSRIs offer the potential advantage of requiring less titration than the TCAs, although studies in the naturalistic environment have found that the rate of titration varies among the SSRIs. Recommended dosages for fluoxetine and paroxetine are 20 mg/day and 50 mg/day for sertraline.[100,101] Based on these recommendations, a cross-sectional study conducted in the UK by Donoghue et al.[102] reported that the rate of titration was the lowest for fluoxetine (6%), followed by paroxetine (17%) and highest for sertraline (52%).

Using a medical record system, Gregor et al.[103] analysed the dosing patterns of SSRIs in the outpatient population of an urban teaching hospital. A cohort of 3350 patients was extracted, of whom 2859 had been prescribed fluoxetine and 460 sertraline. After receipt of the ninth prescription, 23% of patients prescribed fluoxetine required upward titration, compared with 77% of patients prescribed sertraline. The average daily dose for fluoxetine treated patients with depression was 21mg for the first prescription, and 26mg for the ninth. Sertraline treated patients averaged 59mg for the first prescription, and 117mg for the ninth. Cost analyses were not performed with either of these two studies.

4.3 Switching and Augmentation

Although the necessity to switch antidepressants because of lack of response or adverse effects is well acknowledged, particularly with the TCAs, a paucity of data exists documenting the frequency and direction among the antidepressants. Computerised healthcare claims from a large, private health insurer in New England, USA, discerned the frequency of patients who either required augmentation with another antidepressant, or were switched to another antidepressant. During a 12-month follow-up period, the rate of switching and augmenting was minimally lower among patients with fluoxetine compared with patients with sertraline (19.9 *vs* 23.4%, respectively).[104] In a prospective study conducted in an HMO setting, fluoxetine had the lowest switching rate (20.0%) compared with imipramine (43%) and desipramine (48%).[105]

4.4 Concomitant Medication Usage

Rascati[94] retrospectively reviewed the paid claims of more than 30 000 Medicaid beneficiaries to determine the extent of concomitant use of antidepressants (clomipramine, fluoxetine, paroxetine, sertraline) with medication known to counteract anxiety or insomnia. Overall, 35.0% of patients received concomitant *'antianxiety/sleep'* medications:

- paroxetine 41.7%

- sertraline 35.8%
- clomipramine 33.3%
- fluoxetine 33.1%.

In addition, the concomitant use of trazodone with either SSRIs or clomipramine was found to be 7.7% overall:

- paroxetine 8.7%
- sertraline 8.5%
- fluoxetine 7.6%
- clomipramine 5.6%.

Using a more restrictive criteria, Gregor and colleagues[106] conducted a retrospective utilisation review (n = 117 319) to compare concomitant use of anxiolytics and/or hypnotics among patients prescribed SSRIs. Patients were not to have used an antidepressant, anxiolytic or hypnotic for 60 days prior to initiation of SSRI pharmacotherapy, and were to have remained on the initial SSRI prescribed. During the 60-day period following initiation of an SSRI, the percentage of patients using concomitant anxiolytics was 9.5% for fluoxetine and sertraline, and 11.4% for paroxetine (p ≤ 0.05 for paroxetine compared with fluoxetine and sertraline). Concomitant hypnotic use was 2.5% for fluoxetine, 2.8% for sertraline and 3.5% for paroxetine (p ≤ 0.05 for paroxetine compared with fluoxetine and sertraline). The majority of concomitant anxiolytic and hypnotic use was initiated on the same day as the SSRI. As in the Rascati study,[94] use rates for patients using fluoxetine and sertraline were significantly lower than for patients initiating pharmacotherapy with paroxetine. The economic implications of the findings were not addressed.

4.5 Pharmacoeconomic Outcomes

4.5.1 Simulation Models

Using data from controlled clinical trials, Bentkover and Feighner[107] used decision analysis to estimate the effects of paroxetine versus imipramine on total direct medical expenditures over a 6-month treatment period for major depression. Total medical costs were slightly lower with paroxetine ($US2348) compared with imipramine ($US2448) in spite of a significantly higher acquisition cost for paroxetine. The nonsignificant cost difference was attributed to a higher patient drop-out rate because of adverse effects, resulting in increased relapse and hospitalisation rates in the imipramine group. Similarly, Jonsson and Bebbington[108] found cost offsets for paroxetine over imipramine using a simulation model, as did McFarland.[87] While valuable in directing further research, these analytic techniques are limited because they: (i) are based from information from various clinical trials; (ii) use a univariate approach to sensitivity analyses; and (iii) may not accurately reflect practice patterns in the naturalistic setting.

4.5.2 Naturalistic Inquiry

Since McCombs and colleagues[34] investigated the economic consequences of antidepressant treatment failure among TCA recipients, there have been several pharmacoeconomic studies conducted in the naturalistic environment. Using computerised claims data from an HMO, Sclar et al.[109] compared the direct depression-related expenditures for patients initially prescribed, and remaining exclusively on, either fluoxetine or 1 of 3 TCAs (amitriptyline, nortriptyline or desipramine) [n = 701]. Multivariate modelling discerned that receipt of fluoxetine was associated with a significantly (p ≤ 0.05) higher rate of initial prescribing by psychiatrists, an increase in the number of prescriptions for antidepressant pharmacotherapyobtained (30-day supplies) and a reduction in the number of monthly intervals during which time antidepressant pharmacotherapy was not procured.

For patients with a diagnosis of single-episodic depression, receipt of a TCA resulted in a significant ($p \le 0.05$) increase in the use of physician and psychiatric services, hospitalisations and psychiatric hospital services and a significant ($p \le 0.05$) reduction in expenditures for antidepressant pharmacotherapy, for a total increase in health service utilisation of $US313 per patient (31%), 1 year post-initiation of antidepressant pharmacotherapy.

Using a similar methodology in an HMO setting, Skaer et al.[110] contrasted total depression related direct costs among patients prescribed either sertraline or 1 of the 3 TCAs (amitriptyline, desipramine or nortriptyline) for the treatment of single-episodic depression. One year after initiation of treatment, expenditures for patients prescribed a TCA increased for physician and psychiatric services, laboratory tests, hospitalisations and psychiatric hospitalisations, concurrent with a reduction in expenditures for antidepressant pharmacotherapy, for a total increase of $US167 per patient (21%).

Smith and Sherrill[111] retrospectively evaluated the direct medical costs of treating Medicaid patients diagnosed with major depression in a managed care setting. Claims data were randomly selected for patients receiving TCAs (n = 76; amitriptyline, desipramine, imipramine, nortriptyline or doxepin), or SSRIs (n = 76; fluoxetine, paroxetine or sertraline) for at least 3 consecutive months. Total medical costs were found to be similar between the two groups. Higher medication acquisition costs for the SSRIs ($US28 260 versus $US4916) were offset by lower medical utilisation costs ($US25 904 versus $US50 922).

Thompson et al.[104] reviewed computerised claims data from a staff model HMO to assess the cost of care among patients initiating treatment for depression with either fluoxetine, sertraline or paroxetine (n = 1200). Patients were grouped by drug use patterns. During a 1-year follow-up period, overall costs of direct medical care were highest for patients in the switching/augmenting group ($US7590) and early discontinuation group (60 days or less) ($US5610), followed by partial compliance ($US4479), upward titration ($US3822), and were lowest for the '3-month use group' ($US3393). The latter group received at least 90 days of therapy with the initial SSRI, and did not require augmentation or titration. Patients on fluoxetine were more likely than patients on sertraline to be in the '3-month use group.' Patients on fluoxetine were less likely than patients on sertraline to drop-out prematurely, switch or augment their medication or require upward titration.

A retrospective intent-to-treat analysis utilised data from an HMO to contrast financial expenditure patterns stemming from receipt of an SSRI or a TCA.[111a] Cohort assignment was based on initial receipt of either amitriptyline, fluoxetine or nortriptyline for the treatment of single-episodic depression. Patients prescribed amitriptyline were over three times more likely to require a change in antidepressant pharmacotherapy (OR = 3.27, 95% CI = 2.31-5.49), while patients prescribed nortriptyline were nearly four times more likely to require a change in medication (OR = 3.82, 95% CI = 2.74-6.83) relative to patients initially prescribed fluoxetine. Consistent with the intent-to-treat design, all accrued health service expenditures were assigned to the pharmacotherapeutic option initially prescribed. Multivariate analyses revealed initiation of antidepressant pharmacotherapy with amitriptyline resulted in a 25.7% increase in per capita depression-related health service expenditures per year, while initiation of antidepressant pharmacotherapy with nortriptyline resulted in a 28.1% increase in per capita depression-related health service expenditures per year relative to patients initially prescribed fluoxetine. A financial break-even point was achieved at the conclusion of month five, at which time all three intent-to-treat cohorts had comparable health service expenditures in total.

In another retrospective evaluation by Sclar et al.[112] (n = 744), patients who were prescribed paroxetine or sertraline were reported to require dosage titration to a far greater extent (28.1% and 40.3%, respectively) than did patients prescribed fluoxetine (16.1%). Health service expenditures were found to increase significantly (p ≤ 0.05) with an increasing requirement of dosage titration.

Sclar and colleagues[113] evaluated paid-claims data for 1258 HMO beneficiaries prescribed and remaining on either one of the TCAs (amitriptyline, desipramine or nortriptyline), or one of three SSRIs (fluoxetine, paroxetine or sertraline). Cost outcomes, as well as dosage titration and compliance (as measured by the number of antidepressant prescriptions obtained) were examined. Adjusted mean costs for depression-related health service utilisation were not significantly different among patients prescribed the TCAs, but were significantly greater than that of the SSRIs (p ≤ 0.05). Multivariate findings indicated that receipt of fluoxetine was associated with the lowest adjusted 1 year expenditure for depression-related health service utilisation (p ≤ 0.0001) among the 6 antidepressants examined. The authors concluded that an evidence-based algorithm for the selection of antidepressant pharmacotherapy which considers the adverse effect profile, a requirement of dosage titration, and the effect on direct health service expenditures in the first year post-diagnosis appears in rank order of preference as follows: fluoxetine > paroxetine > sertraline > either amitriptyline, desipramine or nortriptyline.

Only one prospective study using naturalistic inquiry has been conducted. Simon et al.[105] compared the clinical, functional and economic outcomes of 536 patients randomised to receive either fluoxetine, desipramine or imipramine for depression in a staff model HMO. Results were reported for the first 6 months of follow up. Although not statistically significant, total healthcare costs were lowest for those initiating pharmacotherapy with fluoxetine ($US1967), followed by imipramine ($US2105) and desipramine ($US2361). The higher acquisition costs of fluoxetine were balanced by lower outpatient visit and inpatient costs. Patients assigned to receive fluoxetine reported fewer adverse effects than for TCAs (9% versus 27%, respectively), were more likely to continue the original medication and were more likely to reach adequate dosages than patients beginning treatment with either TCA medication. Clinical and quality-of-life outcomes in the three groups did not differ at 6 months.

Experience with antidepressant pharmacotherapy within the context of clinical practice is requisite to understanding the benefit(s) of a given pharmacotherapeutic option. Recent studies suggest that access to antidepressant pharmacotherapy is influenced by a variety of factors, including the nature of the physician-patient relationship (e.g. initial encounter or follow-up; duration of encounter; physician specialty); patient expectations as regards the disease state and pharmacotherapy; patient characteristics such as age, gender and race; and the wider social context in which the physician-patient encounter occurs, inclusive of the effect of pharmaceutical advertising and the financial incentives or disincentives intrinsic in a given health insurance programme.[114,115]

5. Conclusions

Controlling depression-related healthcare costs while optimising patient outcomes is a challenge faced by both clinicians and third party payers. The medical literature indicates that a significant number of individuals with depression are either undiagnosed, misdiagnosed and/or suboptimally managed. Pharmacotherapy represents a first-line option in the management of major depressive illness. To maximise the potential for achieving desired patient outcomes, pharmacoeconomic research suggests clinicians and third party payers need to focus beyond the procurement cost of medication and consider the impact of pharmacotherapy on aggregate health service expenditures (direct and indirect). At the same time, further research is warranted to assess the cost-effectiveness of nonpharmacological interventions such as ECT and psychotherapy, and their potential to synergise with pharmacotherapy.

References

1. Hall RC, Wise MG. The clinical and financial burden of mood disorders: cost and outcome. Psychosomatics 1995; 36: S11-8
2. Keller MB. Depression: a long-term illness. Br J Psychiatry 1994; 26 Suppl.: 9-15
3. Thase ME. Relapse and recurrence in unipolar major depression: short-term and long-term approaches. J Clin Psychiatry 1990; 51 Suppl.: 51-7
4. Ormel J, VonKorff M, Ustun B, et al. Common mental disorders and disability across cultures. JAMA 1994; 272: 1741-8
5. Klerman GL, Weissman MM. Increasing rates of depression. JAMA 1989; 261: 2229-35
6. The Cross-National Collaborative Group. The changing rate of major depression: cross-national comparisons. JAMA 1992; 268: 3098-105
7. Nolan-Hoeksema S. Sex differences in unipolar depression: evidence and theory. Psychol Bull 1987; 101: 259-82
8. Kessler RC, McGonagle KA, Swartz M, et al. Sex and depression in the National Comorbidity Survey. I: lifetime prevalence, chronicity and recurrence. J Affect Disord 1993; 29: 85-96
9. Klerman GL. The current age of youthful melancholia: evidence for increase in depression among adolescents and young adults. Br J Psychiatry 1988; 152: 4-14
10. Wittchen HU, Knauper B, Kessler RC. Lifetime risk of depression. Br J Psychiatry 1994; 26 Suppl.: 16-22
11. Spitzer RL, Endicott J, Robins E. Research diagnostic criteria: rationale and reliability. Arch Gen Psychiatry 1978; 35: 773-82
12. American Psychiatric Association. Diagnostic and statistical manual of mental disorders: DSM-III. 3rd ed. Washington, DC: American Psychiatric Association, 1980
13. American Psychiatric Association. Diagnostic and statistical manual of mental disorders: DSM-III-R. 3rd rev. ed. Washington, DC: American Psychiatric Association, 1987
14. American Psychiatric Association. Diagnostic and statistical manual of mental disorders. 4th ed. Washington, DC: American Psychiatric Association, 1994
15. Fleming JE, Offord DR. Epidemiology of childhood depressive disorders: a critical review. J Am Acad Child Adolesc Psychiatry 1990; 29: 571-80
16. Kessler RC, McGonagle KA, Zhao S, et al. Lifetime and 12-month prevalence of DSM-III-R psychiatric disorders in the United States: results from the National Comorbidity Survey. Arch Gen Psychiatry 1994; 51: 8-19
17. Greenberg PE, Stiglin LE, Finkelstein SN, et al. Depression: a neglected major illness. J Clin Psychiatry 1993; 54: 419-24
18. Burvill PW. Recent progress in the epidemiology of major depression. Epidemiol Rev 1995; 17: 21-31
19. Angst J. Epidemiology of depression. Psychopharmacol 1992; 106 Suppl.: S71-4
20. Katon W, Schulberg H. Epidemiology of depression in primary care. Gen Hosp Psychiatry 1992; 14: 237-47
21. Nemeroff CB. Introduction. Am J Med 1994; 97 Suppl. 6A: 1S-2S
22. Stokes PE. Current issues in the treatment of major depression. J Clin Psychopharmacol 1993; 13 Suppl. 2: 2S-9S
23. Brugha TS, Bebbington PE. The undertreatment of depression. Eur Arch Psychiatry Clin Neurosci 1992; 242: 103-8
24. Hirschfeld RMA, Keller MB, Panico S, et al. The National Depressive and Manic-Depressive Association consensus statement on the undertreatment of depression. JAMA 1997; 277: 333-40
25. Keller MB. Depression. Underrecognition and undertreatment by psychiatrists and other health care professionals. Arch Intern Med 1990; 150: 946-8
26. Regier DA, Hirschfeld RM, Goodwin FK, et al. The NIMH Depression Awareness, Recognition, and Treatment Program: structure, aims, and scientific basis. Am J Psychiatry 1988; 145: 1351-7
27. Knauper B, Wittchen HU. Diagnosing major depression in the elderly: evidence for response bias in standardized diagnostic interviews? J Psychiatr Res 1994; 28: 147-64
28. Wells KB, Hays RD, Burnam A, et al. Detection of depressive disorder for patients receiving prepaid or fee-for-service care: results from the Medical Outcomes Study. JAMA 1989; 262: 3298-302
29. Gerber PD, Barrett J, Barrett J, et al. Recognition of depression by internists in primary care: a comparison of internist and 'gold standard' psychiatric assessments. J Gen Intern Med 1989; 4: 7-13
30. Shapiro S, German PS, Skinner A, et al. An experiment to change detection and management of mental morbidity in primary care. Med Care 1987; 25: 327-39
31. Block M, Schulberg HC, Coulehan JC, et al. Diagnosing depression among new patients in ambulatory training settings. J Am Board Fam Pract 1988; 1: 91-7
32. Spitzer RL, Williams JBW, Kroenke K, et al. Utility of a new procedure for diagnosing mental disorders in primary care: the PRIME-MD 1000 study. JAMA 1994; 272: 1749-56
33. Keller MB, Harrison W, Fawcett JA, et al. Treatment of chronic depression with sertraline or imipramine: preliminary blinded response rates and high rates of undertreatment in the community. Psychopharmacol Bull 1995; 31: 205-12
34. McCombs JS, Nichol MB, Stimmel GL, et al. The cost of antidepressant drug therapy failure: a study of antidepressant use patterns in a Medicaid population. J Clin Psychiatry 1990; 51 Suppl. 6: 60-9
35. Donoghue JM, Tylee A. The treatment of depression: prescribing patterns of antidepressants in primary care in the UK. Br J Psychiatry 1996; 168: 164-8

36. Greenberg PE, Stiglin LE, Finkelstein SN, et al. The economic burden of depression in 1990. J Clin Psychiatry 1993; 54: 405-18
37. Conti DJ, Burton WN. The economic impact of depression in a workplace. J Occup Med 1994; 36: 983-8
38. Lim HL. A practical approach to the management of depression. Singapore Med J 1993; 34: 449-51
39. Lader M. Quality of treatment: what do new antidepressants offer? Int Clin Psychopharmacol 1995; 10 Suppl. 1: 5-9
40. Song F, Freemantle N, Sheldon TA, et al. Selective serotonin reuptake inhibitors: meta-analysis of efficacy and acceptability. BMJ 1993; 306: 683-7
41. Nemeroff CB. Evolutionary trends in the pharmacotherapeutic management of depression. J Clin Psychiatry 1994; 55 Suppl. 12: 3-15
42. Burke MJ, Preskorn SH. Short-term treatment of mood disorders with standard antidepressants. In: Bloom F, Kupfer D, editors. Psychopharmacology: the fourth generation of progress. New York: Raven Press, 1994; 1053-65
43. Stimmel GL. How to counsel patients about depression and its treatment. Pharmacotherapy 1995; 15: 100S-4S
44. Franco K, Tamburino M, Campbell N, et al. The added costs of depression to medical care. Pharmacoeconomics 1995; 7: 284-91
45. Preskorn SH. Comparison of the tolerability of bupropion, fluoxetine, imipramine, nefazodone, paroxetine, sertraline and venlafaxine. J Clin Psychiatry 1995; 56 Suppl. 6: 12-21
46. Facts and comparisons. St. Louis (MO): Facts and Comparisons, Inc., 1996 Jul: 262K, 264J-K
47. Milne RJ, Goa KL. Citalopram: a review of its pharmacodynamic and pharmacokinetic properties, and therapeutic potential in depressive illness. Drugs 1991; 41: 450-77
47a. Sclar DA, Robison LM, Skaer TL, et al. Trends in the prescribing of antidepressant pharmacotherapy: office-based visits 1990-1995. Clin Ther 1998; 20: 871-84
48. Sussman N, Stahl S. Update in the pharmacotherapy of depression. Am J Med 1996; 101 Suppl. 6A: 26S-36S
49. Risby E, Donnigan D, Nemeroff CB. Pharmacotherapeutic considerations for psychiatric disorders: depression. Formulary 1997; 32: 46-59
50. Ereshefsky L. Antidepressants: a pharmacologic rationale for treatment and product selection. Formulary 1995; 30 Suppl. 1: S10-9
51. Gardner DM, Shulman KI, Walker SE, et al. The making of a user friendly MAOI diet. J Clin Psychiatry 1996; 57: 99-104
52. Potter WZ, Rudorfer MV, Manji H. The pharmacologic treatment of depression. N Engl J Med 1991; 325: 633-42
53. DeVane CL. Pharmacokinetics of the newer antidepressants: clinical relevance. Am J Med 1994; 97: 13S-23S
54. Möller HJ, Volz HP. Drug treatment of depression in the 1990s: an overview of achievements and future possibilities. Drugs 1996; 52: 625-38
55. Sternbach H. The serotonin syndrome. Am J Psychiatry 1991; 148: 705-13
56. Riesenman C. Antidepressant drug interactions and the cytochrome P450 system: a critical appraisal. Pharmacotherapy 1995; 15: 84S-99S
57. Brosen K. Are pharmacokinetic drug interactions with the SSRIs an issue? Int Clin Psychopharmacol 1996; 11 Suppl. 1: 23-7
58. Schweizer E, Weise C, Clary C, et al. Placebo-controlled trial of venlafaxine for the treatment of major depression. J Clin Psychopharmacol 1991; 11: 233-6
59. Muth EA, Haskins JT, Moyer JA, et al. Antidepressant biochemical profile of the novel bicyclic compound W4-45,030: an ethyl cyclohexamol derivative. Biochem Pharmacol 1986; 35: 4493-7
60. Preskorn SH. Antidepressant drug selection: criteria and options. J Clin Psychiatry 1994; 55 Suppl. A: 6-22
61. Nierenberg AA, Adler LA, Peselow E, et al. Trazodone for antidepressant-associated insomnia. Am J Psychiatry 1994; 151: 1069-72
62. Fink M. Indications for the use of ECT. Psychopharmacol Bull 1994; 30: 269-75
63. Weiner RD, Coffey CE. Electroconvulsive therapy in the United States. Psychopharmacol Bull 1991; 27: 9-15
64. Weiner RD. Treatment optimization with ECT. Psychopharmacol Bull 1994; 30: 313-20
65. Khan A, Mirolo MH, Hughes D, et al. Electroconvulsive therapy. Psychiatr Clin North Am 1993; 16: 497-513
66. Khan A, Cohen S, Stowell M, et al. Treatment options in severe psychotic depression. Convuls Ther 1987; 3: 93-9
67. Persad E. Electroconvulsive therapy in depression. Can J Psychiatry 1990; 35: 175-82
68. Banazak DA. Electroconvulsive therapy: a guide for family physicians. Am Fam Physician 1996; 53: 273-8, 281-2
69. Scott AI. Contemporary practice of electroconvulsive therapy. Br J Hosp Med 1994; 51: 334-8
70. Dubovsky SL, Thomas M. Approaches to the treatment of refractory depression. J Pract Psychiatry Behav Health 1996; 2: 14-22
71. Consensus Conference. Electroconvulsive therapy. JAMA 1985; 254: 2103-8
72. Pary R, Tobias CR, Lippman S. Pharmacologic treatment strategies for the depressed, poorly responsive patient. South Med J 1992; 85: 1122-6, 1130
73. Coryell W. Psychotic depression. J Clin Psychiatry 1996; 57 Suppl. 3: 27-31
74. Franco-Bronson K. The management of treatment-resistent depression in the medically ill. Psychiatr Clin North Am 1996; 19: 329-50
75. American Psychiatric Association. The practice of electroconvulsive therapy: recommendations for treatment, training and privileging: a Task Force Report. Washington, DC: American Psychiatric AssociationPress, 1990
76. Depression Guideline Panel. Clinical practice guideline number 5: depression in primary care, 2: treatment of major depression. Rockville (MD): US Dept of Health and Human Services, Agency for Health Care Policy and Research, 1993. AHCPR publication 93-0551
77. American Psychiatric Association. Practice guidelines for major depressive disorder in adults. Am J Psychiatry 1993; 150 Suppl. 40: 1-26
78. Persons JB, Thase ME, Crits-Christoph P. The role of psychotherapy in the treatment of depression. Arch Gen Psychiatry 1996; 53: 283-90
79. Munoz RF, Hollon SD, McGrath E, et al. On the AHCPR depression in primary care guidelines. Am Psychol 1994; 49: 42-61
80. Schulberg HC, Rush AJ. Clinical practice guidelines for managing major depression in primary care: implications for psychologists. Am Psychol 1994; 49: 34-41
81. Jarrett RB. Psychosocial aspects of depression and the role of psychotherapy. J Clin Psychiatry 1990; 51 Suppl.: 26-35

82. Robinson LA, Berman JS, Neimeyer RA. Psychotherapy for the treatment of depression: a comprehensive review of controlled outcome research. Psychol Bull 1990; 108: 30-49
83. Hollon SD, Shelton RC, Loosen PT. Cognitive therapy and pharmacotherapy for depression. J Consult Clin Psychol 1991; 59: 88-99
84. Scott J. Cognitive therapy of affective disorders: a review. J Affect Disord 1996; 37: 1-11
85. Kendall PC, Lipman AJ. Psychological and pharmacological therapy: methods and modes for comparative outcome research. J Consult Clin Psychol 1991; 59: 78-87
86. Kamlet MS, Paul N, Greenhouse J, et al. Cost utility analysis of maintenance treatment for recurrent depression. Control Clin Trials 1995; 16: 17-40
87. McFarland BH. Cost-effectiveness considerations for managed care systems: treating depression in primary care. Am J Med 1994; 97 Suppl. 6A: 47S-57S
88. McLean PD, Hakstain AR. Relative endurance of unipolar depression treatment effects: longitudinal follow-up. J Consult Clin Psychol 1990; 58: 482-8
89. Kupfer DJ. Long-term treatment of depression. J Clin Psychiatry 1991; 52 Suppl. 5: 28- 34
90. Burke MJ. The search for value: pharmacoeconomic issues in the treatment of depression. J Pract Psychiatry Behav Health 1996; 2: 2-13
91. Sturm R, Wells KB. How can care for depression become more cost-effective? JAMA 1995; 273: 51-8
92. Judd LL, Rapaport MH. Economics of depression and cost-benefit comparisons of selective serotonin reuptake inhibitors and tricyclic antidepressants. Depression 1994/1995; 2: 173-7
93. Mitchell J, Greenberg J, Finch K, et al. Effectiveness and economic impact of antidepressant medications: a review. Am J Managed Care 1997; 3: 323-30
94. Rascati K. Drug utilization review of concomitant use of specific serotonin reuptake inhibitors or clomipramine with antianxiety/sleep medications. Clin Ther 1995; 17: 786-90
95. Nelson C. Are the SSRIs really better tolerated than the TCAs for treatment of major depression? Psychiatr Ann 1994; 24: 628-31
96. Lin EHB, Von Korff M, Katon W, et al. The role of the primary care physician in patients' adherence to antidepressant therapy. Med Care 1995; 33: 67-74
97. Montgomery SA, Henry J, McDonald G, et al. Selective serotonin reuptake inhibitors: meta-analysis of discontinuation rates. Int Clin Psychopharmacol 1994; 9: 47-53
98. LePen C, Levy E, Ravily V, et al. The cost of treatment dropout in depression: a cost-benefit analysis of fluoxetine vs. tricyclics. J Affect Disord 1994; 31: 1-18
99. Anderson IM, Tomenson BM. Treatment discontinuation with selective serotonin reuptake inhibitors compared with tricyclic antidepressants: a meta-analysis. BMJ 1995; 310: 1433-8
100. Physician's Desk Reference. 51st ed. Montvale (NJ): Medical Economics Company, 1996: 935, 2053, 2686
101. Fabre LF, Abuzzahab FS, Amin M, et al. Sertraline safety and efficacy in major depression: a double-blind fixed-dose comparison with placebo. Biol Psychiatry 1995; 38: 593-602
102. Donoghue J, Tylee A, Wildgust H. Cross sectional database analysis of antidepressant prescribing in general practice in the United Kingdom, 1993-5. BMJ 1996; 313: 861-2
103. Gregor KJ, Overhage JM, Coons SJ, et al. Selective serotonin reuptake inhibitor dose titration in the naturalistic setting. Clin Ther 1994; 16: 306-14
104. Thompson D, Buesching D, Gregor KJ, et al. Patterns of antidepressant use and their relation to costs of care. Am J Managed Care 1996; 2: 1239-46
105. Simon GE, VonKorff M, Heiligenstein JH, et al. Initial antidepressant choice in primary care: effectiveness and cost of fluoxetine vs tricyclic antidepressants. JAMA 1996; 275: 1897-902
106. Gregor KJ, Riley JA, Downing DK. Concomitant use of anxiolytics and hypnotics with selective serotonin reuptake inhibitors. Clin Ther 1996; 18: 521-7
107. Bentkover JD, Feighner JP. Cost analysis of paroxetine versus imipramine in major depression. Pharmacoeconomics 1995; 8: 223-32
108. Jonsson B, Bebbington PE. What price depression? The cost of depression and the cost-effectiveness of pharmacological treatment. Br J Psychiatry 1994; 164: 665-73
109. Sclar DA, Robison LM, Skaer TL, et al. Antidepressant pharmacotherapy: economic outcomes in a health maintenance organization. Clin Ther 1994; 16: 715-30
110. Skaer TL, Sclar DA, Robison LM, et al. Economic valuation of amitriptyline, desipramine, nortriptyline, and sertraline in the management of patients with depression. Curr Ther Res 1995; 56: 556-67
111. Smith W, Sherrill A. A pharmacoeconomic study of the management of major depression: patients in a TennCare HMO. Med Interface 1996; 7: 88-92
111a Sclar DA, Skaer TL, Robison LM. Economic outcomes with antidepressant pharmacotherapy: a retrospective intent-to-treat analysis. J Clin Psychiatry 1998; 59 Suppl. 2: 13-7
112. Sclar DA, Robison LM, Skaer TL, et al. Antidepressant pharmacotherapy: economic evaluation of fluoxetine, paroxetine and sertraline in a health maintenance organization. J Int Med Res 1995; 23: 395-412
113. Sclar DA, Skaer TL, Robison LM, et al. Evidence-based algorithm for antidepressant pharmacotherapy. JAMA South East Asia Suppl 1997; 13: 33-40
114. Sclar DA, Robison LM, Skaer TL, et al. What factors influence the prescribing of antidepressant pharmacotherapy? An assessment of national office-based encounters. Int J Psychiatry Med 1998; 28: 447-59
115. Sclar DA, Robison LM, Skaer TL, et al. Ethnicity and the prescribing of antidepressant pharmacotherapy: 1992-1995. Harvard Rev Psychiatry 1999; 7: 29-36

Correspondence: Dr *David A. Sclar*, Director, Pharmacoeconomics and Pharmacoepidemiology Research Unit, Graduate Program in Health Policy and Administration, Washington State University, Pullman, Washington 99164-6510, USA.
E-mail: Sclar@mail.wsu.edu

Dysthymia
Options in Pharmacotherapy - An Update

David S. Baldwin

Department of Mental Health, Faculty of Medicine, Health and Biological Sciences,
University of Southampton, Southampton, UK

Dysthymic disorder (dysthymia) was formally introduced into the psychiatric nomenclature by the American Psychiatric Association with the publication of the DSM-III[1] classification of mental disorders in 1980. Prior to the recognition of dysthymia, patients with chronic mild forms of depressive illness received a variety of diagnoses, including depressive temperament or personality, hysteroid dysphoria, and neurotic or characterological depression.[2] Although ill-defined and open to interpretation, these terms tend to suggest a disorder that is relatively inconsequential, associated with defects of character, and likely to prove resistant to change. It is not surprising, therefore, that earlier classifications, e.g. DSM-II,[3] placed states of prolonged depression within the broad categories of neurosis or personality disorder. In contrast, recent classificatory schemes have avoided speculations as to aetiology and, instead, focused on phenomenology. This has resulted in the inclusion of chronic mild depression within the group of affective disorders.

Little was known of dysthymia at the time of its incorporation within DSM-III. Subsequent research has indicated that many of the assumptions regarding its extent, nature and course are incorrect. Patients with mild but persistent depression are common, both in community and clinical samples.[4,5,6] Chronic minor depression has been found to exert a significant effect on medical outcome and health service utilisation.[7]

The clinical features of dysthymia have been slowly established,[8] and the extent of its comorbidity with other disorders has been determined.[4,9] Finally, an increasing number of controlled clinical trials indicate that patients with dysthymia are not refractory to treatment, but may benefit from a variety of pharmacological approaches to the management of their condition.[10,11,12]

1. Diagnosis

The concept of dysthymia originally evoked considerable controversy amongst academic psychiatrists. Diagnosis rests on establishing that depressive features have been persistent but mild, and is therefore reliant upon accurate recall of symptoms by patients (see tables I and II). The recollection of mood states, however, is notoriously poor. It may be influenced by negative retrospective biases, which are consistent with the other cognitive distortions seen in depressed individuals. Prospective studies in recurrent brief depression, for example, reveal that recollection of affect is reasonably accurate for a period of up to 6 months. However, longer periods of recall are subject to a systematic bias, with over-estimation of duration and under-estimation of symptom-free intervals.[13]

The diagnostic criteria for dysthymia, specified within the DSM-IV[14] classification (table I), represent an improvement over earlier descriptions. In these it was 'too easy to go from a diagnosis of dysthymia to one of major depression'.[15] The ability to accurately diagnose dysthymia has made it easier to distinguish between dysthymia and major depression. As a result, fewer patients will be diagnosed as having 'double depression', in which chronically but mildly depressed patients experience supervening episodes of major depressive illness. The clinical descriptions and diagnostic guidelines for dysthymia contained within ICD-10[16] (table II) and DSM-IV appear less precise than those in DSM-III-R,[17] but delineate an essentially similar syndrome.

2. Epidemiology

For many years, the prevalence of dysthymia in the general population was unclear. Epidemiological investigations[18-22] (table III) have suggested that the point prevalence of dysthymia varies between 1.2 to 3.9%. Differences in both the nature of the chosen population and the study design prevent much comparison of the findings.

The publication of the results of the Epidemiologic Catchment Area (ECA) survey, organised by the US National Institute of Mental Health, provided further data on the epidemiology of dysthymia.[23] The results of this extensive study were similar to those of the earlier studies, and indicated that some 2 to 4% of the general population experience chronic (i.e. more than 2 years duration) depression during their lifetime.[4] The

Table I. DSM-IV[14] criteria for dysthymia (modified)

The patient must present with the following symptoms:

A. Depressed mood for most of the day, more days than not (as indicated either by subjective account or observation by others) for at least 2 years

B. Presence, while depressed, of at least 2 of the following:
   poor appetite or overeating
   insomnia or hypersomnia
   low energy or fatigue
   low self-esteem
   poor concentration or difficulty making decisions
   feelings of hopelessness

C. During a 2-year period of the disturbance, never without the symptoms in 'A' and 'B' for more than 2 months at a time

D. No evidence of an unequivocal major depressive episode during the first 2 years of the disturbance

E. Has never had a manic episode or an unequivocal hypomanic episode

F. Not superimposed on a chronic psychotic disorder, such as schizophrenia or delusional disorder

G. It cannot be established that an organic factor initiated and maintained the disturbance, e.g. prolonged administration of an antihypertensive medication

H. The symptoms cause clinically significant distress, or impairment in social, occupational or other important areas of functioning

Table II. International Classification of Disease (ICD-10)[16] clinical descriptions and diagnostic guidelines for dysthymia

Description:

Chronic depression of mood

Does not fulfil the criteria for recurrent depressive disorder, in terms of either severity or duration of individual episodes (criteria for mild depressive episode may have been fulfilled in the past)

Balance between individual phases of mild depression and intervening periods of comparative normality is very variable

For periods of days or weeks patients may describe themselves as well, but most of the time (often for months at a time) they have the following symptoms:
   depression
   tiredness
   everything is an effort
   anhedonia
   brooding
   complaining
   insomnia
   feelings of inadequacy

Age of onset can be early (in late teenage years or the 20s) or late

Diagnostic guidelines:

Essential feature is a very long-standing depression of mood which is never, or only very rarely, severe enough to fulfil the criteria for recurrent depressive disorder, mild or moderate severity

Usually begins early in adult life

Lasts for at least several years, sometimes indefinitely

When the onset is later in life, the disorder is often the aftermath of a discrete depressive episode and associated with bereavement or other obvious stress

Table III. Prevalence rates for dysthymia

Reference	Year of study	Site	Prevalence rates (%)		
			point	6-month	lifetime
Faravelli & Incerpi[18]	1985	Florence	1.2	2.3	
Kashani[19]	1987	Columbia	3.3		
Wittchen & von Zerssen[20]	1987	Munich	3.9		
Canino et al.[23]	1987	Puerto Rico			4.7
Bland & Newman[21]	1988	Edmonton	3.7	3.7	3.7
Kivelae[22]	1988	Tampere			20.6
Weissman et al.[4]	1988	USA			3.1
Hwu et al.[24]	1989	Taiwan			0.5-1.5
Angst & Wicki[9]	1991	Zurich		2.6	

ECA survey[25] classified all such patients as having dysthymic disorder, failing to take account of the severity of illness, its duration and type of onset. This may therefore represent an overestimate of the true prevalence of dysthymia in the community.

Dysthymia has marked comorbidity with other disorders. The ECA study,[25] for example, indicated that 75% of patients with dysthymia also fulfil the diagnostic criteria for other forms of psychiatric illness, including major depression, substance abuse and a range of anxiety disorders.[4] 'Pure' dysthymia appeared relatively uncommon. Certain authors have suggested that such extensive comorbidity indicates that dysthymia is not a valid independent subtype of depression that can be diagnosed with any degree of reliability.[9]

The ECA study[25] indicates that dysthymia is associated with considerable use of health service resources. When compared with healthy individuals, patients with dysthymia report significantly more contact with general and mental health services, across a variety of treatment settings.

Prescriptions of psychotropic drugs are common in patients with dysthymia, especially for antidepressants, anxiolytics and hypnosedatives.[4] However, a study of 410 patients with DSM-III-R dysthymia without concurrent major depression revealed high levels of under-treatment: only 41.3% had been treated with antidepressant drugs, and only 51.6% had undergone psychotherapy.[26]

3. Pharmacotherapy

3.1 Appropriate Trial Design

Although dysthymic patients may be markedly distressed, and persuasive in their requests for help, drug treatment is likely to be long term, and should only be started after due consideration of the relative risks and benefits.

While much research into the treatment response of dysthymia has been undertaken, methodological flaws (such as insufficient duration and use of open-label designs) characterise some of the earlier published studies. Much of the preliminary research into the clinical response in dysthymia has employed a 'naturalistic' format, in which treatment is uncontrolled but carefully recorded. Such studies provide only limited information, but can allow tentative inferences to be made regarding the value of performing more rigorous investigations in a controlled fashion.

Demonstration of a pharmacological effect of a drug in dysthymia requires a particularly stringent trial design (table IV).[27] Uncontrolled or 'open' studies may be useful in generating hypotheses regarding a likely treatment response, but adequately controlled trials are needed before a therapeutic effect can be confirmed. The lack of a generally accepted treatment of dysthymia necessitates the use of a placebo-controlled design. Although the placebo response in dysthymia appears to be relatively low, studies that employ a placebo control are preferable. These studies are more likely to reveal a true treatment effect and require fewer study participants, thereby reducing the risk of patients being exposed to potentially unhelpful or harmful drugs. Patients included within the study should have sufficient predicted morbidity, both in terms of numbers and the severity of symptoms, to reveal a meaningful clinical response.

Further considerations include the duration of the study and the scales that are employed to measure response. Current diagnostic criteria for dysthymia permit symptom-free periods of up to 2 months (table I). Conventional short term treatment studies (6 to 8 weeks) could therefore produce misleading results. Studies in dysthymia are more likely to yield meaningful findings when treatment is prolonged. There is as yet no consensus on the optimal duration, but periods of around 6 months may be appropriate.

Table IV. Design requirements for treatment studies in dysthymia

Operationally defined diagnostic criteria
Double-blind, placebo-controlled design
Sufficient predicted morbidity
Adequate duration
Reliable and sensitive measures of change
Evaluation of quality of life

Table V. Assessment of severity of symptoms according to the Cornell Dysthymia Rating Scale. Each item is rated on a separate 5-point scale[30]

Depressed mood
Lack of interest or pleasure
Pessimism
Suicidal ideation
Low self-esteem
Guilt
Helplessness
Social withdrawal
Indecisiveness
Low attention and concentration
Psychic anxiety
Somatic anxiety
Worry
Irritability or excessive anger
General somatic symptoms
Low productivity
Low energy
Low sexual interest or activity
Sleep disturbance[a]
Diurnal variation in symptoms[b]

a   Characterised as either the experience of insufficient sleep or sleeping too much.
b   Mood variation is characterised as either worse in the morning or in the evening.

Reliable and accurate measurement of clinical response is mandatory in all pharmacological treatment studies. In major depression, both the Hamilton Depression Rating Scale (HDRS)[28] and the Montgomery-Åsberg Depression Rating Scale (MADRS)[29] are used widely, having sufficient validity and sensitivity to change. Although dysthymia is characterised by typical depressive psychopathology, the threshold for diagnosis is lower, and the relative fixity of symptoms is such that other scales may be rather more sensitive in revealing therapeutic effects. The Cornell Dysthymia Rating Scale (CDRS)[30] [table V] has been developed with the specific aim of accurately measuring change in chronic depression of mild to moderate severity. Preliminary research suggests that the CDRS is a reliable and valid measure of symptom severity in dysthymia.

3.2 Results of Treatment Studies

Various classes of psychotropic drugs have been studied as treatments for dysthymia, including tricyclic antidepressants (such as imipramine and amitriptyline), monoamine oxi-

Table VI. Placebo-controlled studies of drug treatments in patients with dysthymia

Reference	Diagnosis	Year of study	Duration	No. of patients	Treatment	Result
Guy et al.[31]	Chronic dysphoria	1983	6 wks	60	Mianserin Placebo	Mianserin > placebo
Stewart et al.[32]	RDC intermittent depression	1983	6 wks	16	Desipramine Placebo	Desipramine = placebo
Stewart et al.[33]	DSM-III dysthymia	1985	6 wks	16	Desipramine Placebo	Desipramine = placebo
Kocsis et al.[34]	Chronic depression	1996	2y	104	Desipramine Placebo	Desipramine> placebo
Kocsis et al.[35]	DSM-III dysthymia	1988	6 wks	76	Imipramine Placebo	Imipramine> placebo
Versiani et al.[36]	DSM-III dysthymia	1977	8 wks	315	Moclobemide Imipramine Placebo	Moclobemide= imipramine> placebo
Lecrubier et al.[37]	DSM-III-R dysthymia, or major depression in partial remission	1977	6mo	219	Amisulpride Imipramine Placebo	Amisulpride= imipramine> placebo
Thase et al.[38]	DSM-III-R dysthymia	1994	12 wks	416	Sertraline Imipramine Placebo	Sertraline= imipramine > placebo
Bakish et al.[39]	DSM-III dysthymia	1995	7 wks	50	Ritanserin Imipramine Placebo	Ritanserin = imipramine > placebo
Keller et al.[40]	DSM-III-R double depression or chronic major depression	1998	12 wks	635	Sertraline Imipramine	Sertraline = imipramine
Salzmann et al.[41]	DSM-III dysthymia	1995	6 wks	67	Minaprine Imipramine	Minaprine = imipramine
Tyrer et al.[42]	DSM-III dysthymia	1988	6 wks	18	Doxepin Placebo	Doxepin > placebo
Paykel et al.[43]	RDC minor depression	1988	6 wks	41	Amitriptyline Placebo	Amitriptyline = placebo
Harrison et al.[44]	DSM-III dysthymia	1986	26 wks	12 12	Phenelzine Placebo	Phenelzine > placebo
Davidson et al.[45]	RDC minor depression	1988	6 wks	35 35	Isocarboxazid Placebo	Isocarboxazid = placebo
Duarte et al.[47]	DSM-III-R double depression	1996	6 wks	42	Moclobemide Fluoxetine	Moclobemide > fluoxetine
Hellerstein et al.[48]	DSM-III dysthymia	1993	8 wks	35 35	Fluoxetine Placebo	Fluoxetine > placebo
Vanelle et al.[49]	DSM-III-R dysthymia	1997	24 wks	140	Fluoxetine Placebo	Fluoxetine < placebo
Bersani et al.[52]	DSM-III dysthymia	1991	6 wks	30 30	Ritanserin Placebo	Ritanserin > placebo
Costa-e-Silva[54]	DSM-III dysthymia	1990	4 wks	39 39	Amisulpride Placebo	Amisulpride > placebo
Boyer et al.[55]	Primary dysthmia	1999	3mo	323	Amisulpride Amineptine Placebo	Amisulpride = amineptine > placebo
Leon et al.[58]	DSM-III-R dysthymia	1994	4 wks	?	Amisulpiride Viloxazine	Amisulpiride > viloxazine
Bloch et al.[60]	Midlife-onset dysthmia	1999	3 wks	17	DHEA Placebo	DHEA > placebo
Salmaggi et al.[61]	DSM-III-R major depression or dysthymia	1993	4 wks	80	SAMe Placebo	SAMe < placebo

DHEA = dehydroepiandrosterone; **RDC** = Research Diagnostic Criteria; **SAMe** = S-adenosyl-L-methionine; **>** indicates significantly more effective than other treatment; **=** indicates equivalent to other treatment.

dase (MAO) inhibitors (MAOIs), reversible inhibitors of MAO-A (RIMAs), selective serotonin (5-hydroxytryptamine; 5-HT) reuptake inhibitors (SSRIs), lithium, ritanserin, amineptine, minaprine and amisulpiride.[11,12] Despite variations in inclusion criteria and the duration of treatment, most studies have revealed evidence of a clinical response, although usually less than that typically seen in major depression. Confident demonstration of a pharmacological effect in dysthymia, however, requires studies that utilise a placebo-controlled design.

There have been a number of double-blind, placebo-controlled treatment studies in patients with dysthymia (table VI). Tricyclic antidepressants, including imipramine and amitriptyline, have been evaluated a little more extensively than the traditional, older, MAOIs, such as phenelzine or isocarboxazid. Much recent research has focused on the potential utility of SSRIs and moclobemide (a RIMA). Further studies have involved amineptine, a novel anti-depressant, amisulpride, an antipsychotic, and the serotonin 5-HT$_2$ receptor antagonist ritanserin. Many of the earlier studies are flawed, either through the use of small numbers of patients or through other deficiencies in trial design.

3.2.1 Tri- and Tetracyclic Antidepressants

The efficacy of tricyclic and tetracyclic antidepressants in states of prolonged depression has been examined by a number of authors. An early study, in patients with 'chronic dysphoria' (a syndrome rather similar to dysthymia), indicated that mianserin was significantly more effective than placebo, both on global measures of improvement and in reducing depressive psychopathology as measured by the HDRS.[31]

In contrast, three placebo-controlled treatment studies with the tricyclic antidepressant des-ipramine have produced rather disappointing results. In the first,[32] a small group of patients fulfilling Research Diagnostic Criteria (RDC)[40] for intermittent minor depression appeared to derive no benefit from treatment with desipramine. A second investigation, with similar numbers of patients with DSM-III–diagnosed dysthymia,[33] also revealed no clear evidence of a drug-placebo difference. It is possible that the inclusion of only small numbers of patients within these studies may have caused a type II error, i.e. a failure to demonstrate a real differ-ence as a result of deficiencies in trial design. The third study, of maintenance desipramine therapy in chronically depressed patients (105 with dysthymia or double depression) who had previously remitted with open-label desipramine treatment, found that desipramine was sig-nificantly more effective than placebo in preventing relapse of depressive symptoms.[34]

More recent studies of the treatment of dysthymic patients with tricyclic antidepressants have produced rather more encouraging results. Kocsis et al.[35] investigated a large group of patients (n = 76) with DSM-III–diagnosed dysthymia, who were treated with imipramine, and an otherwise matched group of controls allocated to placebo. They were able to demonstrate both a signif-icant reduction in depression and an improvement in social function in drug-treated patients.

Further placebo-controlled treatment studies of imipramine, with comparator drugs in-cluding moclobemide,[36] amisulpride,[37] sertraline[38] and ritanserin[39] have already revealed significant advantages for imipramine over placebo in reducing depressive symptoms. In addition, some studies show advantages for imipramine over placebo in reducing 'negative symptoms'[37] and improving social adjustment and quality of life.[38] Two further, comparator-controlled studies, also found significant improvements in depressive symptoms in dysthymic patients treated with imipramine.[40,41]

Similarly, a rather complex study of patients with DSM-III–diagnosed dysthymia[42] indi-cated that the tricyclic antidepressant doxepin was significantly more effective than placebo in relieving depression, as measured by both subjective assessment and the MADRS. A study in which amitriptyline was found to be of little benefit in minor depression[43] is of limited value to considerations of the management of dysthymia, as it is unclear whether the patients had been chronically depressed.

3.2.2 Monoamine Oxidase Inhibitors

The potential utility of traditional MAOIs in dysthymia has been investigated in two double-blind, placebo-controlled studies. Harrison et al.[44] reported a significant drug-placebo difference for phenelzine, when a group of 12 patients who had responded well to short term treatment were allocated to either drug or placebo for a 6-month continuation period. Although encouraging, the results of this study require replication in a larger group of patients before the long term efficacy of phenelzine in dysthymia can be assumed.

A second study,[45] involving a group of patients who fulfilled RDC criteria for minor depression and who had marked 'atypical' features (such as hypersomnia and hyperphagia), was unable to reveal any differences between placebo and isocarboxazid over a period of 6 weeks.

Moclobemide appears to have a number of advantages over traditional MAOIs such as phenelzine.[46] A study has examined the efficacy of moclobemide, imipramine or placebo in patients with DSM-III-R–diagnosed dysthymia, both in short term treatment and in continuation therapy.[37] Approximately two-thirds of the recruited patients were diagnosed as having pure dysthymia, with the remainder having double depression. The efficacy of moclobemide and imipramine was largely similar, and significantly greater than that of placebo, across a range of outcome variables, including clinical global improvement and measures of depression. Response rates were consistently greater in patients with double depression than in those with pure dysthymia. The study involved over 300 patients, was of good design and reported in a clear fashion.

In a subsequent study, which compared fluoxetine and moclobemide in 42 patients with double depression (DSM-III-R dysthymia plus superimposed major depressive episode), there were significant reductions in depressive symptoms with both drugs, but more patients who received moclobemide showed a 50% or greater reduction in HDRS score.[47]

Taken together, these results provide convincing evidence for the value of antidepressant medication in the management of dysthymia.

3.2.3 Selective Serotonin Reuptake Inhibitors

The SSRIs appear as effective as established antidepressants in the treatment of major depression, and may have certain advantages in particular groups of patients such as those with obsessional features or suicidal thoughts. The efficacy of SSRIs in the treatment of patients with dysthymia has not yet been studied extensively, although the results of a number of placebo-controlled investigations suggest that SSRIs may come to have a role in the management of dysthymic disorder.

In a randomised, double-blind, placebo-controlled study, fluoxetine was found to be significantly more effective than placebo in relieving the symptoms of depression in patients with pure dysthymia, over an 8-week period.[48] However, this significant difference was seen only in the scores on the HDRS and in the Clinical Global Impression of Improvement, and not in the CDRS,[30] or in the subject-completed 58-item Hopkins Symptom Check-List. A subsequent placebo-controlled study of 140 patients with DSM-III-R dysthymia found significant advantages for fluoxetine 20 mg/day over placebo in the number of responders after 3 months of treatment.

Furthermore, 50% of the non-responders at 3 months had responded when the daily dose of fluoxetine was increased to 40mg.[49]

It is not possible to predict which dysthmic patients will respond to treatment with fluoxetine, but an early review of the therapeutic uses of SSRIs in the management of patients with dysthymia indicated that a good clinical response was associated with female gender, a late-onset illness, and evidence of nonsuppression in the dexamethasone suppression test.[50]

The efficacy and tolerability of sertraline has been compared to that of imipramine, within the context of a large, multicentre, randomised, double-blind, placebo-controlled study.[38] In this investigation, 416 patients who fulfilled DSM-III-R criteria for early-onset dysthymia received either sertraline, imipramine or placebo over an initial phase of 12 weeks, followed by a continuation phase of up to 9 months. All of the patients had illnesses of at least 5 years' duration, and none had evidence of concurrent major depression. During the initial 12-week period, both sertraline and imipramine were significantly more effective than placebo in relieving the symptoms of depression. Although there were no differences between the two active treatments in terms of efficacy, sertraline was better tolerated, there being significantly fewer dropouts from treatment during the early phase of the study.

3.2.4 Ritanserin

Many authors have suggested that the pathophysiology of depression may involve a hypersensitivity of postsynaptic 5-HT$_2$ receptors. Evidence for this hypothesis comes from the observation that long term treatment with antidepressant drugs leads to the downregulation and reduces the sensitivity of 5-HT$_2$ receptors.[51]

The novel psychotropic compound ritanserin acts as an antagonist at 5-HT$_2$ receptors, both in animal models and human volunteers.[52] In double-blind, placebo-controlled trials in patients with anxiety and depressive disorders, the first observed effects of ritanserin appear to include a reduction in fatigue and irritability, and an improvement in perceived coping skills. This 'thymosthenic' effect suggests that the drug may have a role in the treatment of mood disorders such as dysthymia.[53]

In a double-blind, placebo-controlled study, ritanserin was found to be effective in relieving the symptoms of depression.[52] After a single-blind placebo run-in period of 7 days, 30 patients fulfilling DSM-III criteria for dysthymic disorder were randomised to receive either placebo or ritanserin 10 mg/day over a 5-week period. In the 23 patients who completed the study, ritanserin was found to be significantly more effective than placebo, both on the HDRS[28] and the Hamilton Anxiety Rating Scale. The overall clinical effect was considered to be marked or moderate in 75% of the ritanserin-treated patients, but in only 18% of those receiving placebo. Unfortunately, the baseline severity of depression was similar to that seen in studies in major depression, which suggests that many of the participating patients probably had double depression, rather than pure dysthymia. Furthermore, the small size of the sample and the short duration of treatment represent additional flaws in the design of the study.

A subsequent investigation of the efficacy of ritanserin in dysthymia was able to support the findings of the earlier study. 50 outpatients fulfilling DSM-III criteria for dysthymic disorder were randomly assigned to treatment with imipramine, ritanserin or placebo over a 7-week period.[39] By the end of the study, both imipramine and ritanserin were significantly more effective than placebo in relieving the symptoms of depression. Imipramine appeared to have an earlier onset of action than ritanserin, being significantly more effective than placebo at week 6. However, the overall tolerability of ritanserin was greater than that of imipramine, with significantly more adverse effects and a higher dropout rate from treatment with imipramine.[39]

Ritanserin would therefore appear to be relatively well tolerated by dysthymic patients, who may not respond to treatment as quickly as patients with major depressive disorder, but nevertheless show a significant improvement given sufficient time.

3.2.5 Amisulpride

Amisulpride is a substituted benzamide derivative, which selectively enhances dopaminergic neurotransmission. Placebo-controlled treatment studies in patients with primary dysthymia, double depression, or major depression in partial remission indicate that amisulpride 50 mg/day is more effective than placebo,[54] and as efficacious as imipramine 100 mg/day[37] or amineptine 200 mg/day.[55] Although amisulpride can cause hyperprolactinaemia, with menstrual dysfunction and galactorrhoea, in around 10% of patients, it is otherwise reasonably well tolerated, and could have a role in the treatment of some patients with dysthymia.[56]

3.2.6 Other Drug Treatments

A number of other psychotropic drugs have been studied in the treatment of patients with dysthymia, including the antidepressant drugs venlafaxine[57] and viloxazine[58] and the benzodiazepine anxiolytic lorazepam.[59] In addition, the antidepressant effects in dysthymia of both dehydroepiandrosterone[60] and S-adenosyl-L-methionine[61] have been evaluated.

An open-label preliminary investigation of the efficacy and tolerability of venlafaxine in patients with dysthymia found that treatment was associated with a 50% reduction in HRSD scores in 73.3% of patients.[57] However, this study involved only 15 patients, and there is a need for placebo-controlled investigations. An amisulpride-controlled study of viloxazine in dysthymia has suggested that viloxazine is less efficacious than amisulpride.[58] In an open-label investigation lasting 8 weeks, the effects of lorazepam at a daily dose of 3mg have been compared with those of amisulpride or fluoxetine: lorazepam appeared significantly less effective than either fluoxetine or amisulpride.[59]

Two other pharmacological approaches to the management of dysthymia have been investigated. A recent placebo-controlled crossover study of dehydroepiandrosterone in 17 patients with 'mid-life dysthymia' suggests that the adrenal androgen was significantly more efficacious than placebo,[60] but the results require confirmation in a larger parallel-group study. Finally, the antidepressant effects of the naturally-occurring amino-acid S-adenosyl-L-methionine at a daily dose of 1.6g have been evaluated in a placebo-controlled study of 80 post-menopausal women with DSM-III-R major depression or dysthymia. S-Adenosyl-L-methionine was significantly more efficacious, with beneficial effects being seen from day 10 of the study.[61] Again, these results require confirmation in further studies.

4. Practical Recommendations

In beginning any attempt to manage a patient with dysthymia, it is essential to make a careful history and examination. Obtaining entirely accurate information is often difficult as a patient's recall of affective symptoms of long standing may be overestimated. Essentially, the clinician should look for chronic depression of mood of more than 2 years duration (the symptoms rarely being severe enough to fulfil the criteria for a major depressive episode). It is useful to gain further information from a key informant. A picture of the severity of symptoms over time should be obtained, so as to exclude such alternative diagnoses as recurrent depression or recurrent brief depression.

Evidence from recent studies has found a high incidence of comorbid psychiatric illness in those with dysthymia.[11] It is vital to search for signs and symptoms of major depression, panic disorder, generalised anxiety disorder, alcohol (ethanol) and substance misuse and personality disorder in the history and examination. Obviously, the identification of any of these comorbid illnesses will have a significant impact on later treatment strategies.

The chronic nature of the low grade affective symptoms present in dysthymia is extremely disabling in the patient, leading to difficulties in social and interpersonal functioning. In managing the whole patient it is therefore important to address such issues as work adjustment, marital and relationship difficulties and withdrawal from social activities.

Suicidal behaviour is a particular problem in dysthymia.[11] A history of suicide attempts, episodes of deliberate self-harm and any current suicidal feelings should be sought.

Treatment strategies should be multifaceted. Whilst recent placebo-controlled trials have demonstrated the beneficial effects of antidepressant medication in the management of dysthymia, these should not be used alone but in conjunction with psychological therapies and related social work.[11] Obviously, any treatment regimen should account for any comorbid illness, and treatment of dysthymia may also alleviate the associated conditions.[62,63] Antidepressants of proven benefit include tricyclic antidepressants (doxepin, desipramine and imipramine), phenelzine, moclobemide, fluoxetine, sertraline, amineptine and ritanserin. The dosages used should be similar to those prescribed for major depressive disorders.

In terms of psychological therapies, more extensive research is required before formal recommendations for treatment can be made. However, once symptoms have been alleviated with pharmacological approaches, the underlying psychosocial disability common in this disorder needs to be addressed. A comparative 16-week treatment study of fluoxetine and cognitive psychotherapy found relatively more dropouts with fluoxetine (33%) than cognitive therapy (9%). Both treatments were efficacious in relieving depressive symptoms, but there were no differences in the overall response to treatment, the authors suggesting that combining treatment approaches may be optimal in the overall management of dysthymia.[64] This notion has received some confirmation in a controlled study in 26 inpatients with double depression, which suggested that combination treatment (i.e. drug treatment plus cognitive-behavioural psychotherapy) was more effective than drug treatment alone at the end of acute treatment, although there was no evidence for lasting additional benefit at 6- and 12-month follow-up assessments.[65] The importance of psychotherapy in the provision of social skills has been stressed.[66] The beneficial effects of marital therapy, particularly with regard to marital intimacy, in these patients has been demonstrated.[67]

There is evidence for the benefit of interpersonal psychotherapy in this group. However, as is strue for cognitive behavioural approaches, more extensive research is necessary to evaluate the benefit in patients with dysthymia alone. Other approaches would include the development of a range of individual coping skills with improved self-management and problem solving techniques.

In conclusion, the practical management of dysthymia involves careful identification of the specific disorder, assessment and appropriate treatment of comorbid psychiatric illness and probably the combined use of antidepressants and psychosocial therapies.

5. Conclusion

As a result of substantial progress in investigations of the management of patients with dysthymia over the last 10 years, it now seems possible to conclude that certain antidepressant drugs (including imipramine, fluoxetine, sertraline and moclobemide) are effective in short term treatment, and possibly also in long term treatment. Much of the early published research in dysthymia was flawed, either through the inclusion of small and heterogeneous groups of patients or through recurring faults in study design that limit analysis of any findings. These flaws apply as much to studies of psychological therapies as to investigations of physical treatments.[68]

There is a clear need for further research. This should include studies involving sufficient numbers of syndromally defined groups of patients with predicted morbidity, who are randomly allocated in a double-blind fashion to either active medication or placebo. The patients should then be followed closely over long periods. During assessment, depressive psychopathology should be elicited in a detailed manner, using scales of proven reliability that are sufficient sensitive to detect small but clinically significant changes in mental state and overall function.

Acknowledgements

This article is an update of a earlier review, written with my previous colleagues Shauna Rudge and Sally Thomas and published in *CNS Drugs* in 1995. I remain grateful to both of them, and also wish to thank Jon Birtwistle of the Primary Care Medical Group in the University of Southampton, for his help with the literature search.

References

1. American Psychiatric Association. Diagnostic and statistical manual of mental disorders. 3rd ed. Washington, DC: American Psychiatric Association, 1980
2. Akiskal HS. Towards a definition of dysthymia: boundaries with personality and mood disorders. In: Burton SW, Akiskal HS, editors. Dysthymic disorder. London: Gaskell, 1990: 1-12
3. American Psychiatric Association. Diagnostic and statistical manual of mental disorders. 2nd ed. Washington, DC: American Psychiatric Association, 1968
4. Weissman MM, Leaf PJ, Bruce ML, et al. The epidemiology of dysthymia in five communities: rates, risks, co-morbidity, and treatment. Am J Psychiatry 1988; 145: 815-9
5. Markowitz JC, Moran ME, Kocsis JH, et al. Prevalence and co-morbidity of dysthymic disorder among psychiatric outpatients. J Affect Disord 1992; 24: 63-71
6. Kocsis JH. Geriatric dysthymia. J Clin Psychiatry 1998; 59 (suppl. 10): 13-5
7. Wells KB, Stewart A, Hays RD, et al. The functioning and well-being of depressed patients: results from the medical outcomes study. JAMA 1989; 262: 914-9
8. Frances A, Hall W. Work in progress on the DSM-IV mood disorders. In: Feighner JP, Boyer WF, editors. Diagnosis of depression. Perspectives in psychiatry. Vol. 2. Chichester: John Wiley & Sons, 1991
9. Angst J, Wicki W. The Zurich Study. XI. Is dysthymia a separate form of depression? Results of the Zurich cohort study. Eur Arch Psychiatry Clin Neurosci 1991; 240: 349-54
10. Howland RH. Pharmacotherapy of dysthymia: a review. J Clin Psychopharmacol 1991; 11: 83-92
11. WPA Dysthymia Working Group. Dysthymia in clinical practice. Br J Psychiatry 1995; 166: 174-88
12. Baldwin DS, Rudge SE, Thomas SC. Dysthymia: options in pharmacotherapy. CNS Drugs 1995; 4: 422-31
13. Montgomery SA. Recurrent brief depression. In: Montgomery SA, Corn TH, editors. Psychopharmacology of depression. Oxford: Oxford Medical Publications, 1994: 129-40
14. American Psychiatric Association. Diagnostic and statistical manual of mental disorders. 4th ed. Washington, DC: American Psychiatric Association, 1994
15. Kocsis JH, Frances AJ. A critical discussion of DSM-III dysthymic disorder. Am J Psychiatry 1987; 144: 1534-42
16. World Health Organization. The ICD-10 classification of mental and behavioural disorders. Clinical descriptions and diagnostic guidelines. Geneva: WHO, 1992
17. American Psychiatric Association. Diagnostic and statistical manual of mental disorders. 3rd rev. ed. Washington, DC: American Psychiatric Association, 1987
18. Faravelli C, Incerpi G. Epidemiology of affective disorders in Florence: preliminary results. Acta Psychiatr Scand 1985; 72: 331-3
19. Kashani J, Carlson GA, Beck NC, et al. Depression, depressive symptoms and depressed mood among a community sample of adolescents. Am J Psychiatry 1987; 144: 931-4
20. Wittchen HU, von Zerssen D. Veläufe behandelter und unbehandelter Depressionen und Angststörungen: eine klinisch-psychiatrische und epidemiologische Verlaufsuntersuchung. Berlin: Springer, 1987
21. Bland RC, Newman SC. Lifetime prevalence of psychiatric disorders in Edmonton. Acta Psychiatr Scand 1988; 77: 24-32
22. Kivelae SL, Pahkala K, Laippala P. Prevalence of depression in an elderly population in Finland. Acta Psychiatr Scand 1988; 78: 401-13
23. Canino GJ, Bird HR, Shrout PE, et al. The prevalence of specific psychiatric disorders in Puerto Rico. Arch Gen Psychiatry 1987; 44: 727-35
24. Hwu HG, Yeh EK, Chang LY. Prevalence of psychiatric disorders in Taiwan defined by the Chinese Diagnostic Interview Schedule. Acta Psychiat Scand 1989; 79: 136-47
25. Robins LN, Helzer JE, Weissman MM, et al. Lifetime prevalence of specific psychiatric disorders in three sites. Arch Gen Psychiatry 1984; 41: 949-58

26. Shelton RC, Davidson J, Yonkers K, et al. The undertreatment of dysthymia. J Clin Psychiatry 1997; 58: 59-65
22. Klerman GL, Weissman MM, Frank E, et al. Evaluating drug treatments of depressive disorders. In: Prien RF, Robinson DS, editors. Clinical evaluation of psychotropic drugs. Principles and guidelines. New York: Raven Press, 1994: 281-325
28. Hamilton M. A rating scale for depression. J Neurol Neurosurg Psychiatry 1960; 23: 56-65
29. Montgomery SA, Asberg M. A new depression scale designed to be sensitive to change. Br J Psychiatry 1979; 134: 382-9
30. Mason BJ, Kocsis JH, Frances AJ. The Cornell Dysthymia Rating scale. New research abstract no. 231. Presented at the 142nd Annual Meeting of the American Psychiatric Association; 1989 May: San Francisco (CA)
31. Guy W, Ban TA, Schaffer JD. Differential treatment responsiveness among mildly depressed patients. In: Clayton PJ, Barrett JE, editors. Treatment of depression: old controversies and new approaches. New York: Raven Press, 1983: 229-36
32. Stewart JW, Quitkin FM, Liebowitz MR, et al. Efficacy of desipramine in depressed outpatients: response according to research diagnostic criteria diagnoses and severity of illness. Arch Gen Psychiatry 1983; 40: 202-7
33. Stewart JW, McGrath PJ, Liebowitz MR, et al. Treatment outcome validation of DSM-III depressive sub-types: clinical usefulness in outpatients with mild to moderate depression. Arch Gen Psychiatry 1985; 42: 148-53
34. Kocsis JH, Friedman RA, Markowitz JC, et al. Maintenance therapy for chronic depression: a controlled clinical trial of desipramine. Arch Gen Psychiatry 1996; 53: 769-76
35. Kocsis JH, Frances AJ, Voss C, et al. Imipramine treatment for chronic depression. Arch Gen Psychiatry 1988; 45: 253-7
36. Versiani M, Amrein R, Stabl M, et al. Moclobemide and imipramine in chronic depression (dysthymia): an international double-blind, placebo-controlled trial. Int Clin Psychopharmacol 1997; 12: 183-93
37. Lecrubier Y, Boyer P, Turjanski S, et al. Amisulpride versus imipramine and placebo in dysthymia and major depression. J Affect Disorders 1997; 43: 95-103
38. Thase ME, Fava M, Halbreich U, et al. A placebo-controlled clinical trial comparing sertraline and imipramine for the treatment of dysthymia. Arch Gen Psychiatry 1996; 53: 777-84
39. Bakish D, Lapierre YD, Weinstein C, et al. Ritanserin, imipramine and placebo in the treatment of dysthymic disorder. J Clin Psychopharmacol 1995; 13: 409-14
40. Keller MB, Gelenberg AJ, Hirschfeld RMA, et al. The treatment of chronic depression, part 2: a double-blind, randomized trial of sertraline and imipramine. J Clin Psychiatry 1998; 59: 598-607
41. Salzmann E, Robin JL. Multicentric double-blind study comparing efficacy and safety of minaprine and imipramine in dysthymic disorders. Neuropsychobiol 1995; 31: 68-75
42. Tyrer P, Murphy S, Kingdon D, et al. The Nottingham study of neurotic disorder: comparison of drug and psychological treatments. Lancet 1988; ii 235-40
43. Paykel ES, Hollyman JA, Freeling P, et al. Predictors of therapeutic benefit from amitriptyline in mild depression: a general practice placebo controlled trial. J Affect Disord 1988; 14: 83-95
44. Harrison W, Rabkin J, Stewart JW, et al. Phenelzine for chronic depression: a study of continuation treatment. J Clin Psychiatry 1986; 47: 346-9
45. Davidson JRT, Giller EL, Zisook S, et al. An efficacy study of isocarboxazid and placebo in depression, and its relationship to depressive nosology. Arch Gen Psychiatry 1988; 45: 120-7
46. Baldwin DS, Rudge SE. The tolerability of moclobemide. Rev Contemp Pharmacother 1994; 5: 57-65
47. Duarte A, Mikkelsen H, Delini-Stula A. Moclobemide versus fluoxetine for double depression: a randomized double-blind study. J Psychiatr Res 1996; 30: 453-8
48. Hellerstein DJ, Yanavitch D, Rosenthal J, et al. A randomised double-blind study of fluoxetine versus placebo in the treatment of dysthymia. Am J Psychiatry 1993; 150: 1169-75
49. Vanelle J-M, Atta-Levy D, Poirier M-F, et al. Controlled efficacy study of fluoxetine in dysthymia. Br J Psychiatry 1997; 170: 345-50
50. Ravindran AV, Biasik RJ, Lapierre YD. Therapeutic efficacy of serotonin reuptake inhibitors (SSRIs) in dysthymia. Can J Psychiatry 1993; 39: 21-6
51. Fluxe K, Ogren SO, Agnati LF, et al. Chronic antidepressant treatment and central 5-HT synapses. Neuropharmacology 1983; 22: 1203-9
52. Bersani G, Pozzi F, Marini S, et al. 5-HT2 receptor antagonism in dysthymic disorder: a double-blind placebo-controlled study with ritanserin. Acta Psychiatr Scand 1991; 83: 244-8
53. Reyntjens A, Gelden YG, Hopperbrouwers HJA, et al. Thymosthenic effects of ritanserin (R 5667), a centrally acting serotonin S-2 receptor blocker. Drug Dev Res 1986; 8: 205-11
54. Costa-e-Silva JA. Treatment of dysthymic disorder with low-dose amisulpride. A comparative study of 50 mg/day amisulpride versus placebo. Ann Psychiatry 1990; 5: 242-9
55. Boyer P, Lecrubier Y, Stalla-Bourdillon A, et al. Amisulpride versus amineptine and placebo for the treatment of dysthymia. Neuropsychobiol 1999; 39: 25-32
56. Noble S, Benfield P. Amisulpride. A review of its clinical potential in dysthymia. CNS Drugs 1999; 12: 471-83
57. Ravindran A, Charbonneau Y, Zaharia MD, et al. Efficacy and tolerability of venlafaxine in the treatment of primary dysthymia. J Psychiatry Neurosci 1998; 23: 288-92
58. Leon CA, Vigoya J, Conde S, et al. Therapeutic efficacy of amisulpride and viloxazine in the treatment of dysthymia: a comparison. Acta Psiquiatr Psicol Am Lat 1994; 40: 41-49
59. Bogetto F, Barzega G, Bellino S, et al. Drug treatment of dysthymia: a clinical study. Riv Psichiatr 1997; 32: 1-5
60. Bloch M, Schmidt PJ, Danaceau MA, et al. Dehydroepiandrosterone treatment of midlife dysthymia. Biol Psychiatry 1999; 45: 1533-41
61. Salmaggi P, Bressa GM, Nicchia G, et al. Double-blind, placebo-controlled study of S-adenosyl-L-methionine in depressed postmenopausal women. Psychother Psychosom 1993; 59: 34-40
62. Bech P, Mellergard M, Ottoson JO. Secondary depression in panic disorder: an indicator of severity with a weak effect on outcome in alprazolam and imipramine treatment. Acta Psychiatr Scand 1987; 365 Suppl.: 39-45
63. Cummins JL. Depression and Parkinson's disease: a review. Am J Psychiatry 1992; 149: 443-54
64. Dunner DL, Schmaling KB, Hendrickson H, et al. Cognitive therapy versus fluoxetine in the treatment of dysthymic disorder. Depression 1996; 4: 34-41
65. Miller IW, Norman WH, Keitner GI. Combined treatment for patients with double depression. Psychother Psychosom 1999; 68: 180-5
66. Markovitz JC. Psychotherapy of the post dysthymic patient. J Psychother Prac Res 1993; 2: 157-63
67. Waring EM, Chamberlaine CH, McCrank EW, et al. Dysthymia: a randomised study of cognitive marital therapy and anti-depressants. Can J Psychiatry 1988; 33: 96-9
68. McCullough JP. Psychotherapy for dysthymia. A naturalistic study of ten patients. J Nerv Ment Dis 1991; 179: 734-40

Correspondence: Dr *David Baldwin*, University Department of Psychiatry, Royal South Hants Hospital, Graham Road, Southampton, Hampshire, SO14 0YG, England.

Recurrent Brief Depression
Diagnosis, Epidemiology and Potential Pharmacological Options

Siegfried Kasper, Mara Stamenkovic and *L Pezawas*

Department of General Psychiatry, University of Vienna, Vienna, Austria

Depressive episodes that are short in duration have been consistently neglected by investigators conducting research into psychiatric disorders. This is astonishing since the concept of recurrent brief depression (RBD) has been described for more than a century. Angst[1] has recently conducted a review of the literature of the history of RBD, and the main findings of this review are summarised in table I.

1. Diagnosis of Recurrent Brief Depression

Although the term RBD has been introduced only recently into the literature, this disorder is considered of such importance that it is already included in the tenth revision of the International Classification of Diseases (ICD-10).[16] In contrast, DSM-IV[17] still categorises

Table I. Important historical findings from investigations of recurrent brief depression (RBD) [summarised from Angst[1]]

Reference	Date	Finding
Pohl[2]	1852	Described cases of multiple brief depressive episodes that lasted from hours to days; introduced the term 'periodic melancholia'
Head[3]	1901	Described cases of multiple brief depressive episodes that lasted from hours to days; frequently linked to ideas of suicide or with an impulse for self-destruction
Gregory[4]	1915	Described brief depressive episodes that were independent of menstruation; many patients committed sudden and unexpected suicide
Paskind[5]	1929	Observed episodes of RBD in elderly patients
Busse et al.[6]	1955	Found that around 14% of patients with manic depression had a symptomatology lasting from a few hours to a few days
Clayton et al.[7]	1980	Described a syndrome of 'very brief depression' in which depressed mood lasted 3 to 7 days; not systematically associated with the premenstrual phase
Montgomery et al.[8-10]	1983, 1989, 1990	Studied psychiatric patients with a history of several suicide attempts; during long term treatment, patients experienced irregular episodes of brief depression that lasted around 3 days; most episodes were severe; sometimes associated with suicidal intentions
Angst & Dobler-Mikola;[11,12] Angst et al.[13]	1984, 1985, 1990	Studied RBD in an epidemiological cohort; defined criteria for RBD (see table II); approximately 90% of RBD episodes last on average 1 to 3 days, and recur irregularly and frequently
Kasper et al.[14,15]	1992, 1994	Found a sizeable subgroup (up to 30%) of patients with diagnosed autumn/winter depressions (e.g. seasonal affective disorder or its subsyndromal form) who can be characterised as having a seasonal type of RBD; termed 'RBD-seasonal'

RBD as a subcategory of depressive disorders 'not otherwise specified', together with minor and other depression, although Appendix B gives a description of RBD and a set of research criteria for further studies. The diagnostic criteria for RBD in ICD-10 are based on those proposed by Angst et al.[13] in 1990 from their epidemiological study of a cohort of 591 individuals in Zurich, Switzerland (see table II). Compared with the criteria of Angst et al.,[13] a slightly softer frequency criterion is required in ICD-10 (i.e. at least one to two episodes per month over 1 year versus approximately one episode per month in the last year). Table III summarises the criteria for RBD from both ICD-10 and DSM-IV.

It is noteworthy that these criteria for a diagnosis of RBD have not been used in most of the published studies, specifically not in the epidemiological studies published by Weiller et al.[18,19] and Maier et al.,[20,21] and also not in the psychopharmacological studies published by Montgomery et al.[8,22-24] The diagnostic criteria used in the studies of Weiller et al.[18,19] were modified in so far as the duration of the depressive episodes was required to be less than 1 week and RBD had to be present 'nearly' every month over 1 year. On the other hand, an impairment criterion was specifically outlined in these studies. In the studies of Maier et al.[20,21] the duration criterion was the same as that of the criteria of Angst et al.,[13] i.e. less than 2 weeks, but the

Table II. Diagnostic criteria for recurrent brief depression as proposed by Angst et al.[13] (reproduced with permission)

Dysphoric mood or loss of interest or pleasure

Duration less than 2 weeks

Four of the following symptoms:

• poor appetite or significant weight loss (when not dieting) or increased appetite or significant weight gain

• insomnia or hypersomnia

• psychomotor agitation or retardation

• loss of interest or pleasure in usual activities, or decrease in sexual drive

• loss of energy; fatigue

• feelings of worthlessness, self-reproach, or excessive or inappropriate guilt

• diminished ability to think or concentrate, slowed thinking, or indecisiveness

• recurrent thoughts of death, suicidal ideation, wishes to be dead, or suicide attempt

Impairment in usual occupational activities

At least 1-2 episodes per month over 1 year

Table III. ICD-10 (F38.1)[16] and DSM-IV [311 (depressive disorder not otherwise specified[a])][17] criteria for recurrent brief depression

1. Symptomatology criterion
Diagnostic criteria for depressive episode (ICD-10) or major depression (DSM-IV) concerning mood and number of symptoms

2. Duration criterion
Duration of depressive episodes less than 2 weeks (ICD-10)
Duration of depressive episodes at least 2 days, but less than 2 weeks (DSM-IV)

3. Frequency criterion
Approximately 1 episode/month in the last year (ICD-10)
Frequency of at least 1 episode/month over 1 year (DSM-IV)

4. Impairment criterion[b]
Symptomatology presents a change of previous functioning (subjective work impairment)

a   Also see section 1 of text for more detailed explanation of inclusion and exclusion criteria.

b   Not specifically included in ICD-10 and DSM-IV definitions, but outlined in DSM-IV research criteria and in the criteria of Angst et al.[13] (see table II).

frequency criterion was modified so that patients had to have experienced an episode of RBD each month with only 'minor exceptions'. Also, in this study, 'impairment' was not required for the definition of RBD. In the two early studies of Montgomery et al.,[8,22] no formal diagnosis of RBD was established and patients were described as having a history of three or more suicide attempts and no major depression. In the most recent study of Montgomery et al.,[24] RBD was defined as an episode of depression satisfying DSM-III-R[25] criteria for major depression, but which lasted less than 2 weeks. The diagnostic criteria of these latter studies did not include an impairment nor a frequency criterion.

With the inclusion of RBD in ICD-10, it can be hoped that future studies will use similar diagnostic criteria and, as a result, more comparable results will be obtained. The diagnostic criteria proposed by Angst et al.[13] (see table II) might help researchers to standardise their protocols according to the diagnosis of RBD. The frequency criterion of Angst et al.[13] could be helpful for epidemiological studies. However, since depressive symptomatology is dependent to some extent on the coping style of the individual, the stringent frequency criterion proposed by Angst et al.[13] might not be applicable to clinical practice and should be replaced with that proposed in ICD-10 (i.e. approximately once per month in the last year).

The research criteria for RBD from DSM-IV specify eight areas, of which four (symptomatology, duration, frequency, impairment) are comparable to those of Angst et al.[13] The remaining four criteria are exclusion criteria: (i) that there is no association with a substance-induced or general medical condition; (ii) that the patient has never met the criteria of major depression or dysthymia; (iii) that the patient has never met the criteria for manic episode, mixed episode, hypomanic episode or cyclothymic disorder; and (iv) the disturbance does not exclusively occur during schizophrenia, schizophreniform disorder, schizoaffective disorder or delusional disorder. The use of these exclusion criteria is likely to be problematic, since epidemiological data revealed a high comorbidity rate of RBD with other diseases (see section 3). Specifically, the exclusion of major depression and dysthymia are not helpful for further research into RBD, and these exclusion criteria need to be revised in light of present epidemiological data.

2. Clinical Characteristics

The most prominent clinical feature in patients with RBD is that depression lasts only a few days, usually between 2 to 4 days, with a high rate of recurrence (nearly every month over a 1-year period). During the episode, patients experience either depressed mood or loss of interest and at least four additional symptoms listed in the definition of major depression according to DSM-IV. There is no hint that RBD is linked to bipolar disorder, since the Zurich epidemiological study[11] reported fewer episodes of mania or hypomania in those patients with RBD than are seen in the general population. Epidemiological studies indicated that RBD often is unrecognised, even by the patients themselves, and is most likely erroneously attributed to physical ailment or personality problems. Further clinical characteristics, detected in a primary care sample assessed by Weiller et al.[18] are summarised in table IV.

Kasper et al.[14,15] established a relationship between RBD and seasonal affective disorder (SAD), which can be considered as a variant of major depression. Patients with SAD experience depression only in autumn and winter, and have a remission of these symptoms, or even hypomania, in spring and summer.[26] The duration and symptomatology of depressive episodes in patients with seasonal-type RBD were comparable to those of the patients with non-seasonal RBD described in the literature,

Table IV. Characteristics of patients with recurrent brief depression as identified in a primary care setting in Paris[18]

Sex ratio (female : male)	1.7 : 1
Mean age (years)	38 (SD ± 11; range 18-62)
Married (%)	30
Employed (%)	75
Completed high school (%)	61
Duration of episodes (days)	3-4
History of suicide attempts (%)	23
Most frequent comorbid disorder	Major depression, generalised anxiety disorder, panic disorder
Prevalence in primary care (%)	10

but the former patients experienced seasonal changes more markedly and reported a lower percentage of first-degree relatives with a history of depression than the nonseasonal RBD group.

3. Epidemiology

Angst and Dobler-Mikola[11] reported the results of a longitudinal, epidemiological cohort study of young adults that was initiated in Zurich, Switzerland in 1978. Based on this sample, the authors showed the frequent occurrence of depressive episodes lasting no more than 8 days. This study demonstrated the clinical relevance of RBD, its social consequences, the high risk of attempted suicide, the social disability associated with RBD, and the incidence of attempted treatment. Furthermore, this study demonstrated that patients with RBD have a positive family history of RBD and that they share comorbidity with anxiety disorders and substance abuse. These findings suggest that RBD and major depression are often present in the same individuals from a longitudinal point of view; however, there is no systematic preference as to the sequence of occurrence of the disorders.

Recent community studies,[18,21] as well as the comprehensive World Health Organization (WHO) study of primary care patients carried out in 15 treatment centres in 14 countries worldwide,[19] have confirmed the existence of RBD. These studies indicate that: (i) more women than men are affected by RBD; (ii) the duration of episodes is between 3 and 4 days; (iii) these patients have a high rate of suicide attempts; and (iv) the most frequent comorbidity is with major depression, generalised anxiety disorder and panic disorder.

The overall point prevalence rate of RBD (without current dysthymia or depressive episode) was found to be 6.4%.[18,19] However, in this sample the point prevalence rates for current depressive episodes and dysthymia were 12.2% and 1.8%, respectively. Furthermore, the prevalence rates of RBD varied from centre to centre, ranging from 1.9% in Groningen (The Netherlands) and 4% in Paris (France) to 8.4% in Seattle (US) and 13.2% in Rio de Janeiro (Brazil).

The frequency of RBD was also studied in a consecutive outpatient population (n = 704; patients actively seeking help) of a psychiatric university hospital in Vienna, Austria (Meszaros et al., personal communication). The preliminary results revealed a rate of RBD of 12.5% within the group of patients diagnosed as having affective disorders.

The results of these studies indicate that RBD is an important health problem, and it is surprising that such a condition has not received more scientific attention over the past century.

4. Treatment Studies

Patients with RBD have a history of inadequate response to previous treatments, mostly that offered in primary care.[10,13,14] Due to the nature of RBD, with its intermittent bursts of quite severe but short-lasting episodes of depression, it is difficult to establish research protocols. Such protocols need to be of a duration of at least 6 months to detect group differences.

Table V summaries the studies that have assessed the drug treatment of patients with RBD. The treatment studies in the field of RBD were carried out by Montgomery and co-workers.[8,22-24] In the first of these studies,[8,22] the authors studied whether different forms of treatment were able to reduce suicide attempts in a group of patients with a history of suicidal behaviour. In these studies, patients were not formally diagnosed as having RBD, but those

Table V. Summary of double-blind, placebo-controlled studies that have investigated the treatment of patients with recurrent brief depression

Reference	No. of patients	Duration of treatment (mo)	Treatment [dosage (mg/day); route]	Results
Montgomery et al.[8]	58[a]	6	Mianserin [30 PO]	Reduction of suicide attempts: mianserin ≥ placebo
Montgomery et al.[22]	37[a]	6	Flupenthixol [20 mg/4 weeks IM]	Reduction of suicidal behaviour: flupenthixol > placebo
Montgomery et al.[23]	148	6	Paroxetine [20 PO]	Paroxetine ≡ placebo
Montgomery et al.[24]	107[b]	6	Fluoxetine [60mg twice weekly PO]	Number of episodes and suicide attempt rate: fluoxetine ≡ placebo (33 vs 34%, respectively)
Stamenkovic et al.[24a]	2	4	Mirtazapine [30 PO]	Successful reduction of symptomatology

a No formal diagnosis of recurrent brief depression was established, as proposed by Angst et al.[13] Patients had a history of three or more suicide attempts and no major depression.

b Recurrent brief depression was defined as an episode of depression satisfying DSM-III-R[25] criteria for major depression, but which lasted < 2 weeks (no impairment or frequency criteria used).

IM =intramuscular; **mo** = months; **PO** = oral; > indicates significantly more effective than other treatment; ≥ indicates more effective than other treatment, but not a significant difference; ≡ indicates equivalent efficacy to other treatment.

with major depression were excluded. Patients were studied in a prophylactic design lasting 6 months. Active treatment (intramuscular flupenthixol 20 mg/month or, in a parallel study, oral mianserin 30 mg/day) was compared with placebo.

From these studies it became apparent that patients with brief episodes of depression [as measured by the Montgomery-Åsberg Depression Rating Scale (MADRS)[27]] were at a high risk of suicide attempts. These prophylactic studies also revealed that the suicide attempts seemed to occur only during brief episodes of depression that lasted less than 2 weeks. Furthermore, antipsychotic, but not antidepressant, drug therapy appeared to be effective in reducing suicidal behaviour. There was a significant advantage for low dose flupenthixol over placebo in reducing suicidal behaviour.[22] In contrast, while there was a reduction in suicide attempts in patients receiving mianserin compared with placebo, the difference was not statistically significant.[8] Although both these studies were designed to reduce suicidal behaviour, neither were specifically designed to treat brief depressive episodes. However, since brief depressive episodes were linked to suicidal behaviour, it seems logical to conclude that pharmacological treatment might be a possible strategy to treat both conditions.

In a comparative, placebo-controlled study, Montgomery et al.[24] studied 107 patients diagnosed with RBD who did not have major depression and who were treated with either fluoxetine 60mg (given twice weekly) or placebo. Patients were assessed over an interval of approximately 2 to 4 weeks. The dosage of fluoxetine was chosen because of the long elimination half-life of fluoxetine and its active metabolite norfluoxetine. It was thought that this dosage regimen would achieve a blood drug concentration that would be in line with that achieved using the recommended dosage for the treatment of depression (20 mg/day).

In this study, there was no difference in the recurrence rate of brief depression and the rate of suicide attempts occurring during the 6-month observation period between fluoxetine- and placebo-treated patients. The authors, therefore, speculated that selective serotonin (5-hydroxy-tryptamine; 5-HT) reuptake inhibitors (SSRIs) are probably not effective in RBD. This study also addresses the question of whether suicidal behaviour can be induced by antidepressant treatment regimens. In this large study of patients with a high suicide attempt rate prior to entering the study, suicidality was not increased over the placebo rate in the fluoxetine group. This study, therefore, contradicts the suggestion, based on anecdotal reports,[28] that fluoxetine induces suicidal behaviour.

Two available studies that have assessed the effect of antidepressants (mianserin or fluoxetine) in patients with RBD do not demonstrate the efficacy of these drugs in this disorder. However, it should be noted that mianserin itself is considered to be a weak antidepressant[14] and, furthermore, the dosage of 30 mg/day is certainly too low to achieve an antidepressant effect. On the other hand, at a dosage of 20 mg/day (equivalent to that used in the study of Montgomery et al.[24]) fluoxetine has been shown to be an effective antidepressant (for an overview see Kasper et al.[29]). Nevertheless, the notion that SSRIs might not be the treatment of choice is corroborated by other findings of Montgomery's group.[23] In a preliminary study, the effects of another SSRI, paroxetine (at a dosage of 20 mg/day), were also found to be not significant different to placebo. Recently our group[24a] reported on the beneficial effects of mirtazapine (30 mg/day) in 2 patients with RBD. Although encouraging, these results need to be substantiated in a controlled trial.

In a group of patients with seasonal-type RBD (see section 2), there was a hint that light therapy, given in a manner that has been shown to be effective in patients with SAD,[26] might be beneficial. However, this observation needs to be corroborated in future studies.

5. Conclusions and Future Treatment Options

The few studies that are currently available do not indicate that antidepressants are the treatment of choice for patients with RBD. Nevertheless, these studies should be viewed as preliminary, since no dose-finding studies have been carried out and since it is possible that the dosage chosen for patients with major depression might not be appropriate for those with RBD.

According to the literature, it would be logical to infer that patients with low serotonergic activity have a high likelihood of future suicide attempts,[30] a characteristic that is prominent in patients with RBD. It could therefore be concluded that these patients are candidates for treatment with SSRIs. However, the studies conducted with fluoxetine[24] and paroxetine[23] are not indicative of such a treatment response. Nevertheless, it could well be that a more specific approach, such as influencing distinct serotonergic receptor subtypes, might help to clarify the treatment options in this group of patients.

RBD has a high comorbidity with major depression. Since there is presently no evidence that antidepressants are effective in RBD, it seems worthwhile to differentiate between patients with RBD who do or do not have major depression. This is important because patients with combined depression (RBD plus major depression) might be responsive to antidepressants.

The antipsychotic flupenthixol has been shown to be beneficial in patients with recurrent suicidal acts, some of whom can probably be classified as having RBD.[22] This is significant, since general practitioners in Germany frequently use another antipsychotic, fluspirilene, at a dosage comparable with that used in the flupenthixol study, for the treatment of different states that they identify as 'psychic cases'. Since the epidemiological data indicate the high prevalence rate of RBD in primary care settings, it is likely that a substantial number of these patients might have RBD. It would, therefore, be interesting to further study the underlying biological abnormalities of RBD in an attempt to clarify whether the neuroendocrine or biochemical profile of patients with the disorder shows a pattern consistent with a hyperdopaminergic state. However, this question has, as yet, not been thoroughly studied. The study of Staner et al.[31] aimed to evaluate the validity of RBD by means of clinical and biological data. The results of their investigation suggest that RBD could be viewed as a subtype of affective disorder, since it shares many characteristics with major depression. The authors found that patients with RBD did not differ significantly from age-matched patients with major depression on the basis of dexamethasone nonsuppression, blunted thyroid-stimulating hormone response to thyrotropin-releasing hormone and shortening of REM sleep latency.

Lithium might be another option for the treatment of patients with RBD, since suicidality is a prominent clinical feature that has been shown to be positively influenced by lithium treatment.[32] However, this possibility should be pursued with caution since lithium itself has a low therapeutic range and a high toxicity if taken in overdose.

Another approach to the treatment of RBD would be to compare these patients with those who have rapid-cycling bipolar disorder. In these latter patients, antidepressants have also been reported to be ineffective and, moreover, have even been cited as inducing ultra-rapid cycling.[33] The treatment of choice for patients with rapid-cycling bipolar disorder is anti-convulsants, such as carbamazepine and valproic acid (sodium valproate), or calcium ant-agonists, such as nimodipine.[34] It would, therefore, be worthwhile to study these agents as candidates for the treatment of RBD.

In the evaluation of treatment outcome of brief depressive episodes, traditional measurements (such as the Hamilton Depression Rating Scale or MADRS) should not be the only assessment criteria. Other important efficacy criteria are the duration and severity of the episodes and the interval between episodes.

To date, there are limited data on the treatment of RBD. Of the antidepressants that are currently available, only fluoxetine, paroxetine and mianserin (at a low dosage) have been as-sessed in a large patient sample. A placebo-controlled treatment study has also been carried out with moclobemide, but the results are not yet available. Mirtazapine seems to be an option as demonstrated in a preliminary clinical observation.[24a] It is, therefore, premature to con-clude that antidepressants have no therapeutic effect in patients with RBD. Further studies are necessary to establish treatment recommendations. As for other treatments, exploratory open-label studies in carefully selected patient populations are needed before double-blind trials are carried out, a strategy that has not been forwarded sufficiently for this treatment indication. However, since patients with RBD have a substantial risk of suicide attempts, psychotropic agents that have a high toxicity (such as tri- or tetracyclic antidepressants[35]) can be ruled out as future treatments.

References

1. Angst J. The history and concept of recurrent brief depression. Eur Arch Psychiatry Clin Neurosci 1994; 244: 171-3
2. Pohl E. Die Melancholie nach dem neuesten Standpunkte der Physiologie und auf Grundlage klinischer Beobachtungen. Prague: Verlag JG Calve'schen Buchhandlung, 1852
3. Head H. Certain mental changes that accompany visceral disease. Brain 1901; 24: 345-429
4. Gregory MS. Transient attacks of manic-depressive insanity. Med Rec 1915; 88: 1040-4
5. Paskind HA. Brief attacks of manic-depressive depression. Arch Neurol Psychiatry (Chicago) 1929; 22: 123-34
6. Busse EW, Barnes RH, Silverman AJ, et al. Studies of the processes of aging, X: the strengths and weaknesses of psychic functioning in the aged. Am J Psychiatry 1955; 111: 896-901
7. Clayton PJ, Marten S, Davis MA, et al. Mood disorder in women professionals. J Affect Disord 1980; 2: 37-46
8. Montgomery SA, Roy D, Montgomery DB. The prevention of recurrent suicidal acts. Br J Clin Pharmacol 1983; 15: 183S-8S
9. Montgomery SA, Montgomery D, Baldwin D, et al. Intermittent 3-day depressions and suicidal behaviour. Neuropsychobiology 1989; 22: 128-34

10. Montgomery SA, Montgomery D, Baldwin D, et al. The duration, nature and recurrence rate of brief depressions. Prog Neuropsych Biol Psychiatry 1990; 14: 729-35
11. Angst J, Dobler-Mikola A. The Zurich Study. II. The continuum from normal to pathological depressive mood swings. Eur Arch Psychiatry Neurol Sci 1984; 234: 21-9
12. Angst J, Dobler-Mikola A. The Zurich Study. A prospective epidemiological study of depressive, neurotic and psychosomatic syndromes. IV. Recurrent and nonrecurrent brief depression. Eur Arch Psychiatry Neurol Sci 1985; 235: 408-16
13. Angst J, Merikangas KR, Scheidegger P, et al. Recurrent brief depression: a new subtype of affective disorder. J Affect Disord 1990; 19: 87-98
14. Kasper S, Ruhrmann S, Haase T, et al. Recurrent brief depression and its relationship to seasonal affective disorder. Eur Arch Psychiatry Clin Neurosci 1992; 242: 20-6
15. Kasper S, Ruhrmann S, Haase T, et al. Evidence for a seasonal form of recurrent brief depression (RBD-seasonal). Eur Arch Psychiatry Clin Neurosci 1994; 244: 205-10
16. World Health Organization. The ICD-10 classification of mental and behavioural disorders. Clinical descriptions and diagnostic guidelines. Geneva: World Health Organization, 1992
17. American Psychiatric Association. Diagnostic and statistical manual of mental disorders. 4th ed. Washington, DC: American Psychiatric Association, 1994
18. Weiller E, Boyer P, Lepine J-P, et al. Prevalence of recurrent brief depression in primary care. Eur Arch Psychiatry Clin Neurosci 1994; 244: 174-81
19. Weiller E, Lecrubier Y, Maier W, et al. The relevance of recurrent brief depression in primary care. A report from the WHO project on psychological problems in general health care conducted in 14 countries. Eur Arch Psychiatry Clin Neurosci 1994; 244: 182-9
20. Maier W, Herr R, Gänsicke M, et al. Recurrent brief depression in general practice. Clinical features, comorbidity with other disorders and need for treatment. Eur Arch Psychiatry Clin Neurosci 1994; 244: 196-204
21. Maier W, Herr R, Lichtermann D, et al. Brief depression among patients in general practice. Prevalence and variation by recurrence and severity. Eur Arch Psychiatry Clin Neurosci 1994; 244: 190-5
22. Montgomery SA, Montgomery D, McAuley R, et al. Maintenance therapy in repeat suicidal behaviour: a placebo controlled trial. Proceedings of the 10th International Congress for Suicide Prevention and Crisis Intervention; 1979 Jun 19; Ottawa, 227-9
23. Montgomery SA, Montgomery DB, Evans R. Pharmacological differences between brief and major depressions. Eur Neuropsychopharmacol 1993; 3 Suppl. 3: 214-5
24. Montgomery DB, Roberts A, Green M, et al. Lack of efficacy of fluoxetine in recurrent brief depression and suicidal attempts. Eur Arch Psychiatry Clin Neurosci 1994; 244: 211-5
24a. Stamenkovic M, Pezawas L, de Zwaan M, et al. Mirtazapine in recurrent brief depression. Int Clin Psycopharmacol 1998; 13: 39-40
25. American Psychiatric Association. Diagnostic and statistical manual of mental disorders. 3rd ed. rev. Washington, DC: American Psychiatric Association, 1987
26. Rosenthal NE, Sack DA, Gillin JC, et al. Seasonal affective disorder, a description of the syndrome and preliminary findings with light therapy. Arch Gen Psychiatry 1984; 41: 72-80
27. Montgomery SA, Asberg M. A new depression scale designed to be sensitive to change. Br J Psychiatry 1979; 134: 382-9
28. Teicher MH, Glod C, Cole JO. Emergence of intense suicidal preoccupation during fluoxetine treatment. Am J Psychiatry 1990; 147: 207-10
29. Kasper S, Fuger J, Möller HJ. Comparative efficacy of antidepressants. Drugs 1992: 43 Suppl. 2: 11-23
30. Kasper S, Schindler S, Neumeister A. Le risque de suicide dans la dépression et ses implications pour le traitement psychopharmacologique. Neuro-psy 1994 (numero special - Dec): 46-55
31. Staner L, De La Fuente JM, Kerkhofs M, et al. Biological and clinical features of recurrent brief depression: a comparison with major depressed and healthy subjects. J Affect Disord 1992; 26: 241-6
32. Thies-Flechtner K, Seibert W, Walther A, et al. Suizide bei rezidivprophylaktisch behandelten Patienten mit affektiven Psychosen. In: Müller-Oerlinghausen B, Berghöfer A, editors. Ziele und Ergebnisse der medikamentösen Prophylaxe affektiver Psychosen. Stuttgart: Georg Thieme Verlag, 1994: 61-4
33. Wehr TA, Goodwin FK. Rapid cycling in manic-depressives induced by tricyclic antidepressants. Arch Gen Psychiatry 1979; 36: 555-9
34. Post RM, Ketter TA, Pazzaglia PJ, et al. New developments in the use of anticonvulsants as mood stabilizers. Neuropsychobiology 1993; 27: 132-7
35. Henry JA. A fatal toxicity index for antidepressant poisoning. Acta Psychiatr Scand 1989; 80: 37-45

Correspondence: Prof. *Siegfried Kasper*, Department of General Psychiatry, University of Vienna, Währinger Gürtel 18-20, A-1090 Vienna, Austria.

Seasonal Affective Disorder
A Guide to Diagnosis and Management

Timo Partonen and *Jouko Lönnqvist*

National Public Health Institute, Department of Mental Health and Alcohol Research, Helsinki, Finland

1. Definition

Seasonal affective disorder (SAD) is characterised by recurrent depressive episodes. The subtypes described are winter SAD and summer SAD. Winter SAD occurs more frequently and constitutes a group of patients with more atypical than classical symptoms of depression. The episodes coincide with reduced hours of daylight during the winter season and disappear in summer. Given the greater frequency of winter SAD compared with the summer variant, this article will focus on winter SAD.

2. Pathogenesis

The lifetime prevalence of affective disorders is about 8%. Since 10% of all affective disorders and 15% of recurrent variants show seasonal recurrences, the risk of SAD is approximately 0.8% to 1.2% in the general population,[1] which agrees with recent findings from a community-based sample of 8098 interviewed individuals.[2] The seasonal changes in mood and behaviour tend to run in families and have a marked genetic predisposition.[3]

The decrease in the amount of daylight that occurs in winter can result in there being an insufficient amount of daylight to maintain optimal mood in some people. In healthy individuals, atypical symptoms of depression, such as an increased duration of sleep, increased appetite, bodyweight gain and carbohydrate craving, can be induced by low levels of illumination, such as those to which people are ordinarily exposed indoors.[4] The decreasing photoperiod is thought to induce the onset of a depressive episode in predisposed individuals. Patients with winter SAD in particular are assumed to be deprived of light and to crave it. The atypical symptoms that they experience in response to low light levels are closely associated with the recurrence of depressive episodes, as they often precede the onset of each episode.[5] In contrast, the development of common or typical symptoms of depression is not related to the onset nor influenced by unfavourable local weather conditions.[6] Atypical symptoms of depression may hence represent the key element of winter SAD.

In patients with winter SAD, the circadian cycle appears to be more variable across days, deviating more from 24 hours and peaking at more unstable times, than in healthy individuals.[7] There is additional evidence of phase delay in the timing of circadian rhythms in some patients with winter SAD. The circadian disturbances are thought to be a consequence of less consistent resetting of the circadian clock by light, being intensified by the relative shortage of light during winter and with aging.

3. Diagnosis

Winter SAD can be diagnosed using either the ICD-10 Classification of Mental and Behavioural Disorders[8] or the DSM-IV[9] system.

3.1 ICD-10

In ICD-10, SAD is recognised as a form of recurrent affective disorder (codes F31 orF33). For a diagnosis of SAD to be made, an individual should have had three or more episodes in consecutive years (table I).

3.2 DSM-IV

SAD was originally defined by Rosenthal et al.[10] as a syndrome in which depression developed during the autumn or winter and remitted the following spring or summer in at least 2 successive years. In addition to the recurrent depressive episodes, the patient had to show a history of major depressive or bipolar disorder. These operational formulations for the concept of SAD were ultimately transformed into the DSM-based diagnostic criteria for affective disorders with a seasonal pattern. For the diagnosis, two severe depressive episodes must have occurred in the previous 2 years (table II).

Table I. Diagnostic criteria for seasonal affective disorder (as defined in the tenth edition of the International Classification of Diseases)[8]

1. Three or more episodes of mood (affective) disorder must occur, with onset within the same 90-day period of the year, for 3 or more consecutive years
2. Remissions also occur within a particular 90-day period of the year
3. Seasonal episodes substantially outnumber any nonseasonal episodes that may occur

Table II. Diagnostic criteria for affective disorders with a seasonal pattern specifier (as defined in DSM-IV)[9]

Mood disorders, seasonal pattern specifier:

A. There has been a regular temporal relationship between the onset of major depressive episodes in bipolar I or bipolar II disorder or major depressive disorder, recurrence and a particular time of the year [e.g. regular appearance of the major depressive episode in the autumn (fall) or winter][a]

B. Full remissions (or a change from depression to mania or hypomania) also occur at a characteristic time of the year (e.g. depression disappears in the spring)

C. In the last 2 years, two major depressive episodes have occurred that demonstrate the temporal seasonal relationships defined in criteria A and B, and no nonseasonal major depressive episodes have occurred during that same period

D. Seasonal major depressive episodes (as described above) substantially outnumber the nonseasonal major depressive episodes that may have occurred over the individual's lifetime

a   Cases in which there is an obvious effect of seasonal-related psychosocial stressors (e.g. regularly being unemployed every winter) should not be included.

4. Clinical Picture

Similar to other types of depressive illness, winter SAD predominantly affects women. However, winter SAD is unlike most severe forms of major depressive disorder in that patients seldom require hospitalisation, have psychotic symptoms or are at risk of suicide.

The clinical features of winter SAD are rather consistent across series of patients from diverse cultures.[11-16] Not infrequently, patients with winter SAD present with somatic symptoms. Besides common depressive symptoms, more than half of patients have atypical symptoms of depression. Patients with winter SAD paradoxically report activation following carbohydrate ingestion, whereas healthy individuals often complain of sedation.[17] In addition, decreased activity and social withdrawal are frequent signs among patients with winter SAD (table III).

The onset of the first episode of winter SAD typically occurs between 20 and 30 years of age, but patients do not usually seek psychiatric attention until they are 35 to 45 years old. After the diagnosis and treatment, during a follow-up period of 2 to 11 years, less than half (35 to 42%) of patients will continue to have winter SAD and over a third (33 to 44%) will develop a nonseasonal pattern to their subsequent episodes.[18-20] The rest will have only mild symptoms or the disorder will resolve completely. The atypical symptoms of depression present early in the course of illness best predict the regular recurrence of seasonal episodes.[21]

Table III. Clinical picture of winter seasonal affective disorder as described by a number of studies[11-16]

Symptom	Subtype of symptom	No. of patients assessed	% of patients with symptom
Mood	Sadness	678	92
	Irritability	457	63
	Anxiety	632	87
Sleep	Increased	678	63
	Decreased	69	38
	Poor quality	360	65
Appetite	Increased	678	55
	Decreased	678	29
	Increased intake of carbohydrates	678	70
Bodyweight	Increased	632	57
	Decreased	632	18
Decreased activity		678	96
Decreased libido		490	65
Social withdrawal		142	98
Suicidal thoughts		74	43

The functional impairment associated with winter SAD is often worse than that associated with most chronic medical conditions.[22] Despite the depressive episodes seldom being severe enough to require absence from work, most individuals with winter SAD do experience disability at work and in their social relations. Frequent symptoms, such as daytime tiredness and fatigue, are of concern not only for work performance but also for public safety (as they may adversely affect, for example, driving ability). Hence, the efforts put into the detection and treatment of winter SAD are justified in primary and occupational healthcare settings.

5. Treatment

5.1 Drug Therapies

There have been 15 double-blind trials and 11 uncontrolled trials, involving a total of 646 patients, of drug therapies for winter SAD (tables IV and V).

5.1.1 Antidepressants

Four double-blind, placebo-controlled parallel trials have assessed the efficacy of anti-depressant drugs. Moclobemide,[50] a reversible inhibitor of monoamine oxidase A (RIMA), was no more effective than placebo in a 3-week trial of 31 patients.[23] In contrast, fluox-etine,[51] a selective serotonin (5-hydroxytryptamine; 5-HT) reuptake inhibitor (SSRI), was more effective than placebo when the clinical response to the 2 treatments was compared in a 5-week trial of 66 patients.[27] However, the drug was no more effective than placebo when assessed using the change in continuous outcome scores. Sertraline,[52] another SSRI, was more effective than placebo in an 8-week trial of 142 patients.[28] Citalopram,[53] also an SSRI, resulted in greater clinical benefit than placebo in a trial of 8 patients who were observed over 1 year.[54]

Table IV. Double-blind pharmacological trials in patients with winter seasonal affective disorder

Active drug	Design	No. of patients		Duration (wks)	Response rate (%)[a]			Ref.
		active drug	placebo		active drug	placebo	difference	
Placebo-controlled trials								
Moclobemide	Parallel	16	15	3	44	53	−9	23
Levodopa (+ carbidopa)	Parallel	11	12	2	36	42	−6	24
Propranolol	Parallel	12	11	2	NR	NR		25
Cyanocobalamin	Parallel	14	13	2	NR	NR		26
Fluoxetine	Parallel	34	32	5	59	34	25	27
Sertraline	Parallel	70	72	8	62	46	16	28
Melatonin	Parallel	3	5	3	100	20	80	29
Extracts of Maidhenhair tree	Parallel	9	8	10	NR	NR		30
Citalopram	Parallel	4	4	52	NR	NR		54
Melatonin	Crossover	6	6	1	NR	NR		31
Dexfenfluramine	Crossover	7	7	3	57	29	28	32
Atenolol	Crossover	19	19	1	21	16	5	33
Dexfenfluramine	Crossover	18	18	4	72	17	55	34
Tryptophan	Crossover	13	13	1	NR	NR		35
Direct comparative trial[b]								
Fluoxetine *vs* moclobemide	Parallel	18	11	6	44	64	−20	36

a Percentage of patients reaching a pre-set response criteria by study end.
b Figures for fluoxetine are given first, followed by those for moclobemide.
NR = not reported.

Table V. Uncontrolled pharmacological trials in patients with winter seasonal affective disorder

Active drug	No. of patients	Duration (wk)	Response rate (%)[a] of active drug	Ref.
Melatonin	17	1	18	37
Tranylcypromine	14	5	86	40
Moclobemide	5	4	100	41
Amfebutamone (bupropion)	15	5	68	42
Extracts of St John's wort	20	4	NR	43
Fluoxetine	10	6	NR	44
Tryptophan	14	2	64	45
Tryptophan	13	4	38	46
Fluoxetine	19	5	65	47
Mirtazapine	8	4	75	48
Reboxetine	11	6	100	49

a Percentage of patients reaching a pre-set response criteria by study end.
NR = not reported.

In addition, a double-blind active-control parallel trial compared 6 weeks' of treatment with fluoxetine or moclobemide in 29 patients (table IV).[36] The results suggest that both fluoxetine and moclobemide might be effective in treating winter SAD.

There have also been 7 uncontrolled trials that have investigated the effect of anti-depressants from a number of classes in patients with SAD (see table V). In a 6-week trial, fluoxetine was compared with light therapy.[47] The results of this study indicate that both treatments are equally effective in patients with winter SAD. Open trials of tranylcypromine[40] and amfebutamone (bupropion)[42] reported a very good response rate, while a trial of moclobemide suggested an excellent response in a small sample of patients.[41] The results of open trials of St John's wort[43] and fluoxetine[44] were promising and indicate that further investigation of these agents is warranted.

There have been five case reports of treatments for winter SAD, describing a good response within 2 weeks of initiation of treatment with the TCA nortriptyline[55] and the SSRI citalopram.[56] In contrast, there was no response to monotherapy with the TCA doxepin, but a response was achieved 5 days after the addition of lithium.[55] A trial of the tricyclic antidepressant (TCA) desipramine found an initial response, followed by a relapse 2 to 4 months later.[39] Alprazolam, a short-acting triazolo-benzodiazepine, alleviated symptoms in about 3 days, with initial elevation of mood followed by euthymia about 2 weeks later.[38] In a postal survey of 301 patient association members, St John's wort improved the quality of sleep after 8 weeks.[57]

5.1.2 Other Drugs

In a double-blind, placebo-controlled parallel trial of 23 patients, propranolol, a short-acting nonselective β-adrenoceptor blocker, was effective at reducing depressive symptoms and maintaining the remission obtained.[25] In contrast, atenolol, a long-acting but less lipophilic β-blocker, failed to reduce the depressive symptoms in 19 patients in a double-blind, placebo-controlled crossover trial.[33]

Six other double-blind, placebo-controlled crossover trials, involving a total of 69 patients, have assessed the efficacy of a number of other drugs in patients with winter SAD. Efficacy was demonstrated in only half of these trials, pointing to efficacy for dexfenfluramine, a serotonin-releasing agent (table IV).[32,34] However, given recent concerns about the safety of this agent, it is unlikely to become a standard treatment for winter SAD.

The efficacy of melatonin has been studied in a 3-week, double-blind, placebo-controlled trial of 8 patients[29] and in a 1-week open trial of 17 patients.[37] The former study (0.125mg twice, 4 hours apart, in the afternoon) showed that melatonin improved mood, but the latter one demonstrated that melatonin has no therapeutic effect on depressive symptoms in patients with winter SAD when given at the same dosage (i.e. 5 mg/day) as is used in the treatment of circadian rhythm–related sleep disorders.

In summary, there is evidence to suggest that several drugs might be effective in the treatment of winter SAD. However, most of the pharmacological trials have involved relatively small sample sizes and short periods of assessment. In general, the results of these trials should be interpreted with caution. Specifically, there are confounding factors related to the design of the trials, including an ordering effect in five of the 15 controlled trials, differences in expectations after the crossover, and relapses during the washout. As a result, there is no consensus about the drug of choice for winter SAD. Nevertheless, results from the controlled trials can

Table VI. Summary of recommendations for the use of drugs that have been assessed for the treatment of winter seasonal affective disorder

Recommended	Efficacy unresolved	Rejected
Sertraline	Amfebutamone	Atenolol
Fluoxetine	(bupropion)	Cyanocobalamin
Moclobemide	Citalopram	Extracts of
		Maidenhair tree
	Extracts of St John's wort[a]	Levodopa (+ carbidopa)
	Melatonin	
	Mirtazapine	
	Tryptophan[a]	
	Propranolol	
	Reboxetine	
	Tranylcypromine	
a Probably best as an adjunct to another active treatment.		

be used to form some treatment recommendations (see table VI).

In recent studies, there has been no evidence of abnormal hormonal responses to 5-hydroxytryptophan[58] (a precursor of serotonin), fenfluramine,[59] or ipsapirone (a partial agonist at serotonin 5-HT$_{1A}$ receptors)[60] in patients with winter SAD. However, the administration of *m*-chlorophenylpiperazine, a metabolite of the antidepressant drug trazodone, results in abnormally exaggerated hormonal responses, and activation and euphoria, and that of sumatriptan, a 5-HT$_{1D}$ receptor agonist, in abnormally blunted hormonal responses among such patients.[61,62] Short term tryptophan depletion rapidly leads to a depressive relapse in patients with treated (remitted) winter SAD.[63,64] The depletion results similarly in a rapid relapse in untreated (recovered) patients with recurrent major depression,[65] but a different, more inert, response among untreated (depressed) patients with major depressive disorder.[66] These findings suggest that serotonergic drugs such as the SSRIs may be effective in the treatment of winter SAD.

The efficacy of propranolol in winter SAD is suggested to depend on the resulting suppression of melatonin synthesis in the pineal gland. On the other hand, the effects could be mediated via the action of the drug on serotonergic receptors.[67] Similarly, the rapid response to alprazolam[38] might be related to its serotonergic effects rather than simply to the suppression of plasma melatonin levels[68] or its binding to benzodiazepine receptors. There is experimental evidence to suggest that alprazolam facilitates serotonergic neurotransmission and decreases the activity of β-adrenergic receptors in the CNS.[69]

A depressive disorder that has atypical symptoms, such as SAD, has a unique profile and may have a distinct treatment response. Patients with atypical symptoms of depression show a more pronounced hormonal response to desipramine than patients with common symptoms, suggesting less impairment of the noradrenergic system in the former.[70] Noradrenergic drugs might therefore be less effective in the treatment of patients with atypical symptoms. This suggestion is in agreement with the results from the pharmacological trial with desipramine.[39] Whether other relatively selective noradrenaline (norepinephrine) reuptake inhibitors or noradrenergic drugs in general would or would not be clinically useful in the treatment of winter SAD remains to be investigated.

5.2 Light Therapies

Bright light treatment is a mode of therapy that has various medical applications and is rapidly gaining in popularity. It involves the administration of artificial visible light with illuminance of at least 2500lx at eye level. Lux is a unit of illumination, with 1lx being equal to the illumination produced by luminous flux of 1 lumen falling perpendicularly on a surface 1m². Illumination is usually 100lx or less in houses and 300 to 500lx in workplaces. Outdoors, the level of illumination varies greatly with the latitude, season, time of day and weather conditions, ranging from 1000lx or less on a rainy day, through 1000 to 10 000lx in unsettled weather to 10 000lx or more in direct sunshine.

The effects of light therapy are thought to be mediated exclusively by the eyes. The patient's face therefore needs to be bathed in the light and he/she needs to keep his/her eyes open during the treatment session.

A meta-analysis was performed of light therapy in 332 patients with winter SAD.[71] The most effective regimen tested was morning light of 2500lx administered from a light box device in at least 2-hour daily sessions for at least 1 week. Recent studies on the use of higher intensity (up to 10 000lx) and shorter duration (down to 0.5 hour) of light exposure have resulted in an equivalent response rate.[72] The administration of light in the morning is more effective than at other times of the day.[73]

According to the review by Terman et al.,[71] morning bright light therapy resulted in a clinical response in 67% of patients with mild depressive episodes and in 40% of those with moderate to severe episodes. This effect corresponded to the efficacy of antidepressant drugs in the treatment of depression. The clinical response rate of dim light (a control condition) was 11%.[71] Adverse effects, such as eyestrain and headache, appear to be frequent, but are temporary and well tolerated and seldom result in the cessation of therapy. Patients aged over 40 years are most likely to experience adverse effects of light therapy.[74]

The efficacy of recently developed light devices, such as the dawn simulator or the light visor, has been disappointing, but they may be of use as options for augmentation strategies.

5.3 Psychological Therapies

There are no studies on the efficacy of psychological therapies in patients with winter SAD. From a theoretical point of view, the most effective treatments are likely to include behavioural, cognitive, interpersonal and problem-solving therapies. All four therapies have been used for the management of depressed patients. Problem-solving therapy, with a short duration,[75] could be useful for the clinician working in primary care.

6. Management

6.1 First-Line Option

Light therapy is the treatment of choice for the management of patients with winter SAD. The clinical response to the daily administration of light is usually observed within 1 to 2 weeks of the onset of treatment. Continuing light therapy throughout the season is recommended to prevent relapse and optimise outcome.[76] The light therapy need not necessarily be administered daily over the winter: sessions carried out at least 5 times a week can maintain the therapeutic effect.[77]

The presence of atypical symptoms of depression, rather than the severity of a depressive episode, best predict treatment outcome.[78] A good response to light therapy is best predicted by the pre-treatment presence of an increased level of sleepiness[74] and an increased duration of sleep,[78-80] increased appetite,[79,80] carbohydrate craving,[78,81] variation in energy or mood (being worse in the evenings than mornings)[78] and a small extent of variation,[82] and an increased level of melatonin late in the evening.[83] In addition, patients who are susceptible to motion sickness are likely to respond better to light therapy than those who are resistant to this disorder.[84]

Bright light is easily administered with a standard light box in the patient's home. The therapeutic effect of light therapy needs to be ascertained before patients are encouraged to purchase a light therapy apparatus for their own use. Alternatively, light therapy can be administered at outpatient services in a room that is furnished specially for the treatment.

Because of the well recognised adverse effects of long term exposure to ultraviolet radiation, light therapy is recommended using sources that do not emit ultraviolet radiation or that have had this band of the spectrum filtered. As light therapy is becoming increasingly popular, patients who use light therapy devices at home and those without close supervision need to be informed about the possibility of adverse effects. No eye damage has been reported with treatment of up to 6 years duration,[85] and therefore light therapy seems to be fairly well tolerated. However, the occurrence of subthreshold photochemical damage in the eyes cannot be ruled out when light sources are used for long periods of time. Therefore, patients at risk of light-induced lesions, such as those with pre-existing retinal or eye disease (e.g. retinal detachments, retinitis pigmentosa, glaucoma), systemic illnesses that affect the retina (e.g. diabetes mellitus), or previous cataract surgery and lens removal, should be advised to consult an ophthalmologist for follow-up examinations during light therapy.

6.2 Second-Line Options

If there is no therapeutic response to light therapy or the patient prefers another treatment, the prescription of an antidepressant drug is recommended as the second-line treatment for winter SAD. The most appropriate choice would be an SSRI or moclobemide. If the patient has insomnia, he/she should be prescribed a drug that does not reduce levels of melatonin, e.g. fluvoxamine is preferred to fluoxetine.[44]

The dosages of antidepressants should be similar to those used in the treatment of major depression. However, the duration of treatment in patients with SAD is often shorter than that required in other indications.

It is possible to combine light therapy with an antidepressant, and no adverse interactions with this combination have been reported.[86,87] Indeed, the risk of ocular phototoxicity is relatively low with the use of antidepressant drugs, such as fluoxetine or imipramine, as measured by the degree of experimental photodestruction of lens proteins.[88]

In the rare instance when a patient needs to be hospitalised, he/she would greatly benefit from a brightly lit room, since the stay in a sunny hospital room may expedite recovery from a severe depressive episode.[89] A daily morning walk in the sunshine might also be helpful.[90] If necessary, all methods applied to the treatment of affective disorders should be available for the treatment of hospitalised patients with winter SAD. For example, as in the treatment of the most severe depressive episodes, electroconvulsive therapy should be considered for severe cases of SAD. However, no specific data on the efficacy of ECT in winter SAD are available.

6.3 Comorbid Disorders

Comorbidity of disorders is a frequent phenomenon in medicine in general and psychiatry in particular. Such mixed disorders usually make the search for the primary disorder more difficult and management more complicated. Comorbid disorders influence the clinical picture of winter SAD by modulating the course of illness, and each may require specific intervention.

Patients with winter SAD who also have a personality disorder are less likely to respond to light therapy than patients without any pathology in personality.[91] Patients with comorbid personality disorders should be referred to a psychiatrist at the beginning of treatment. In contrast, a comorbid anxiety disorder predicts a good response to light therapy in patients with winter SAD.[92] These patients can be treated very well in primary care, and the effective use of light therapy can often obviate the need for benzodiazepines.

7. Conclusion

The most effective treatment for patients with winter SAD is exposure to light of 2500lx or over in the morning. This treatment is usually administered using a light box. New innovative light devices have been developed, but their clinical advantages are unclear at present. The presence of atypical symptoms of depression predicts a good response to light therapy. Continuing treatment throughout the winter season is advisable to prevent relapse. Those patients at risk of light-induced eye damage should consult an ophthalmologist for follow-up examinations during light treatment. Antidepressant drugs are a relatively unexplored treatment for winter SAD, but preliminary data from controlled trials suggest that several pharmaceuticals may be effective. While the treatment of choice for winter SAD is light therapy, all methods of treatment should be considered, when the treatment response is not optimal.

References

1. Faedda GL, Tondo L, Teicher MH, et al. Seasonal mood disorders: patterns of seasonal recurrence in mania and depression. Arch Gen Psychiatry 1993; 50: 17-23
2. Blazer DG, Kessler RC, Swartz MS. Epidemiology of recurrent major and minor depression with a seasonal pattern: the National Comorbidity Survey. Br J Psychiatry 1998; 172: 164-7
3. Madden PAF, Heath AC, Rosenthal NE, et al. Seasonal changes in mood and behavior: the role of genetic factors. Arch Gen Psychiatry 1996; 53: 47-55
4. Espiritu RC, Kripke DF, Ancoli-Israel S, et al. Low illumination experienced by San Diego adults: association with atypical depressive symptoms. Biol Psychiatry 1994; 35: 403-7
5. Young MA, Watel LG, Lahmeyer HW, et al. The temporal onset of individual symptoms in winter depression: differentiating underlying mechanisms. J Affect Disord 1991; 22: 191-7
6. Molin J, Mellerup E, Bolwig T, et al. The influence of climate on development of winter depression. J Affect Disord 1996; 37: 151-5
7. Teicher MH, Glod CA, Magnus E, et al. Circadian rest-activity disturbances in seasonal affective disorder. Arch Gen Psychiatry 1997; 54: 124-30
8. World Health Organization. The ICD-10 classification of mental and behavioural disorders: diagnostic criteria for research. Geneva: World Health Organization, 1993
9. American Psychiatric Association. Diagnostic and statistical manual of mental disorders. 4th ed. Washington, DC: American Psychiatric Press, 1994
10. Rosenthal NE, Sack DA, Gillin JC, et al. Seasonal affective disorder: a description of the syndrome and preliminary findings with light therapy. Arch Gen Psychiatry 1984; 41: 72-80
11. Thompson C, Isaacs G. Seasonal affective disorder: a British sample: symptomatology in relation to mode of referral and diagnostic subtype. J Affect Disord 1988; 14: 1-11
12. Boyce P, Parker G. Seasonal affective disorder in the southern hemisphere. Am J Psychiatry 1988; 145: 96-9
13. Hellekson C. Phenomenology of seasonal affective disorder: an Alaskan perspective. In: Rosenthal NE, Blehar MC, editors. Seasonal affective disorders and phototherapy. New York: The Guilford Press, 1989: 33-45
14. Lam RW, Buchanan A, Remick RA. Seasonal affective disorder: a Canadian sample. Ann Clin Psychiatry 1989; 1: 241-5
15. Sakamoto K, Kamo T, Nakadaira S, et al. A nationwide survey of seasonal affective disorder at 53 outpatient university clinics in Japan. Acta Psychiatr Scand 1993; 87: 258-65
16. Rosenthal NE. Diagnosis and treatment of seasonal affective disorder. JAMA 1993; 270: 2717-20
17. Rosenthal NE, Genhart MJ, Caballero B, et al. Psychobiological effects of carbohydrate- and protein-rich meals in patients with seasonal affective disorder and normal controls. Biol Psychiatry 1989; 25: 1029-40
18. Leonhardt G, Wirz-Justice A, Kräuchi K, et al. Long-term follow-up of depression in seasonal affective disorder. Compr Psychiatry 1994; 35: 457-64
19. Thompson C, Raheja SK, King EA. A follow-up study of seasonal affective disorder. Br J Psychiatry 1995; 167: 380-4
20. Schwartz PJ, Brown C, Wehr TA, et al. Winter seasonal affective disorder: a follow-up study of the first 59 patients of the National Institute of Mental Health seasonal studies program. Am J Psychiatry 1996; 153: 1028-36
21. Sakamoto K, Nakadaira S, Kamo K, et al. A longitudinal follow-up study of seasonal affective disorder. Am J Psychiatry 1995; 152: 862-8
22. Schlager D, Froom J, Jaffe A. Winter depression and functional impairment among ambulatory primary care patients. Compr Psychiatry 1995; 36: 18-24
23. Lingjaerde O, Reichborn-Kjennerud T, Haggag A, et al. Treatment of winter depression in Norway: II: a comparison of the selective monoamine oxidase A inhibitor moclobemide and placebo. Acta Psychiatr Scand 1993; 88: 372-80
24. Oren DA, Moul DE, Schwartz PJ, et al. A controlled trial of levodopa plus carbidopa in the treatment of winter seasonal affective disorder: a test of the dopamine hypothesis. J Clin Psychopharmacol 1994; 14: 196-200
25. Schlager DS. Early-morning administration of short-acting β-blockers for treatment of winter depression. Am J Psychiatry 1994; 151: 1383-5
26. Oren DA, Teicher MH, Schwartz PJ, et al. A controlled trial of cyanocobalamin (Vitamin B$_{12}$) in the treatment of winter seasonal affective disorder. J Affect Disord 1994; 32: 197-200
27. Lam RW, Gorman CP, Michalon M, et al. Multicenter, placebo-controlled study of fluoxetine in seasonal affective disorder. Am J Psychiatry 1995; 152: 1765-70
28. Moscovitch A, Blashko C, Wiseman R, et al. A double-blind, placebo-controlled study of sertraline in the treatment of outpatients with seasonal affective disorder [abstract]. 148th Annual Meeting of the American Psychiatric Association, 1995 May 20-25; Miami
29. Lewy AJ, Bauer VK, Cutler NL, et al. Melatonin treatment of winter depression: a pilot study. Psychiatry Res 1998; 77: 57-61

30. Lingjaerde O, Foreland AR, Magnusson A. Can winter depression be prevented by *Ginkgo biloba* extract? A placebo-controlled trial. Acta Psychiatr Scand 1999; 100: 62-6
31. Sherer MA, Weingartner H, James SP, et al. Effects of melatonin on performance testing in patients with seasonal affective disorder. Neurosci Lett 1985; 58: 277-82
32. O'Rourke DA, Wurtman JJ, Brzezinski A, et al. Serotonin implicated in etiology of seasonal affective disorder. Psychopharmacol Bull 1987; 23: 358-9
33. Rosenthal NE, Jacobsen FM, Sack DA, et al. Atenolol in seasonal affective disorder: a test of the melatonin hypothesis. Am J Psychiatry 1988; 145: 52-6
34. O'Rourke D, Wurtman JJ, Wurtman RJ, et al. Treatment of seasonal depression with *d*-fenfluramine. J Clin Psychiatry 1989; 50: 343-7
35. McGrath RE, Buckwald B, Resnick EV. The effect of L-tryptophan on seasonal affective disorder. J Clin Psychiatry 1990; 51: 162-3
36. Partonen T, Lönnqvist J. Moclobemide and fluoxetine in treatment of seasonal affective disorder. J Affect Disord 1996; 41: 93-9
37. Wirz-Justice A, Graw P, Kräuchi K, et al. Morning or night-time melatonin is ineffective in seasonal affective disorder. J Psychiatr Res 1990; 24: 129-37
38. Teicher MH, Glod CA. Seasonal affective disorder: rapid resolution by low-dose alprazolam. Psychopharmacol Bull 1990; 26: 197-202
39. Dilsaver SC, Del Medico VJ, Quadri A, et al. Pharmacological responsiveness of winter depression. Psychopharmacol Bull 1990; 26: 303-9
40. Dilsaver SC, Jaeckle RS. Winter depression responds to an open trial of tranylcypromine. J Clin Psychiatry 1990; 51: 326-9
41. Lingjaerde O, Haggag A. Moclobemide in winter depression: some preliminary results from an open trial. Nord J Psychiatry 1992; 46: 201-3
42. Dilsaver SC, Qamar AB, Del Medico VJ. The efficacy of bupropion in winter depression: results of an open trial. J Clin Psychiatry 1992; 53: 252-5
43. Martinez B, Kasper S, Ruhrmann S, et al. Hypericum in the treatment of seasonal affective disorders. J Geriatr Psychiatry Neurol 1994; 7 Suppl. 1: S29-33
44. Childs PA, Rodin I, Martin NJ, et al. Effect of fluoxetine on melatonin in patients with seasonal affective disorder and matched controls. Br J Psychiatry 1995; 166: 196-8
45. Lam RW, Levitan RD, Tam EM, et al. L-tryptophan augmentation of light therapy in patients with seasonal affective disorder. Can J Psychiatry 1997; 42: 303-6
46. Ghadirian A-M, Murphy BEP, Gendron M-J. Efficacy of light versus tryptophan therapy in seasonal affective disorder. J Affect Disord 1998; 50: 23-7
47. Ruhrmann S, Kasper S, Hawellek B, et al. Effects of fluoxetine versus bright light in the treatment of seasonal affective disorder. Psychol Med 1998; 28: 923-33
48. Heßelmann B, Habeler A, Praschak-Rieder N, et al. Mirtazapine in seasonal affective disorder (SAD): a preliminary report. Hum Psychopharmacol 1999; 14: 59-62
49. Hilger E, Willeit M, Praschak-Rieder N, et al. Rapid remission of atypical depressive symptoms with selective noradrenalin reuptake inhibitor reboxetine in SAD patients. Eur Neuropsychopharmacol 1999; 9 Suppl. 5: S243
50. Fitton A, Faulds D, Goa KL. Moclobemide: a review of its pharmacological properties and therapeutic use in depressive illness. Drugs 1992; 43: 561-96
51. Gram LF. Drug therapy: fluoxetine. N Engl J Med 1994; 331: 1354-61
52. Murdoch D, McTavish D. Sertraline: a review of its pharmacodynamic and pharmacokinetic properties, and therapeutic potential in depression and obsessive-compulsive disorder. Drugs 1992; 44: 604-24
53. Milne RJ, Goa KL. Citalopram: a review of its pharmacodynamic and pharmacokinetic properties, and therapeutic potential in depressive illness. Drugs 1991; 41: 450-77
54. Thorell LH, Kjellman B, Arned M, et al. Light treatment of seasonal affective disorder in combination with citalopram or placebo with 1-year follow-up. Int Clin Psychopharmacol 1999; 14 Suppl. 2: S7-11
55. Pande AC. Pharmacological treatments of SAD [letter]. Can J Psychiatry 1990; 35: 721-2
56. Wirz-Justice A, van der Velde P, Bucher A, et al. Comparison of light treatment with citalopram in winter depression: a longitudinal single case study. Int Clin Psychopharmacol 1992; 7: 109-16
57. Wheatley D. Hypericum in seasonal affective disorder (SAD). Curr Med Res Opin 1999; 15: 33-7
58. Jacobsen FM, Sack DA, Wehr TA, et al. Neuroendocrine response to 5-hydroxytryptophan in seasonal affective disorder. Arch Gen Psychiatry 1987; 44: 1086-91
59. Yatham LN, Michalon M. Hormonal responses to *dl*-fenfluramine challenge are not blunted in seasonal affective disorder. Psychoneuroendocrinology 1995; 20: 433-8
60. Schwartz PJ, Turner EH, Garcia-Borreguero D, et al. Serotonin hypothesis of winter depression: behavioral and neuroendocrine effects of the 5-HT1A receptor partial agonist ipsapirone in patients with seasonal affective disorder and healthy control subjects. Psychiatry Res 1999; 86: 9-28
61. Schwartz PJ, Murphy DL, Wehr TA, et al. Effects of *meta*-chlorophenylpiperazine infusions in patients with seasonal affective disorder and healthy control subjects. Arch Gen Psychiatry 1997; 54: 375-85
62. Yatham LN, Lam RW, Zis AP. Growth hormone response to sumatriptan (5-HT1D agonist) challenge in seasonal affective disorder: effects of light therapy. Biol Psychiatry 1997; 42: 24-9
63. Lam RW, Zis AP, Grewal A, et al. Effects of rapid tryptophan depletion in patients with seasonal affective disorder in remission after light therapy. Arch Gen Psychiatry 1996; 53: 41-4
64. Neumeister A, Praschak-Rieder N, Hesselmann B, et al. Effects of tryptophan depletion on drug-free patients with seasonal affective disorder during a stable response to bright light therapy. Arch Gen Psychiatry 1997; 54: 133-8
65. Smith KA, Fairburn CG, Cowen PJ. Relapse of depression after rapid depletion of tryptophan. Lancet 1997; 349: 915-9
66. Delgado PL, Price LH, Miller HL, et al. Serotonin and the neurobiology of depression: effects of tryptophan depletion in drug-free depressed patients. Arch Gen Psychiatry 1994; 51: 865-74
67. Pazos A, Engel G, Palacios JM. β-Adrenoceptor blocking agents recognize a subpopulation of serotonin receptors in brain. Brain Res 1985; 343: 403-8
68. McIntyre IM, Burrows GD, Norman TR. Suppression of plasma melatonin by a single dose of the benzodiazepine alprazolam in humans. Biol Psychiatry 1988; 24: 105-8
69. Sevy S, Brown SL, Wetzler S, et al. Effects of alprazolam on increases in hormonal and anxiety levels induced by meta-chlorophenylpiperazine. Psychiatry Res 1994; 53: 219-29
70. Asnis GM, McGinn LK, Sanderson WC. Atypical depression: clinical aspects and noradrenergic function. Am J Psychiatry 1995; 152: 31-6

71. Terman M, Terman JS, Quitkin FM, et al. Light therapy for seasonal affective disorder: a review of efficacy. Neuropsychopharmacology 1989; 2: 1-22
72. Terman JS, Terman M, Schlager D, et al. Efficacy of brief, intense light exposure for treatment of winter depression. Psychopharmacol Bull 1990; 26: 3-11
73. Terman M, Terman JS, Ross DC. A controlled trial of timed bright light and negative air ionization for treatment of winter depression. Arch Gen Psychiatry 1998; 55: 875-82
74. Partonen T. Effects of morning light treatment on subjective sleepiness and mood in winter depression. J Affect Disord 1994; 30: 47-56
75. Mynors-Wallis LM, Gath DH, Lloyd-Thomas AR, et al. Randomised controlled trial comparing problem solving treatment with amitriptyline and placebo for major depression in primary care. BMJ 1995; 310: 441-5
76. Partonen T, Lönnqvist J. Prevention of winter seasonal affective disorder by bright-light treatment. Psychol Med 1996; 26: 1075-80
77. Partonen T, Lönnqvist J. The influence of comorbid disorders and of continuation light treatment on remission and recurrence in winter depression. Psychopathology 1995; 28: 256-62
78. Terman M, Amira L, Terman JS, et al. Predictors of response and nonresponse to light treatment for winter depression. Am J Psychiatry 1996; 153: 1423-9
79. Oren DA, Jacobsen FM, Wehr TA, et al. Predictors of response to phototherapy in seasonal affective disorder. Compr Psychiatry 1992; 33: 111-4
80. Lam RW. Morning light therapy for winter depression: predictors of response. Acta Psychiatr Scand 1994; 89: 97-101
81. Kräuchi K, Wirz-Justice A, Graw P. High intake of sweets late in the day predicts a rapid and persistent response to light therapy in winter depression. Psychiatry Res 1993; 46: 107-17
82. Meesters Y, Jansen JHC, Lambers PA, et al. Morning and evening light treatment of seasonal affective disorder: response, relapse and prediction. J Affect Disord 1993; 28: 165-77
83. Partonen T, Vakkuri O, Lamberg-Allardt C, et al. Effects of bright light on sleepiness, melatonin, and 25-hydroxyvitamin D3 in winter seasonal affective disorder. Biol Psychiatry 1996; 39: 865-72
84. Mirabile Jr CS, Glueck BC. Separation of affective disorder into seasonal and nonseasonal types using motion sickness susceptibility as a marker. J Neuropsychiatry Clin Neurosci 1993; 5: 330-4
85. Gallin PF, Terman M, Remé CE, et al. Ophthalmologic examination of patients with seasonal affective disorder, before and after bright light therapy. Am J Ophthalmol 1995; 119: 202-10
86. Levitt AJ, Joffe RT, Kennedy SH. Bright light augmentation in antidepressant nonresponders. J Clin Psychiatry 1991; 52: 336-7
87. Beauchemin KM, Hays P. Phototherapy is a useful adjunct in the treatment of depressed inpatients. Acta Psychiatr Scand 1997; 95: 424-7
88. Roberts JE, Remé CE, Dillon J, et al. Exposure to bright light and the concurrent use of photosensitizing drugs [letter]. N Engl J Med 1992; 326: 1500-1
89. Beauchemin KM, Hays P. Sunny hospital rooms expedite recovery from severe and refractory depressions. J Affect Disord 1996; 40: 49-51
90. Wirz-Justice A, Graw P, Kräuchi K, et al. 'Natural' light treatment of seasonal affective disorder. J Affect Disord 1996; 37: 109-20
91. Reichborn-Kjennerud T, Lingjaerde O. Response to light therapy in seasonal affective disorder: personality disorders and temperament as predictors of outcome. J Affect Disord 1996; 41: 101-10
92. Levitt AJ, Joffe RT, Brecher D, et al. Anxiety disorders and anxiety symptoms in a clinic sample of seasonal and non-seasonal depressives. J Affect Disord 1993; 28: 51-6

Correspondence: Dr *Timo Partonen*, National Public Health Institute, Department of Mental Health and Alcohol Research, Mannerheimintie 166, FIN-00300 Helsinki, Finland.

Mixed Anxiety and Depression
Diagnosis and Treatment Options

David Bakish,[1-3] *Rami Habib*[1,2] and *Cynthia L. Hooper*[2,3]

1   Department of Psychiatry, University of Ottawa, Ottawa, Ontario, Canada
2   Psychopharmacology Unit, Royal Ottawa Hospital, Ottawa, Ontario, Canada
3   Institute of Mental Health Research, Royal Ottawa Hospital, Ottawa, Ontario, Canada

1. Epidemiology

Symptoms of anxiety and depression typically coexist in patients seen in clinical practice. The National Institute of Mental Health Epidemiologic Catchment Area Study[1] found that the majority (75%) of people who had had a depressive episode at sometime during their lifetime also had a history of another psychiatric disorder. This study also demonstrated that major depressive episodes often co-occur with other disorders. The US National Comorbidity Survey[2] also found high rates of comorbidity: 58% of respondents with lifetime depression also had an anxiety disorder, 39% had a substance abuse disorder and 74% had one or more disorders. In fact, 32% of individuals had three or more comorbid disorders. Many other studies of comorbid symptomatology have identified similarly high rates.[3-10] Therefore, it may be suggested that comorbidity is the rule rather than the exception.

There is ample evidence to suggest that patients with symptoms of both anxiety and depression show greater overall psychopathology and are more chronically ill, show greater social and occupational impairment, have a higher statistical probability of suicide and have a poorer prognosis than those who have only a single disorder.[9,11,12] The need for concise diagnosis and appropriate treatment options is clear.

2. Diagnosis

There are several ways of conceptualising the interaction of anxiety and depressive symptoms in patients. Anxiety and depression can be seen as discrete disorders, with differences in diagnosis, prognosis and treatment. Boulenger and Lavallée[13] proposed the following four categories of patients who present with overlapping features of anxiety and depression:
- patients who have both anxiety and depressive symptoms, but who have never fulfilled the criteria for these diagnoses as defined by DSM-III-R[14]
- patients with both an anxiety and depressive disorder diagnosis as defined by DSM-III-R
- patients with either an anxiety or depressive disorder diagnosis as defined by DSM-III-R, associated respectively with depressive or anxiety symptoms
- patients who have chronic anxiety and depressive symptoms and who do not fulfil criteria for these diagnoses as defined by DSM-IV,[15] but who have a history of past anxiety and/or depressive disorders.

This classification of co-existing anxiety and depressive states includes the simultaneous diagnosis of major depression or dysthymia with one of the distinct anxiety disorders [generalised anxiety disorder (GAD), panic disorder, obsessive-compulsive disorder (OCD) or phobic disorder].[13] This classification excludes patients who have chronic and stable features of both anxiety and depression, but in whom neither set of symptoms is of sufficient severity to lead to a diagnosis of either an anxiety or depressive disorder.

There are several problems with this dichotomous conceptualisation, most notably the inconsistency with what is seen in clinical practice. Most clinicians and researchers agree that the majority of patients present with symptoms of both depression and anxiety, and frequently fall into more than one diagnostic category. If a patient is experiencing both depressive and panic symptoms, should a diagnosis of primary depressive disorder and secondary panic disorder be made? Are the disorders equal in importance and impact? Or, are the panic symptoms merely an aspect of the depression? Hamilton[16] clearly identified anxiety symptoms as the rule in depressive illness. They may wane once treatment begins, but residual anxiety symptoms may be indicators of a risk for relapse.[17]

Another option is to consider co-existing depressive and anxiety symptoms as a unique disorder. Instead of considering anxiety symptoms in the depressed patient as a comorbid secondary illness, patients are seen as having both sets of symptoms simultaneously.[18] The concept of 'subsyndromal' symptoms is also considered under this conceptualisation. It posits that people can have long term, stable symptoms of depression and anxiety that never reach a severe enough level to warrant a diagnosis of an anxiety or depressive illness. Only under stress will the symptoms evolve into a specific disorder. This is of interest to researchers as these individuals may be at a higher risk for affective and anxiety problems.

The ICD-10 manual for clinical descriptions and diagnostic instructions[19] introduced the diagnostic category of mixed anxiety and depressive disorder (MADD) for patients who simultaneously exhibit symptoms of anxiety and depression, but who do not meet the defining criteria for another psychiatric disorder. This category is therefore likely to include many patients who would presently be considered to have subsyndromal anxiety or depression. ICD-10 defines MADD as a syndrome consisting of a mixture of anxiety and depressive symptoms of equal importance associated with at least some autonomic symptoms such as tremor, palpitations and stomach churning. It implies that the majority of cases are seen in primary care settings or in the general population.

In concert with ICD-10, the appendix of the DSM-IV defines MADD as a clinical syndrome characterised by the equal presence of both anxiety and depressive symptoms, neither of which reaches diagnostic threshold for an established disorder.[15] At least four of the symptoms shown in table I must be present and accompanied by dysphoric mood of at least 1 month's duration.

Given the recent incorporation of MADD into official classification systems, the prevalence, risk factors, course and outcome of MADD have not been fully evaluated. Some studies have indicated that MADD could be common, with a point prevalence of around 10%,[6] although a recent re-analysis of

Table I. Defining symptoms of mixed anxiety and depressive disorder as outlined in DSM-IV[15]

Concentration problems
Sleep disturbance
Fatigue
Irritability
Worry
Easily moved to tears
Hypervigilance
Anticipating the worst
Hopelessness
Low self-esteem

data produced during a longitudinal epidemiological study indicated that MADD, as described by ICD-10, may have a point prevalence of approximately 1%.[20]

A recent review found that in a general population of patients who had mixed anxiety and depressive symptoms not severe enough to meet psychiatric diagnosis, nevertheless had significant decrements in their social and vocational activities and tended to have many medically unexplained somatic symptoms.[10] These patients tended to overuse medical services and were at significant risk of developing one of the more severe affective or anxiety disorders in the absence of adequate treatment.

In a study involving a large group of patients with psychiatric symptoms,[11] it was found that patients with mixed anxiety and depressive and subsyndromal depressive symptoms did not fit easily into the official psychiatric nosology when assessed with a structured interview, despite definite impairment in occupational or social functioning related to their symptoms. It is likely that some of these patients could fit a diagnosis of MADD.

3. Treatment

Because of the rarity of controlled treatment studies of MADD, this review of treatment options focuses on the treatment of patients with symptoms of both depression and anxiety, regardless of which illness is considered primary, secondary, comorbid or subsyndromal. Where evidence exists specifically for the treatment of MADD, it will be identified.

3.1 Nonpharmacological Treatment

Very little information is available on the nonpharmacological treatment of mixed anxiety and depressive symptoms. Thase et al.[21] suggested using long term psychotherapy as relapse prevention. Fava et al.[17] used cognitive-behavioural treatment following effective pharmacological therapy of primary major depressive disorder. It successfully reduced the level of residual symptoms (primarily generalised and somatic anxiety and irritability) following drug discontinuation. It also resulted in a lower rate of relapse 2 years after the study. Other sources have reported cognitive-behavioural treatment to be an effective adjunct to the treatment of all anxiety disorders.[22,23]

3.2 Psychopharmacological Treatment

Several anxiolytics and antidepressants have shown efficacy in reducing both anxiety and depressive symptoms. Ideally, pharmacotherapy should address both the depression as well as the comorbid or subsyndromal features of the illness. Often this will necessitate the use of more than one drug.

3.2.1 Tricyclic Antidepressants

The tricyclic antidepressants (TCAs) have proved efficacious as both anxiolytic and antidepressant agents.[24] These antidepressants have comparable, if not greater, in anxiolytic efficacy to benzodiazepines.[25] They are particularly effective at reducing symptoms in patients with a mixture of anxiety and depressive symptoms,[18,26-28] and have been recommended for the treatment of depressed patients with comorbid GAD, panic disorder, social phobia and OCD.[22]

Specifically, imipramine and clomipramine are recommended when depression is comorbid with panic disorder.[9,23] However, in some patients, TCAs can exacerbate panic attacks, suggesting that if TCAs are chosen, treatment should start with low dosages (as low as 10 mg/day) that are increased slowly, with monitoring.

Clomipramine is suggested for use in depressed patients who have comorbid OCD.[9,23] If the OCD symptoms remit during therapy, desipramine may be an effective option for treating unremitted symptoms of depression.[23] Furthermore, patients with OCD and depression may require longer terms of treatment before a response is seen, with higher than average dosages.

Table II. Common adverse effects of tricyclic antidepressants

Tremor
Dry mouth
Blurred vision
Constipation
Increased perspiration
Flushing
Postural hypotension
Increased heart rate
Cardiac rhythm disturbance
Oedema
Bodyweight gain

Despite their effectiveness, however, the adverse effect profile of these medications causes problems for some patients. Frequent adverse effects are outlined in table II. In addition, TCAs may interact with other agents including monoamine oxidase inhibitors (MAOIs), alcohol (ethanol), oral contraceptives and anticholinergic drugs, thus limiting their use. For these reasons, TCAs are not considered a first-line treatment option.

3.2.2 Monoamine Oxidase Inhibitors

Classical MAOIs such as phenelzine and tranylcypromine are effective antidepressants and have been shown to have superior efficacy to TCAs in patients with atypical depression.[29,30] Atypical depression is characterised by depression associated with significant anxiety, hyperphagia, hypersomnia, reverse diurnal variation and extreme reaction sensitivity. This profile of effects would suggest that these drugs would be effective in treating patients with mixed symptoms of depression and anxiety, particularly social phobia.

While MAOIs have proven efficacy in treating patients with social phobia,[29,31] there are no studies examining their use in treating patients with social phobia and depression. Liebowitz et al.[32] found that MAOI treatment was preferential in patients with atypical depression and panic attacks, and patients with atypical depression and hysteroid dysphoria. Other researchers have recommended the use of classical MAOIs in the treatment of depression with panic disorder.[23,33]

Despite their efficacy, classical MAOIs are rarely used because of their adverse reactions, particularly the potentially fatal interaction with tyramine-containing foods and some pharmacological agents. The lack of adherence to dietary restriction can result in hypertensive crisis, which has been reported in as many as 8% of patients receiving MAOIs.[22] The classical MAOIs are not considered first-line treatments for depression with anxiety.

The recent introduction of moclobemide, a reversible inhibitor of monoamine oxidase-A (RIMA), provides an alternative to the traditional MAOIs. This drug is generally well tolerated and selectively and reversibly binds to MAO-A, leaving MAO-B free to metabolise tyramine and thus eliminating the need for dietary restriction. Moclobemide has been found to be effective in treating both agitated and retarded forms of depression.[34,35] There is also evidence to suggest it is effective in treating social phobia and panic disorder.[36-39] Although these preliminary results and clinical experience suggest moclobemide may be effective in treating patients with mixed anxiety and depressive features, no studies have yet been completed.

3.2.3 Selective Serotonin Reuptake Inhibitors

The introduction of the selective serotonin (5-hydroxytryptamine; 5-HT) reuptake inhibitors (SSRIs) has significantly affected the treatment of depression. These agents have been found to be effective in the treatment of anxious forms of depression,[40,41] as well as discrete anxiety disorders such as panic disorder,[42,43] social phobia[43] and OCD.[44,45]

Several of the SSRIs have been tested in patients with mixed depressive and anxiety symptoms/ disorders. The greatest experience has been accumulated with fluoxetine, which has been found to be effective in treating depression and panic disorder.[22,46] It has also been effective in treating depression with comorbid OCD[22] and depression with social phobia.[47]

The other SSRIs have demonstrated some efficacy in treating mixed anxiety and depressive symptoms. Paroxetine is suggested as a treatment for depression comorbid with panic disorder, although it has not been tested empirically.[9] It has been shown to decrease anxiety symptoms on the Hamilton Depression Rating Scale (HDRS) compared with active controls and placebo,[41] and compared with fluoxetine.[48] Fluvoxamine has been reported to be effective in treating general practice patients who had symptoms of both depression and anxiety,[49] and in treating patients with a DSM-IV diagnosis of MADD.[50] Sertraline also was effective in reducing both anxiety and depressive symptoms in patients with an ICD-10 diagnosis of MADD.[51] Finally, Lydiard[33] has suggested using fluvoxamine, sertraline or fluoxetine to treat major depression with comorbid OCD.

The advantages of SSRIs as a class include a relatively mild adverse effect profile when compared with TCAs and MAOIs, as well as the fact that they are substantially safer in overdose. The most common adverse events associated with SSRIs are gastrointestinal and CNS, specifically nausea, loss of appetite, diarrhoea, insomnia and tremor.[52] There is a suggestion that these drugs increase anxiety and nervousness, but this usually occurs early in treatment and patients quickly develop tolerance to these effects. They may be more common with fluoxetine and less common with paroxetine.[52]

It has been suggested that when SSRIs are used to treat anxiety disorders, lower than standard dosages should be used.[43,53] This caveat should perhaps be extended to the treatment of patients with mixed anxiety and depressive symptoms.

3.2.4 Azapirones

Research has shown that the azapirones, such as buspirone, are effective in the treatment of patients with GAD, and possibly social phobia and OCD.[43,45,54] There is evidence that buspirone is also effective in treating depression.[55,56] Several studies have examined its use in patients with mixed symptoms. It has been tested extensively in patients with GAD and depressive symptoms and was found to be effective.[22,28,33,57] It may also be useful in treating patients with depression and OCD,[22] and has been recommended for use in patients with mixed anxiety and depression symptoms.[22,23]

The azapirones, including buspirone, have partial agonist activity at serotonin $5-HT_{1A}$ receptors. The specificity of this action results in the drugs lacking sedating effects, interactions with CNS depressants, withdrawal symptoms and negative effects on psychomotor performance and having a positive effect on the core symptoms of anxiety and depression.[58]

The dosages required to treat depression are significantly higher than for anxiety alone, and at these higher dosages adverse effects such as dizziness, headache and nausea may prove intolerable for some patients.[55,56]

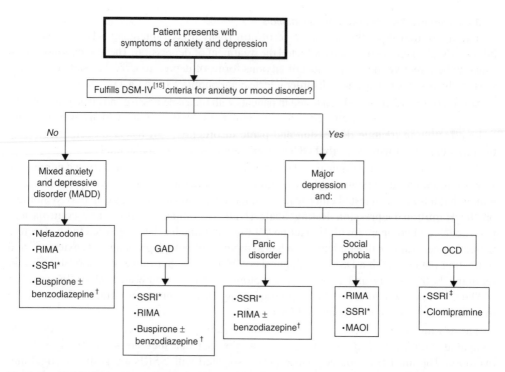

Fig. 1. Algorithm for the treatment of patients with coexisting anxiety and depression. This algorithm has been modified from Lydiard,[33] based on the opinions of the authors.
GAD = generalised anxiety disorder; **MAOI** = monoamine oxidase inhibitor; **OCD** = obsessive-compulsive disorder; **RIMA** = reversible inhibitor of monoamine oxidase A; **SSRI** = selective serotonin (5-hydroxytryptamine; 5-HT) reuptake inhibitor; [†] indicates short term use only; [*] indicates that these drugs may be required at lower than usual dosages; [‡] indicates that these drugs may be required at higher than usual dosages.

3.2.5 Nefazodone

Nefazodone, a new antidepressant, may prove to be particularly effective in treating patients with mixed anxiety and depression. This agent has unique pharmacological properties and acts as a weak inhibitor of serotonin reuptake as well as a potent serotonin 5-HT$_2$ receptor antagonist. Nefazodone is effective in treating depression[59] and has a mild adverse effect profile.[60]

Several studies have found it to be effective in treating patients with depression-related anxiety symptoms, when compared with other antidepressants.[61,62] There is also a report of nefazodone successfully treating panic disorder with comorbid depression or depressive symptoms.[63] Recently, a small open-label trial suggested that nefazodone may relieve anxiety symptoms in patients with mild depression within 2 weeks of the onset of treatment.[64] It is possible that nefazodone acts via two different mechanisms of action on the two sets of symptoms.

3.2.6 Benzodiazepines

The effectiveness of benzodiazepines in the treatment of GAD has been well established.[28] These medications have also proved effective in providing early relief of depression-related anxiety and insomnia.[28] The notion that alprazolam, a triazolo-benzodiazepine, may have specific antidepressant properties remains controversial and it is more likely that these drugs have little or no efficacy in treating the core symptoms of depression.[28] In fact, there is some suggestion that benzodiazepines, in particular clonazepam, may cause the emergence of symptoms of depression.[12,65] Furthermore, patients with bipolar depression may be switched into mania by alprazolam.[12] Certainly, when the primary illness is major depression, benzodiazepines should be used infrequently and with caution.[12]

Benzodiazepines may be best used as adjunctive therapies in patients with depression and comorbid GAD, panic disorder, social phobia and mild MADD.[22,23,33] The benefits of benzodiazepines include a rapid onset of therapeutic effect, few adverse effects and relative safety in overdose.

Adverse effects may include daytime sedation, cognitive impairment and the potential for a withdrawal syndrome.[22] If these drugs are used as adjunctive medication in the acute treatment of anxiety secondary to depression, it is recommended that they be considered for gradual tapering once a full antidepressant effect is achieved.[23]

There is a time/dose dependence relationship with benzodiazepines; the longer the course of treatment, the lower the dosage that can cause dependence. Thus, short courses of treatment are recommended, since the risk of dependence rises significantly after 1 year of continuous treatment.[66]

3.2.7 Antipsychotics

Antipsychotics have been shown to have both anxiolytic and antidepressant properties.[28] These drugs have a role in the short term treatment of psychotic depression; however, their long term use in the treatment of anxiety and depressive disorders is discouraged because of their adverse effect profile, specifically the potential for causing tardive dyskinesia.

3.2.8 Serotonin-Noradrenaline Reuptake Inhibitors

Several studies have appeared recently in the literature that indicate that venlafaxine, a serotonin-noradrenaline (norepinephrine) reuptake inhibitor (SNRI), can effectively treat patients with anxiety and depressive symptoms. Venlafaxine was shown to be more effective than both imipramine and placebo in treating comorbid anxiety associated with major depressive disorder.[67] It also significantly reduced anxiety scores on the HDRS in patients with depression associated with anxiety, as early as 3 weeks after the start of treatment.[68] Finally, Feighner et al.[69] demonstrated, in a series of double-blind controlled trials, that an extended release formulation of venlafaxine significantly reduced moderate to severe anxiety symptoms in patients with DSM-IV–diagnosed major depressive disorder. Clearly, the SNRIs have a role in the treatment of patients with symptoms of both anxiety and depression.

4. Treatment Recommendations and Conclusions

Large long term epidemiological studies have supported the claim that mixed anxiety and depressive symptoms occur quite frequently. It may be suggested that comorbidity is the rule rather than the exception. Furthermore, there are patients, seen by the primary care physician, who have mixed anxiety and depressive symptoms that do not reach a diagnostic threshold. Nevertheless, these patients experience significant social and occupational impairment.

Recognition of this overlap in symptomatology has been parallelled by the introduction of newer agents capable of treating more than a single aspect of an illness. Evidence suggests that these agents can no longer be dichotomised into either antidepressant or anxiolytic categories. Differences in pharmacological properties allow certain drugs to target specific symptom complexes. The newer agents are associated with improved compliance, as a result of a milder adverse effect profile, and are significantly safer in overdose.

When treating patients with comorbid anxiety and depressive symptoms, the clinician should take into account that these problems are likely to be chronic in nature and treatment is likely to be long term.[9] This challenges the clinician to find a medication that is easy to manage and well tolerated in the long term. Figure 1 outlines a proposed algorithm for the treatment of patients with mixed anxiety and depression.

When possible, monotherapy should be attempted first with a drug capable of treating depression as well as the comorbid or subsyndromal mental disorders. SSRIs and buspirone have been used to effectively treat patients with anxiety and depressive symptoms and should be considered as first-line choices. Moclobemide and nefazodone have not been studied as extensively, but clinical and early research experience suggest their potential use in this group of patients.

There are now a number of monotherapy options for the clinician treating patients with mixed anxiety and depressive symptoms. In terms of future research directions, clinicians and researchers need to start considering the total symptomatology, rather than treating the secondary symptoms as just 'noise'. Furthermore, there should be more thorough reporting of patients with difficult to treat disorders: the patients with mixed symptoms or comorbid disorders, and the patients who require more complex treatment plans.

References

1. Robins LN, Locke BZ, Regier DA. An overview of psychiatric disorders in America. In: Robins LN, Regier DA, editors. Psychiatric disorders in America: the Epidemiologic Catchment Area Study. New York: Free Press, 1991: 328-66
2. Kessler RC, Nelson CB, McGonagle KA, et al. Comorbidity of DSM-III-R major depressive disorder in the general population: results from the US National Comorbidity Survey. Br J Psychiatry 1996; 168 Suppl. 30: 17-30
3. Angst J, Merikangas KR, Scheidegger P, et al. Recurrent brief depression: a new subtype of affective disorder. J Affect Disord 1990; 19: 87-98
4. Angst J, Vollrath M, Merikangas KR, et al. Comorbidity of anxiety and depression in the Zurich Cohort Study of young adults. In: Maser JD, Cloninger CR, editors. Comorbidity of mood and anxiety disorders. Washington, DC: American Psychiatric Press, 1990: 123-37
5. Ball SG, Buchwald AM, Waddell MT, et al. Depression and generalized anxiety symptoms in panic disorder: implications for comorbidity. J Nerv Ment Dis 1995; 183: 304-8
6. Blazer D, Schwartz M, Woodbury M, et al. Depressive symptoms and depressive diagnoses in a community population: use of a new procedure for analysis of psychiatric comorbidity. Arch Gen Psychiatry 1988; 45: 1078-84
7. Breslau N, Davis GC. DSM-III generalized anxiety disorder: an empirical investigation of more stringent criteria. Psychiatr Res 1985; 14: 231-8
8. Breslau N, Davis GC. Further evidence on the doubtful validity of generalized anxiety disorder [letter]. Psychiatr Res 1985; 16: 177-9
9. Cassano GB, Michelini S. Pharmacological treatment of depression and comorbid anxiety disorders. Adv Biochem Psychopharmacol 1995; 49: 113-25
10. Katon W, Roy-Byrne PP. Mixed anxiety and depression. J Abnorm Psychol 1991; 100: 337-45
11. Barrett JE, Barrett JA, Oxman TE, et al. The prevalence of psychiatric disorders in a primary care practice. Arch Gen Psychiatry 1988; 45: 1100-6
12. Liebowitz MR. Treating the patient with depression and associated anxiety. In: Serotonin – Reshaping the Treatment of Depression. MEDICINE Publishing Foundation Symposium Series, 32. Toronto: The Medicine Group (Canada) Ltd., 1992: 31-41
13. Boulenger J-P, Lavallée Y-J. Mixed anxiety and depression: diagnostic issues. J Clin Psychiatry 1993; 54 Suppl. 1: 3-8
14. American Psychiatric Association. Diagnostic and statistical manual of mental disorders. 3rd ed. rev. Washington, DC: American Psychiatric Association, 1987
15. American Psychiatric Association. Diagnostic and statistical manual of mental disorders. 4th ed. Washington, DC: American Psychiatric Association, 1994
16. Hamilton M. Frequency of symptoms in melancholia (depressive illness). Br J Psychiatry 1989; 154: 201-6
17. Fava GA, Grandi S, Zielezny M, et al. Cognitive behavioral treatment of residual symptoms in primary major depressive disorder. Am J Psychiatry 1994; 151: 1295-9
18. Stahl SM. Mixed anxiety and depression: clinical implications. J Clin Psychiatry 1993; 54 Suppl. 1: 33-8
19. World Health Organization. The ICD-10 classification of mental and behavioural disorders: clinical descriptions and guidelines. Geneva: WHO, 1992
20. Wittchen HU, Essau CA. Comorbidity and mixed anxiety-depressive disorders: is there epidemiologic evidence? J Clin Psychiatry 1993; 54 Suppl. 1: 9-15
21. Thase ME, Simons AD, McGreary J, et al. Relapse after cognitive behavioral therapy of depression: potential implications for longer course of treatment. Am J Psychiatry 1992; 149: 1046-52

22. Keller MB, Hanks DL. Anxiety symptom relief in depression treatment outcomes. J Clin Psychiatry 1995; 56 Suppl. 6: 22-9
23. Zajecka JM, Ross JS. Management of comorbid anxiety and depression. J Clin Psychiatry 1995; 56 Suppl. 2: 10-3
24. Kahn RJ, McMair DM, Lipman RS, et al. Imipramine and chlordiazepoxide in depressive and anxiety disorders. II. Efficacy in anxious outpatients. Arch Gen Psychiatry 1986; 43: 79-85
25. Hoehn-Saric R, McLeod DR, Zimmerli WD. Differential effects of alprazolam and imipramine in generalized anxiety disorder: somatic versus psychic symptoms. J Clin Psychiatry 1988; 49: 293-301
26. Johnstone EC, Cunningham Owens DG, Frith CD, et al. Neurotic illness and its response to anxiolytic and antidepressant treatment. Psychological Med 1980; 10: 321-8
27. Rickels K, Cdanalosi I, Chung HR, et al. Amitriptyline in anxious-depressed outpatients: a controlled study. Am J Psychiatry 1974; 131 (1): 25-30
28. Rickels K, Schweizer E. The treatment of generalized anxiety disorder in patients with depressive symptomatology. J Clin Psychiatry 1993; 54 Suppl.: 20-3
29. Liebowitz MR, Quitkin FM, Stewart JW, et al. Antidepressant specificity in atypical depression. Arch Gen Psychiatry 1988; 45: 129-37
30. Quitkin FM, Stewart JW, McGrath PJ, et al. Phenelzine versus imipramine in the treatment of probable atypical depression: defining syndrome boundaries of selective MAOI responders. Am J Psychiatry 1988; 145: 306-11
31. Versiani M, Mundim FD, Nardi AE, et al. Tranylcypromine in social phobia. J Clin Psychopharmacol 1988; 8: 279-83
32. Liebowitz MR, Quitkin FM, Stewart JW, et al. Effect of panic attacks on the treatment of atypical depressives. Psychopharmacol Bull 1985; 21 (3): 558-61
33. Lydiard RB. Co-existing depression and anxiety: special diagnostic and treatment issues. J Clin Psychiatry 1991; 52 Suppl. 6: 48-54
34. Angst J, Stabl M. Efficacy of moclobemide in different patient groups: a meta-analysis of studies. Psychopharmacology 1992; 106 Suppl.: 109-3
35. Fitton A, Faulds D, Goa KL. Moclobemide: a review of its pharmacological properties and therapeutic use in depressive illness. Drugs 1992; 43 (4): 561-96
36. Bakish D, Saxena BM, Bowen R, et al. Reversible monoamine oxidase A inhibitors in panic disorder. Clin Neuropharmacology 1993; 16 (2 Suppl.): 77S-82S
37. Johnson MR, Lydiard RB, Ballenger JC. MAOIs in panic disorder and agoraphobia. In: Kennedy SH, editor. Clinical advances in monoamine oxidase inhibitor therapies. Washington, DC: American Psychiatric Press, Inc., 1994: 205-24
38. Versiani M, Nardi AE, Mundim FD, et al. Pharmacotherapy of social phobia: a controlled study with moclobemide and phenelzine. Br J Psychiatry 1992; 161: 353-60
39. Bakish D. The use of the reversible monoamine oxidase-A inhibitor brofaromine in social phobia complicated by panic disorder with or without agoraphobia. J Clin Psychopharmacol 1994; 14 (1): 74-5
40. Wakelin J. Differential effects of fluvoxamine, imipramine and placebo on anxiety in depression [abstract]. 16th Congress Collequium Internationale Neuropsycho-pharmacologicum: 1988; Munich
41. Dunbar GC, Fuell DL. The anti-anxiety and anti-agitation effects of paroxetine in depressed patients. Int Clin Psychopharmacol 1992; 6 Suppl. 4: 81-90
42. den Boer JA, Westenberg GM. Effect of a serotonin and noradrenaline uptake inhibitor in panic disorder: a double-blind comparative study with fluvoxamine and maprotiline. Int Clin Psychopharmacol 1988; 3: 59-74
43. Roy-Byrne P, Wingerson D, Cowley D, et al. Psychopharmacologic treatment of panic, generalized anxiety disorder, and social phobia. Psychiatr Clin North Am 1993; 16 (4): 719-35
44. Montgomery S, McIntrye M, Osterheide R, et al. A double-blind, placebo-controlled study of fluoxetine in patients with DSM-III-R obsessive-compulsive disorder. Eur Neuropsychopharmacol 1993; 3 (2): 143-52
45. McDougle CJ, Goodman WK, Leckman JF, et al. The psychopharmacology of obsessive compulsive disorder: implications for treatment and pathogenesis. Psychiatr Clin North Am 1993; 16 (4): 749-66
46. Louie AK, Lewis TB, Lannon RA. Use of low-dose fluoxetine in major depression and panic disorder. J Clin Psychiatry 1993; 54: 435-8
47. Sternbach H. Fluoxetine treatment of social phobia. J Clin Psychopharmacol 1990; 10 (3): 230-1
48. DeWilde J, Spiers R, Mertens C, et al. A double-blind, comparative, multicentre study comparing paroxetine with fluoxetine in depressed patients. Acta Psychiatr Scand 1993; 87: 141-5
49. Laws D, Ashford JJ, Anstee JA. A multicentre double-blind comparative trial of fluvoxamine versus lorazepam in mixed anxiety and depression treated in general practice. Acta Psychiatr Scand 1990; 81: 185-9
50. Houck C. An open-label study of fluvoxamine in outpatients with mixed anxiety-depressive disorder [poster no. 118]. 37th Annual meeting of the New Clinical Drug Evaluation Unit (NCDEU) program: 1997 May 27-30; Boca Raton
51. Carrasco JL, Diaz-Marsa M, Saiz J. Sertraline in the treatment of mixed anxiety and depression disorder [in Spanish]. Actas Luso Esp Neurol Psiquiatr Cienc Afines 1997; 25 (3): 141-5
52. Boyer WF, Feighner JP. Side effects of the selective serotonin re-uptake inhibitors. In: Feighner JP, Boyer WF, editors. Selective serotonin re-uptake inhibitors. Chichester: John Wiley & Sons, 1991: 109-17
53. Bakish D, Hooper CL, Filteau M-J, et al. A double-blind placebo-controlled trial comparing fluvoxamine and imipramine in the treatment of panic disorder with or without agoraphobia. Psychopharmacol Bull 1996; 32 (1): 135-41
54. Schneier F, Campeas R, Fallon B, et al. Buspirone in social phobia [abstract no. O-12-7-8]. Presented at the 17th Congress of Collegium Internationale Neuro-Psychpharmacologium: 1991 Sep 10-14, Kyoto
55. Schwiezer EE, Amsterdam J, Rickels K, et al. Open trial of buspirone in the treatment of major depressive disorder. Psychopharmacol Bull 1986; 22: 183-5
56. Fabre LF. Buspirone in the management of major depression: a placebo-controlled comparison. J Clin Psychiatry 1990; 51 Suppl. 9: 55-61
57. Sramek JJ, Tansman M, Suri A, et al. Efficacy of buspirone in generalized anxiety disorder with coexisting mild depressive symptoms. J Clin Psychiatry 1996; 57: 287-91
58. Sussman N. How to manage anxious patients who are depressed. J Clin Psychiatry 1993; 54 (5 Suppl.): 8-16
59. Rickels K, Robinson DS, Schweizer E, et al. Nefazodone: aspects of efficacy. J Clin Psychiatry 1995; 56 Suppl. 6: 43-6
60. Robinson DS, Roberts DL, Smith JM, et al. The safety profile of nefazodone. J Clin Psychiatry 1996; 57 Suppl. 2: 31-8
61. Fawcett J, Marcus RN, Anton SF, et al. Response of anxiety and agitation symptoms during nefazodone treatment of major depression. J Clin Psychiatry 1995; 56 Suppl. 6: 37-42
62. Zajecka JM. The effect of nefazodone on comorbid anxiety symptoms associated with depression: experience in family practice and psychiatric outpatient settings. J Clin Psychiatry 1996; 57: 10-5

63. DeMartinis NA, Schweizer E, Rickels K. An open-label trial of nefazodone in high comorbidity panic disorder. J Clin Psychiatry 1996; 57: 245-8
64. Stewart JW, Quitkin FM, McGrath PJ. Nefazodone may relieve anxiety within two weeks in anxious-depressives [poster 119]. 37th Annual meeting of the New Clinical Drug Evaluation Unit (NCDEU) program: 1997 May 27-30; Boca Raton
65. Lydiard RB, Laraia MT, Ballenger JC, et al. Emergence of depressive symptoms in patients receiving alprazolam for panic disorder. Am J Psychiatry 1987; 144: 664-5
66. Marks J. The benzodiazepines. Lancaster: MTP Press Limited, 1985: 100-5
67. Lecrubier Y, Bourin M, Moon CAL, et al. Efficacy of venlafaxine in depressive illness in general practice. Acta Psychiatr Scand 1997; 95: 485-93
68. Khan A, Upton V, Rudolph RL, et al. The use of venlafaxine in the treatment of major depression and major depression associated with anxiety: a dose-response study. J Clin Psychopharmacol 1998; 18: 19-25
69. Feighner JP, Entsuah AR, McPherson MK. Efficacy of once-daily venlafaxine extended release (XR) for symptoms of anxiety in depressed outpatients. J Affect Disord 1998; 47: 55-62

Correspondence: Dr *David Bakish*, Psychopharmacology Unit, Royal Ottawa Hospital, 1145 Carling Avenue, Ottawa, Ontario, K1G 7K4, Canada.
E-mail: dbakish@rohcg.on.ca

Current Perspectives on the Diagnosis and Treatment of Double Depression

David J. Hellerstein[1] and *Suzanne A.S. Little*[2]

1 Psychiatric Outpatient Services, Beth Israel Medical Center and Department of
   Psychiatry, Albert Einstein College of Medicine, New York, New York, USA
2 Mood Disorders Research Unit, Beth Israel Medical Center, New York, New York, USA

The vast majority of individuals who have dysthymic disorder develop a major depression during their lifetime. Concurrent major depression and dysthymia, a condition known as 'double depression', was first described in the literature by Keller and colleagues.[1,2] Broadly defined, double depression is a major depressive episode superimposed on dysthymic disorder. However, clinical researchers are increasingly adhering to a 'stricter' definition of double depression defined as current major depression with a pre-existing, underlying minor depression of at least 2 years in duration *prior to* the onset of major depression.

Double depression belongs to a clinically heterogeneous group of disorders that fall under the rubric of chronic depression. Chronic depression (where chronicity is defined as the persistence of depressive symptoms for at least 2 years) consists of at least four subtypes: (i) chronic major depression; (ii) major depression, with partial remission; (iii) double depression; and (iv) pure dysthymia.

With the establishment, in 1980, of dysthymia as a mood disorder in DSM-III,[3] researchers began to identify dysthymic types. Akiskal et al.[4] distinguished between subaffective dysthymia, which they described as a medication-responsive subtype, and character spectrum or 'characterological' dysthymia, which was considered to involve more neurotic personality factors and to be more resistant to medication treatment. Investigators also began to study the comorbidity of dysthymia with other affective disorders. Individuals with pure dysthymia became differentiated from those whose dysthymia coincided with a major depressive episode.

Historically, the identification of double depression has been hindered by a lack of clear differentiation between dysthymia and major depression. Researchers using DSM-III criteria speculated that the prevalence of double depression might be an artefact of the high degree of overlap between these 2 disorders, which share an arbitrary number of symptoms and differ only in severity and duration.[1,2,5] Modifications introduced into DSM-III-R[6] helped to differentiate dysthymia as a diagnostic entity in terms of early and late onset and primary and secondary type (the latter distinction has been discontinued in DSM-IV[7]).

However, the debate continues as to whether dysthymia is a separate psychiatric disorder, a mild manifestation of major depressive disorder, or the consequence of untreated or partially resolved episodes of major depression that have become chronic. Given the discrepancies in terminology, it is not surprising that many studies investigating 'double depression' continue to report findings on patients for whom the onset of chronic depression has not been clearly established.[4,8,9] In addition, these studies do not distinguish between the differing typologies of double depression. As a result, medication strategies for these patients often fail to differentiate between acute and chronic symptomatology, in terms of individual responsiveness to treatment as well as differing rates of recovery, both of which can significantly affect clinical outcome.

Although research on double depression is still in the early stage, its clinical significance as a public health problem is abundantly clear. Patients with double depression, when compared with patients who have episodic major depression, have:

- a more pernicious course of illness[1,2,10]
- a lower rate of recovery[1,2,10]
- a higher rate of relapse[1,2,10]
- an earlier age of onset of mood disturbance[11]
- more major depressive episodes[11]
- more frequent concurrent anxiety disorders[11]
- more severe depressive symptoms[10]
- more personality disturbance[10]
- greater comorbidity[10]
- lower levels of social support[10]
- greater deficits and impairments.[10]

Given the debilitating chronicity of this depressive condition, long term treatment strategies that address the full range and differential severity of its symptomatology are indicated.

1. Double Depression: Incidence and Prevalence

Although prevalence rates of chronic depression from community samples (3 to 5%) are somewhat lower than rates derived from treatment studies (9 to 31%),[12,13] the community data support the clinical finding that dysthymic disorder is a significant risk factor for major depression. The National Institute of Mental Health Epidemiological Catchment Area (ECA) study,[13] a collaborative study of the rates and risks of psychiatric disorders in five US communities, found a 3.1% mean lifetime prevalence rate of dysthymia, and a high lifetime comorbidity with major depression (38.9%, $p < 0.001$), using the Diagnostic Interview Schedule. Only anxiety disorder (46.2%, $p < 0.001$) had a higher co-occurrence.[13] A significantly higher comorbidity of major depression (58%) was also found in 150 adolescents diagnosed with dysthymic disorder than in non-dysthymic adolescents.[14]

Further support for the relationship between dysthymia and major depression is based on evidence that persons diagnosed with dysthymia who have never had major depression are at increased risk for developing major depression over time. Using longitudinal data from the ECA study, Horwath and colleagues[15] have shown that persons with dysthymia were found to be 5.5 times more likely than persons with no prior history of either major depression or dysthymia to develop a first onset major depression within a 1-year follow-up period.

Family studies, which are often used to demonstrate the genetic contribution to psychiatric disorders, suggest there is a significant biological relationship between dysthymia and major depression.[10] A high risk of dysthymia has been found in first-degree relatives of probands with major depression.[13] As Howland points out,[12] patients whose depression develops at an early age may have a high genetic loading for severe mood disturbance. Such genetic vulnerability may explain why dysthymic patients, particularly when the disorder has an early onset, show a greater likelihood of developing acute depressive episodes.

Several biological studies have shown that chronic depression and major depression are related. Sleep investigations of dysthymia show relatively consistent reductions in rapid eye movement (REM) sleep latency. Similar reductions have been detected in studies of patients with major depressive disorder.[16] Studies of electrodermal activity have also found similar reductions in skin conduction in dysthymia and major depressive disorder.

There also appears to be a relationship between chronic depression and bipolar disorder. Klein et al.[10] have shown that patients with double depression have higher rates of bipolar II disorder, as well as nonbipolar affective disorders, in first-degree relatives. In addition, a greater percentage of patients with double depression in this sample had two parents with affective disorders (16%) than patients diagnosed with episodic major depression (2%, p < 0.02).

2. Psychosocial Functioning

Chronic depression has been implicated as a major factor in poor social function, increased use of health resources, suicide risk, and increased psychiatric comorbidity, including Axis II personality disturbances and anxiety disorders.[12,17-19] Patients with double depression, when compared with patients with episodic major depression[6] and patients with pure dysthymia,[20] fare considerably worse on measures of overall social dysfunction, as evaluated by the Global Assessment Scale (GAS)[21] and the Social Adjustment Scale (SAS).[22]

In a naturalistic treatment study, Klein and colleagues[10] examined the clinical and psychosocial characteristics of patients with double depression. In their sample of 81 patients, those with double depression (n = 31) had greater impairment, more severe depressive symptoms, more personality disturbances and lower levels of social support than patients with episodic major depression (n = 50). A significantly greater proportion of patients with double depression met criteria for lifetime DSM-III diagnoses of eating disorders (22.6% *vs* 6%, p < 0.05) and severe personality disorders, such as borderline, antisocial and schizotypal (48.4% *vs* 22%, p < 0.01). Patients with double depression also reported poorer adolescent social adjustment on the Schedule for Affective Disorders and Schizophrenia instrument. At a 6-month follow-up, 75% of patients with double depression failed to show recovery – again, a significantly higher percentage than the acutely depressed patients (32.4%, p < 0.001). Patients with double depression also showed significantly higher mean levels of depression and poorer social and global functioning.

2.1 Morbidity

Patients who are chronically depressed show a greater global functional impairment (as measured by the GAS and SAS) and use medical health services more frequently than patients who have episodic major depression.[10,14]

Data from the Medical Outcomes Survey (MOS),[23] a 2-year observational study of 1790 patients with depression, diabetes, hypertension, recent myocardial infarction and/or congestive heart failure, indicate that depressed patients have persistent and substantial decrements in multiple domains of functioning and well-being, equalling or exceeding those of patients with chronic medical illnesses. Patients in this study were treated both in community and in medical or mental health settings, and a population of 62 patients with double depression was assessed. After 2 years of observation, the patients had a significant improvement in emotional well-being, role functioning, social functioning, and levels of energy and fatigue; however, both physical and mental functioning in these patients remained significantly more impaired than that of patients with chronic medical illnesses.

Wells and colleagues[24] assessed the health and well-being of several subgroups of depressed patients who participated in the MOS. They found that both dysthymic and double-depressed patients had poor energy, poor general health and impaired physical functioning, comparable to that associated with patients who had major depression.

2.2 Mortality

Affective disorders, including episodic and chronic depression, have been associated with increased mortality due primarily to suicide. A recent paper reported a very high rate of suicide in patients with 'depressive neurosis' (dysthymia).[25] Findings from 17 studies indicate that 15% of patients with a severe major depression of more than 1 month's duration died of suicide.[26]

Very few studies have documented mortality rates in patients with double depression. In the study of Klein et al.,[10] however, a higher percentage of patients with double depression (48.4%, $p < 0.01$) than with episodic depression (24%) had a history of suicide attempts.

3. Naturalistic Studies of the Treatment of Double Depression

The course of double depression has been characterised as 'pernicious' since Keller and colleagues[2] performed a study comparing patients with double depression with those with major depression. In this naturalistic study, the acute major depression in double-depressed patients responded more quickly to treatment (median 13 weeks after starting treatment) than in patients with major depression alone. Yet the chronic depression took a long time to resolve (median >104 weeks). Of 66 patients in whom the major depression responded to treatment, only 38% (25) had also recovered from the chronic minor depression after 1 year of treatment. Not only did chronic depression remain for a significant time, but also, patients with double depression had a significantly higher rate of relapse into major depression than patients with major depression alone. The antidepressant type, dosage or compliance and the relation to outcome were not stated in this study.

Klein et al.[10] also found worse outcome among patients with double depression than those with major depression: only 25% of double-depressed patients recovered by 6 months, compared with 67.6% of major depressed patients.

Several studies[24,27-30] have indicated that the treatment of all forms of depression in the community, both by psychiatrists and internists/primary care physicians, is often grossly ineffective. Furthermore, Kocsis and colleagues[31] suggest that chronic depression is undertreated compared with acute depression. It is not clear to what degree these factors account for the often discouraging outcome of double depression. Problems include:
- underdiagnosis of depression (acute and chronic)
- underprescription of effective antidepressants
- inadequate dosage and duration of treatment
- the use of possibly ineffective or inappropriate medications such as benzodiazepines instead of antidepressants.

Recently, Wells et al.[32] found that less than one-third of depressed outpatients were prescribed antidepressant medications. Of 133 patients with double depression in their study, only

30.1% were prescribed antidepressant medications, whereas 27.8% had been prescribed minor tranquillisers such as benzodiazepines. Although the underprescription of antidepressants for seriously depressed patients was particularly severe among nonpsychiatric physicians and among nonphysician psychotherapists, over half (50.8%) of the most severely depressed patients under the care of psychiatrists were also not receiving antidepressants.

4. Clinical Studies of the Treatment of Double Depression

A number of prospective medication studies have shown that double depression, although perhaps more difficult to treat than uncomplicated major depression, often responds significantly to medication with proper diagnosis and aggressive treatment.

4.1 Initial Treatment

Harrison and Stewart[33] reviewed studies of the treatment of double depression, concluding that a variety of antidepressant medications (including imipramine, ritanserin, phenelzine, moclobemide, amitriptyline and tianeptine) representing several classes of antidepressants [including tricyclic antidepressants (TCAs), irreversible and reversible monoamine oxidase inhibitors (MAOIs), selective serotonin (5-hydroxytryptamine; 5-HT) reuptake inhibitors (SSRIs) and postsynaptic serotonin 5-HT_2 receptor antagonists] are effective in the initial treatment of double depression.[8,34-37] For instance, Kocsis et al.[36] studied 76 patients with chronic depression, of whom 96% (73) had double depression. Patients were treated with imipramine [mean ± standard deviation (SD) dose = 198 ± 59 mg/day] or placebo. Of patients completing the study, 59% responded to drug treatment compared with 13% receiving placebo [response was defined as a Hamilton Depression rating scale (HAM-D)[38] score <7, significant response defined as a HAM-D score <12].

In our small, open-label study,[37] we treated patients who had double depression with fluoxetine or trazodone. Of those patients who completed 3 months' of treatment, 50% (7 of 14) responded to medication and 57.1% were in remission at 5 months [response was defined as a >50% decrease in HAM-D score *and* a score of 1 (very much improved) or 2 (much improved) on the Clinical Global Impressions Improvement scale].

Medication studies of double depression have been limited by several factors, including small sample sizes, brief study periods, lack of comparative drug studies and lack of placebo control groups. In addition, there is a need for crossover studies to determine whether patients with double depression who are unresponsive to one medication will respond to another. It is estimated that a significant percentage would show clinical response if given more appropriate and/or supplemental treatment.

Few studies, as Harrison and Stewart[33] point out, have determined whether patients still meet DSM criteria for dysthymia at the end of treatment. Furthermore, critics have raised the possibility that in many patients the acute (but not the chronic) depression may have responded to treatment. However, a growing body of studies suggest that dysthymia itself (when not accompanied by major depression) responds to antidepressant treatment in the majority of cases. Our double-blind, placebo-controlled study with fluoxetine[39] found that 62.5% (10 of 16) of dysthymic patients responded to medication compared with 18.8% (3 of 16) of placebo recipients.

Marin et al.[40] studied treatment response to desipramine in dysthymic (n = 44) versus double-depressed patients (n = 50), using an open-label design and a mean (± SD) dosage of

221 (± 70.1) mg/day. 20.2% of patients dropped out of treatment before completing the 8-week medication trial. Of 42 patients with double depression, 53% had complete (36%) or partial (17%) remission, compared with 70% of patients with pure dysthymia (who were not in a current major depression). The authors concluded that there was a similar rate of response for both double depression and pure dysthymia, and that patients with pure dysthymia actually respond somewhat better to medication than those with double depression.

4.2 Long Term Treatment

Although there is a paucity of studies of continued treatment of double depression, the existing ones suggest that initial medication response is generally maintained over time.

A follow-up[41] of patients seen in the study of Kocsis et al.[36] determined that of patients initially responding to medication, 89% of those who remained on medication continued responding. In contrast, only 37% of patients who had discontinued medication or who had initially been medication nonresponders were in remission.

Our group[42] performed a naturalistic follow-up study of 40 patients with dysthymia who had been treated in earlier efficacy protocols (mean ± SD of treatment = 37.0 ± 25.7 weeks) with fluoxetine or trazodone. We showed that few (17.4%; 4 of 23) patients remaining on medication relapsed (relapse defined as HAM-D score >13), whereas 50% (7 of 14) of patients who had discontinued medication relapsed.

In a more rigorous ongoing study cited by Harrison and Stewart,[33] Kocsis and colleagues[43] have prospectively studied the discontinuation of TCA medication in 99 patients, of whom 60% were double-depressed. They determined that among patients initially responding to desipramine, relapse occurred in 65% (11 of 17) of patients randomised to placebo continuation, whereas only 5% (1 of 20) of those randomised to desipramine continuation relapsed (relapse was defined as HAM-D score >12 for 3 of 4 weeks and Global Assessment of Functioning score ≤60).

These few studies are complemented by the more extensive literature on major depression, most notably studies by Frank et al.,[44] Montgomery et al.[45] and Doogan and Caillard[46] with imipramine, fluoxetine and sertraline, respectively. These studies demonstrated that maintenance of antidepressant medication is associated with persistent remission in major depressives, and that discontinuation of medication is associated with frequent relapse. The prospective, randomised study of Frank et al.[44] is notable in that it followed depressed patients for a

Table I. Typology of double depression and goals of treatment

Severity of major depression	Severity of dysthymia	Example (DSM IV[7])	Treatment focus	Minimal duration of treatment
+	++	Major depression, single episode, mild *and* dysthymia, early onset, with atypical features	Treat dysthymia	2-year trial
++	+	Major depression, recurrent, moderate severity *and* dysthymia, late onset	Treat major depression, prevent relapse	Varies: 6-12 months for first episode; longer duration if recurrent[49]
++	++	Major depression, recurrent, severe, with melancholia, *and* dysthymia, early onset	Treat dysthymia and major depression	Ongoing (possibly lifelong)

+ indicates the severity of depression/dysthymia [mild (+) or severe (++)].

36-month period, and found that an average dosage of 200 mg/day of imipramine had a highly significant effect in preventing recurrence.

Despite the numerous studies of initial response of double depression to treatment, there are few studies of continued response to medication or of relapse upon discontinuation of medication. Thus, clinicians have inadequate data to conclude how often initial response is maintained over time, how often relapse occurs, and whether continuation treatment is essential to prevent relapse. Studies of major depression have concluded that continued medication treatment is often effective in preventing relapse and that discontinuation of medication is associated with the return of depression. Given these findings, and the high psychosocial morbidity and increased tendency for relapse amongst patients with double depression compared with those with major depression, it appears that ongoing medication treatment will be required for most patients with double depression.

5. Differential Diagnosis

Before initiating treatment, clinicians must rule out a wide range of medical disorders (including endocrinological, haematological, neurological, neoplastic, infectious or cardiovascular) that may alone account for the chronic and acute depressive symptomatology. Alternatively, there may be coexisting acute or chronic medical and psychiatric disorders.

Clinicians must also eliminate various other psychiatric conditions that can present with a similar picture to both acute and chronic depression. In particular, one must rule out the possibility that a patient's chronic dysphoria is a result of an Axis II disorder (e.g. borderline personality disorder), an anxiety disorder, psychoactive substance use, psychosis or other nonaffective condition.

Within the mood disorders, a number of conditions also must be differentiated. While in the midst of a major depressive episode a patient may report that he/she has been depressed 'all his/her life', once recovered the patient may admit that the acute depression led to retrospective falsification of prior experience. A patient with dysthymia alone may appear to be doubly depressed if evaluated during a brief period of additional dysphoria. Clinicians must also determine whether patients experience variants of 'double' depressions not yet systematically researched: for example bipolar mood disorder with concurrent dysthymia; mixed anxiety-depressive disorder with superimposed major depression; or residual major depression with superimposed adjustment disorder with depressed mood.[7]

5.1 Secondary Conditions

Clinicians must be alert to the often present secondary or tertiary psychiatric disorders resulting from double depression. Many dysthymic patients develop avoidant behaviour or dependent relationships, and may meet criteria for avoidant or dependent personality disorder; others attempt to self-medicate with alcohol (ethanol) or other drugs. Still others have concurrent anxiety, which may be either a symptom of mood disorder or an independent anxiety disorder, such as generalised anxiety disorder or panic disorder.[5,47,48]

5.2 Typology of Double Depressions

Once the clinician determines that a patient has double depression, he or she should assess the relative severity of the two disorders. Specific diagnoses should be made according to DSM-IV criteria for both major depression and dysthymic disorder.

In our outpatient clinic at Beth Israel Medical Center, we have observed patients who meet criteria for double depression, but whose depressive symptoms vary considerably with regard to severity and functional impairment. Both dysthymia and major depression may range (often independently) along a continuum of severity. Accordingly, we have described three major patterns in double depression (see table I):

1) Patients in whom the dysthymia is more severe and disabling than the superimposed major depressive episode.

2) Patients in whom the dysthymia is relatively mild, and the major depressive episode more severe.

3) Patients in whom both the dysthymia and the major depression are both severe and disabling.

Although the relative frequency or treatment responsiveness of these three subtypes has not been adequately described in the literature, it is extremely useful to understand the patient's individual pattern of illness in order to set treatment goals and establish medication strategies. Important questions to ask are: How severe is the patient's chronic depression? What impact does it have on social, vocational and interpersonal functioning? How frequent and severe are the major depressive episodes?

6. Treatment

At Beth Israel, we recommend aggressive medication treatment for all patients with double depression, although the goals and duration of their treatment may vary, given the patient's particular typology (see table I).

A patient who is immobilised by chronic depressive symptoms and unable to work or to sustain relationships, and who has brief episodes of major depression following significant losses or stresses (Pattern 1 as outlined in section 5.2), will require ongoing medication treatment. In addition, they should receive psychotherapy and/or social skills training with the goal of alleviating chronic depressive symptoms and addressing the psychosocial damage of chronic depression (see section 6.8). Psychotherapy, in fact, may be all the more beneficial when the dysthymic symptoms remit.

In contrast, a patient who is able to function at work and maintain intimate relationships despite low-level chronic depression, but who becomes unable to work during infrequent episodes of major depression (Pattern 2), will require treatment targeted at the acute depression. Such individuals may not accept a lifetime course of antidepressant treatment, especially when the episodes of major depression are relatively infrequent, and may prefer episodic treatment of acute depressive episodes.

Patients with severe chronic *and* acute depressive disorders (Pattern 3) may be at the highest risk for poor outcome, and are likely to require aggressive treatment on both a short and long term basis. We recommend that such patients stay on antidepressant medication for the long term.

Other important factors influencing treatment include:

Table II. Potential advantages and disadvantages of antidepressant classes proposed as long term treatment of double depression

Class	Drugs studied	Advantages	Disadvantages
TCA	Desipramine, imipramine	Demonstrated efficacy in major and severe depression	High dropout rate in controlled studies, high cardiotoxicity in overdose, high degree of adverse effects (anticholinergic, sedation, bodyweight gain, orthostatic hypotension)
MAOI	Phenelzine, moclobemide	Increased effectiveness in depression with atypical features	Dietary restrictions, risk of hypertensive crisis (typical MAOIs only), adverse effects of long term use (including fluid retention, bodyweight gain, etc.)
SSRI	Fluoxetine, sertraline	Low toxicity, good tolerability	Sexual dysfunction with long term use in some patients
5-HT$_2$ receptor antagonist	Ritanserin Nefazodone[a]	Low toxicity, good tolerability No sexual dysfunction, antianxiety effects	Efficacy unclear
Atypical	Amfebutamone (bupropion)[a] Venlafaxine[a]	No sexual dysfunction, activating Effective in refractory depression	Possibility of increased seizure risk,[b] irritability and agitation in some patients

a Drug has not been studied specifically in patients with double depression.
b Incidence of seizures estimated at 0.24% (dosage range 225-450 mg/day) during an 8-week open trial (n = 3341).[51]
SSRI = selective serotonin (5-hydroxytryptamine; 5-HT) reuptake inhibitor; **MAOI** = monoamine oxidase inhibitor; **TCA** = tricyclic antidepressant.

- age at onset
- past and current history of suicidal and other high-risk behaviours
- presence of post-affective personality changes[50]
- concurrent medical and psychiatric disorders.

6.1 Medication Choice

Definitive studies determining the relative efficacy of different agents in the initial and long term treatment and prophylaxis of double depression have not yet been done. As a result, no single antidepressant class appears to be superior to another in the treatment of double depression. TCAs, MAOIs (including the reversible MAOI moclobemide), ritanserin and the SSRIs fluoxetine and sertraline have all been demonstrated to have some efficacy in the treatment of double depression.[33] It is also likely that other classes of antidepressants [such as the post-synaptic 5-HT$_2$ receptor antagonist and serotonin reuptake inhibitor nefazodone; the serotonin and noradrenaline (norepinephrine) reuptake inhibitor venlafaxine; and the atypical agent amfebutamone (bupropion); and other agents] will also be effective in the treatment of double depression.

Most patients with double depression will require many years of medication treatment, whether continuous or intermittent.[12] Medication choice (see table II) must therefore be influenced by factors such as tolerability to the patient, based on both short and long term adverse effects.

Medication choice is also affected by the patient's specific symptomatology (including the severity of depressed mood, insomnia, lethargy, agitation, cognitive dysfunction, anxiety and psychotic symptoms) and by the presence of other comorbid psychiatric and medical conditions. An agitated patient who cannot sleep may do better on a relatively sedating medication such as imipramine, which may not be tolerated by a patient who complains of continuous lethargy and fatigue.

Patients with major depressive disorder with atypical features of hypersomnia, lethargy, bodyweight gain and rejection sensitivity may respond preferentially to MAOIs,[52] and may also respond well to SSRIs. Patients with double depression presenting with complaints of prominent cognitive dysfunction may do well with medications such as amfebutamone or desipramine. Those with concurrent panic disorder may respond favourably to SSRIs such as sertraline or fluoxetine, to imipramine, or to MAOIs.[53] For patients with comorbid obsessive-compulsive disorder (OCD), SSRIs may also be recommended, along with clomipramine.[54]

Venlafaxine, a newly approved antidepressant that is chemically unrelated to the TCAs and SSRIs, has not been studied in chronic depression. Although recent clinical trials have shown venlafaxine to be effective in the treatment of major depression,[55,56] it is considered a second-line agent due to its problematic adverse effect profile (nausea, sexual dysfunction, elevated blood pressure).[57] However, results from these trials indicate that venlafaxine is effective for treating refractory depression. Patients who fail to respond to other medications often respond to this antidepressant.[56]

For patients experiencing acute major depressive episodes, (e.g. Pattern 2 or 3 in section 5.2), electroconvulsive therapy (ECT) may be necessary as the initial treatment, followed by prophylactic treatment with an antidepressant medication or lithium.

6.2 Tolerability

Short and long term tolerability are not always synonymous. For instance, SSRIs are often tolerated well by patients on a short term basis, and may be the preferred treatment for many outpatients. However, a significant rate of sexual dysfunction including anorgasmia may lead patients to discontinue SSRI medication after acute depressive symptoms have resolved. Sexual dysfunction is now recognised as an important clinical issue, although it is sometimes difficult to discern when the decreased libido is directly related to medication use or is a result of depressive symptomatology. There are also sexual adverse effects, such as decreased libido, reported with the use of MAOIs and TCAs.[58] In general, patients diagnosed with double depression who are afflicted with sexual dysfunction or related adverse effects may benefit from changing medication (to nefazodone or amfebutamone), or adding supplemental medication (such as yohimbine,[59] bethanechol, amantadine, cyproheptadine or amfebutamone).[59]

Regular follow-up visits with medicated patients should be scheduled to enable the treating clinician to monitor drug response and tolerability. The frequency of these visits may be initially weekly or biweekly and may be decreased to monthly or less often once a patient is in remission.

6.3 Partial Responses

Ideally, the primary treatment goal for all patients should be full symptom remission, especially since both psychotherapy and drug treatment studies suggest that residual depressive symptoms are a risk factor for relapse, noncompliance and treatment dropout.[60] Nevertheless, some patients are satisfied with a persistent level of depressive symptoms (e.g. a score of 10 to 15 on the HAM-D) that would be generally considered to be persistent residual symptomatology. In our studies,[39,42] common residual symptoms included mild depressed mood, reduced energy and fatigue, and decreased libido (although the latter may be an adverse effect of SSRI medication). Identifying and characterising such residual symptoms is useful in determining the effectiveness of further treatment options.

Not all patients respond adequately to initial drug treatment. The absolute treatment response rate appears to be 20% lower in chronic depressions than in acute depressions.[34] Approximately 20 to 30% of patients fail to respond substantially, for example, to SSRI medications, despite their low toxicity and favourable adverse effect profile, and of this percentage, those who do respond fail to reach and sustain euthymia.[61]

Kocsis et al.[31] found that the psychosocial functioning of dysthymic patients may improve with medication, but Haykal[62] found that many dysthymic patients can work yet remain isolated and avoidant, with impaired social relationships. According to Thase and Howland,[63] poor response or nonresponse to antidepressants may be partly attributable to specific psychosocial factors. There is evidence that individuals with serious personality pathology have poor short term responses to pharmacotherapy.[63] Similarly, patients with high levels of dysfunctional attitudes and neurotic personality traits show poorer outcomes with antidepressant treatment.[63] In such patients, psychotherapy or social skills training may be particularly helpful (section 6.8).[64]

6.4 Augmentation and Dosage Variation

Clinicians treating patients with double depression often report that medications lose initial efficacy after several months to years of treatment. For patients who begin to relapse, clinicians should prescribe maximum dosages, reinforce medication compliance, and consider monitoring serum antidepressant concentrations where indicated (e.g. with TCAs). Loss of efficacy may be more of a problem with the SSRIs than with other antidepressant medications, but can be addressed with sufficient dose increases.[65]

In cases of relapse and partial response, supplemental medication may be indicated (e.g. adding desipramine, lithium or amfebutamone to an SSRI) or changing to a different class of medication (e.g. from an SSRI to a TCA or venlafaxine for treatment-resistant depression).[66]

Other patients may note cyclical patterns in depression severity. In patients with features of seasonal affective disorder, antidepressant dosage may need to be increased by 25 to 50% during darker winter months, and decreased again in the spring. In women with premenstrual worsening of depression, increasing dosage (e.g. fluoxetine from 40 to 50 mg/day) several days prior to menses may protect against recurrence.

6.5 Refining Treatment Goals

We recommend that the initial goals of psychopharmacology be related to the typology of the patient's double depression (see section 5.2), as well as to other individual characteristics of the patient. Once the acute depression has responded to treatment, and the patient has returned to baseline, treatment goals may require further refinement.

A clinician must ask whether the primary goal is to alleviate major depression, to alleviate the dysthymia, or to alleviate both major depression and dysthymia. Treatment of major depression is generally straightforward: both patient and clinician are trying to obtain a return to the prior baseline of mood, energy, sleep, etc. With dysthymia, however, the alleviation of symptoms may be baffling for clinician and patient alike. A patient who has been depressed since childhood may report never having felt 'normal' until being placed on antidepressant medication.[67] Euthymia may be a novel, even aberrant state for many such patients, and consequently difficult at times for both clinician or patient to objectively assess. A low score on a depression rating inventory such as the HAM-D is only one end-point, and should not be the clinician's sole guide to treatment. In some cases, for example, a patient may appear to be euthymic, when in fact he or she is manifesting a pharmacologically induced hypomanic state.

The alleviation of depression is welcomed by most patients, yet some report feeling disturbed by losing their customary psychological (albeit dysphoric) homeostasis. In such patients, familiar depressive symptoms may have played a significant motivating role in the patient's ability to achieve success and/or cope with stress. In such patients psychotherapy may be particularly useful (section 6.8).

6.6 Duration of Treatment

The pharmacological recommendations for long term treatment of major depression are becoming increasingly clear. Greden,[49] for example, recommends the need for maintenance antidepressant treatment of patients with frequent or severe recurrent episodes, according to the following criteria:
- in patients aged ≥50 years at the first episode of major depression
- in patients ≥40 years with two or more episodes
- in patients of any age with three or more episodes.

In contrast, the pharmacological recommendations for long term treatment of dysthymia have not yet been established on the basis of rigorous studies. However, the low placebo response rate of dysthymia is similar to the low placebo response rate of conditions such as OCD or panic disorder, and these conditions often require 2 or more years of antidepressant treatment in order to lead to sustained remission.

Some clinicians would argue that all patients diagnosed with double depression warrant a lifetime course of antidepressant medication. As of now, there are no published controlled studies offering evidence to support that view. Our recommendation is that the majority of double-depressed patients (at least those with Patterns 1 and 3 as outlined in section 5.2) should remain on pharmacological treatment for a minimum of 2 years once remission is achieved. Generally, a full therapeutic dose of antidepressant is required, although, again, there is insufficient data to determine whether low doses of medications such as SSRIs may prevent relapse. If medication is discontinued, patients should continue to be observed regularly to prevent recurrence.

Given the limited data on maintenance treatment of double depression, ongoing medication treatment should be considered for patients meeting Greden's[49] criteria for major depression. This would be a conservative recommendation, since as discussed in section 2.1 patients with double depression have a generally worse course, more recurrence and more morbidity than the general population of major depressed patients.

6.7 Prophylaxis

The converging data in the epidemiological literature and treatment of dysthymia and double depression suggest the theoretical value of preventing the development of double depression and its associated morbidity. Clinicians are becoming more aggressive in the treatment of dysthymia, and new antidepressant medications are more tolerable for patients requiring long term treatment. An as-yet-unstudied question is whether aggressive treatment of dysthymia would be effective in preventing the development of double depression, and thereby helping to reduce the significant psychosocial morbidity associated with that disorder. On an individual basis, clinicians may decide to pursue that goal when treating dysthymic patients, but with the knowledge that the data for preventive treatment have not yet been obtained.

6.8 Benefits of Psychotherapy

In addition to medication treatment, our belief (yet to be tested with rigorous study) is that psychotherapy (both individual and group modalities) for patients with double depression may help prevent relapse and decrease psychosocial morbidity.

Table III. Goals of psychotherapy in patients with double depression

Building and rebuilding supportive social networks
Changing dysfunctional behavioural and cognitive habits
Reversing secondary avoidance and dependency behaviours
Improving social skills
Developing more satisfying intimate relationships and work lives

Akiskal[50] has described common post-affective personality changes among people who are chronically depressed. These include:

- clinging dependence
- rigidity
- pessimism
- low self-esteem
- social withdrawal
- being easily hurt
- hostility
- mood lability
- impulsivity
- demandingness
- manipulativeness.

Such patterns of thought, behaviour and social interaction may persist even following remission of depressive symptomatology.

A recent review by Markowitz[64] of psychotherapy studies in dysthymia concluded that interpersonal therapy or cognitive therapy may be beneficial for many dysthymic patients. Some patients with dysthymia apparently respond to psychotherapy in the absence of pharmacotherapy. However, given the increased severity of double depression, we recommend a concurrent treatment regimen, with medication as the initial treatment, then adding psychotherapy (when the patient is able to benefit from therapeutic treatment) as a supplemental intervention.

Important psychotherapy goals are shown in table III. Optimally, such skills will help provide an important buffer for patients in remission, forestalling symptom recurrence. Patients who have been chronically depressed often go through a process of 'grieving' for the years of lost opportunities, and may require a period of adjustment to their new euthymia. At the same time, they may find renewed motivation and energy to pursue and achieve personal and career goals seemingly unattainable in the past. It can be gratifying to identify patients with double depression and help them, with efficacious treatment, achieve significant changes in their lives.

7. Conclusion

Patients diagnosed with dysthymia are at increased risk for developing major depression. Double depression is increasingly being viewed as a particularly pernicious illness, associated with personality disturbance, poor health, and impaired social and physical functioning. Clinical studies show that patients with double depression have low rates of recovery and a tendency towards relapse.

However, a substantial portion of these patients, as shown in naturalistic studies, receive inadequate medication treatment, or have not been treated at all. Frequently, treatment fails to differentiate between the various typologies of double depression. We believe that more aggressive medication strategies targeted at both the acute and chronic symptoms can help patients with double depression to make gains in overall psychological functioning, to improve rates of recovery and to decrease relapse.

References

1. Keller MB, Shapiro RW. 'Double depression': superimposition of acute depressive disorders on chronic depressive disorders. Am J Psychiatry 1982; 139: 438-42
2. Keller MB, Lavori PW, Endicott J, et al. 'Double depression': two-year follow-up. Am J Psychiatry 1983; 140: 689-94
3. American Psychiatric Association. Diagnostic and statistical manual of mental disorders. 3rd ed. Washington, DC: American Psychiatric Association, 1980: 220-3
4. Akiskal HS, Rosenthal TL, Radwan F, et al. Characterological depressions: clinical and sleep EEG findings separating 'subaffective' dysthymias from 'character-spectrum disorders.' Arch Gen Psychiatry 1980; 37: 777-83
5. Kocsis JH, Markowitz JC, Prien RF. Comorbidity of dysthymic disorder. In: Maser JD, Cloninger RC, editors. Comorbidity of mood and anxiety disorders. Washington, DC: American Psychiatric Press, 1990: 316-28
6. American Psychiatric Association. Diagnostic and statistical manual of mental disorders. 3rd ed. rev. Washington, DC: American Psychiatric Association, 1987: 230-3
7. American Psychiatric Association. Diagnostic and statistical manual of mental disorders. 4th ed. Washington, DC: American Psychiatric Association, 1994; 623-4
8. Angst J, Stabl M. Efficacy of moclobemide in different patient groups: a meta-analysis of studies. Psychopharmacology 1992; 106 Suppl.: S109-13
9. Rounsaville BJ, Sholomskas D, Prosoff BA. Chronic mood disorders in depressed outpatients: diagnosis and response to pharmacotherapy. J Affect Disord 1980; 2: 73-88
10. Klein DN, Taylor EB, Harding K, et al. Double depression and episodic major depression: demographic, clinical, familial, personality, and socioenvironmental characteristics and short-term outcome. Am J Psychiatry 1988; 145: 1226-31
11. Levitt AJ, Joffee RT, MacDondald C. Life course of depressive illness and characteristics of current episode in patients with double depression. J Nerv Ment Dis 1991; 179: 678-82
12. Howland RH. Chronic depression. Hosp Community Psychiatry 1993; 44: 633-9
13. Weissman MM, Leaf PJ, Bruce ML, et al. The epidemiology of dysthymia in five communities: rates, risks, comorbidity, and treatment. Am J Psychiatry 1988; 145: 815-9
14. Kashani JH, Carlson GA, Beck NC, et al. Depression, depressive symptoms and depressed mood among a community sample of adolescents. Am J Psychiatry 1987; 144: 931-4
15. Horwath E, Johnson J, Klerman GL, et al. Depressive symptoms as relative and attributable risk factors for first-onset major depression. Arch Gen Psychiatry 1992; 49: 817-23
16. Howland RH, Thase ME. Biological studies of dysthymia. Biol Psychiatry 1991; 30: 283-304
17. Howland RH. General health, health care utilization, and medical comorbidity in dysthymia. Int J Psychiatry Med 1993; 23: 211-38
18. Friedman RA. Social impairment in dysthymia. Psychiatr Ann 1993; 23: 632-7
19. Markowitz JC, Moran ME, Kocsis JH, et al. Prevalence and comorbidity of dysthymic disorder. J Affect Disord 1992; 24: 63-71
20. Stewart JW, Quitkin FM, McGrath PJ, et al. Social functioning in chronic depression: effect of six weeks of antidepressant treatment. Psychiatry Res 1988; 25: 213-22
21. Endicott J, Spitzer RL. A diagnostic interview: the schedule for affective disorders and schizophrenia. Arch Gen Psychiatry 1978; 35: 837-44
22. Weissman MM, Bothwell S. Assessment of social adjustment by patient self-report. Arch Gen Psychiatry 1976; 33: 1111-5
23. Hays RD, Wells KB, Sherbourne CD, et al. Functioning and well-being outcomes of patients with depression compared with chronic general medical illnesses. Arch Gen Psychiatry 1995; 52: 11-9
24. Wells KB, Burnam MA, Rogers W, et al. The course of depression in adult outpatients: results from the medical outcomes study. Arch Gen Psychiatry 1992; 49: 788-94
25. Allgulander C. Suicide and mortality patterns in anxiety neurosis and depressive neurosis. Arch Gen Psychiatry 1994; 51: 708-12
26. Keller MB, Hanks DL. The natural history and heterogeneity of depressive disorders: implications for rational antidepressant therapy. J Clin Psychiatry 1994; 55 (9 Suppl. A): 25-31
27. Keller MB. Dysthymia in clinical practice: course, outcome and impact on the community. Acta Psychiatr Scand 1994; 383 Suppl.: 24-34
28. Froom J, Schlager DAS, Steneker S, et al. Detection of major depressive disorder in primary care patients. J Am Board Fam Pract 1993; 6: 5-11
29. Katon W, von Korff M, Lin E, et al. Adequacy and duration of antidepressant treatment in primary care. Med Care 1992; 30: 67-76
30. Simon GE, von Korff M, Wagner EH, et al. Patterns of antidepressant use in community practice. Gen Hosp Psychiatry 1993; 15: 399-408

31. Kocsis JH, Voss C, Mann JJ, et al. Chronic depression: demographic and clinical characteristics. Psychopharmacol Bull 1986; 22: 192-5
32. Wells KB, Katon W, Rogers B, et al. Use of minor tranquilizers and antidepressant medications by depressed outpatients: results from the Medical Outcomes Study. Am J Psychiatry 1994; 151: 694-700
33. Harrison WM, Stewart JW. Pharmacotherapy of dysthymia. Psychiatr Ann 1993; 23: 638-48
34. Howland RH. Pharmacotherapy of dysthymia: a review. J Clin Psychopharmacol 1991; 11: 83-92
35. Harrison W, Rabkin J, Stewart JW, et al. Phenelzine for chronic depressions: a study of continuation treatment. J Clin Psychiatry 1986; 47: 346-9
36. Kocsis JH, Frances AJ, Voss CB, et al. Imipramine for treatment of chronic depression. Arch Gen Psychiatry 1988; 45: 253-7
37. Hellerstein DJ, Yanowitch P, Rosenthal J, et al. Long-term treatment of double depression: a preliminary study with serotonergic antidepressants. Prog Neuropsych Biol Psychiatry 1994; 18: 139-47
38. Hamilton M. A rating scale for depression. J Neurol Neurosurg Psychiatry 1960; 25: 56-62
39. Hellerstein DJ, Yanowitch P, Rosenthal J, et al. A randomized double-blind study of fluoxetine versus placebo in treatment of dysthymia. Am J Psychiatry 1993; 150: 1169-75
40. Marin DB, Kocsis JH, Frances AJ, et al. Desipramine for the treatment of 'pure' dysthymia versus 'double' depression. Am J Psychiatry 1994; 151: 1079-80
41. Kocsis JH, Sutton BM, Frances AJ. Long-term follow-up of chronic depression treated with imipramine. J Clin Psychiatry 1991; 52: 56-9
42. Hellerstein DJ, Little SAS. SSRI medications in the treatment of dysthymia and chronic depression. J Serotonin Res 1994; 1: 181-7
43. Kocsis JH, Friedman RA, Markowitz JC, et al. Maintenance therapy for chronic depression: a controlled clinical trial of desipramine. Arch Gen Psychiatry. In press
44. Frank E, Kupfer DJ, Perel JM, et al. Three-year outcomes for maintenance therapies in recurrent depression. Arch Gen Psychiatry 1990; 47: 1093-9
45. Montgomery SA, Dufour H, Brion S, et al. The prophylactic efficacy of fluoxetine in unipolar depression. Br J Psychiatry 1992; 160: 217-22
46. Doogan DP, Caillard V. Sertraline in the prevention of depression. Br J Psychiatry 1992; 160: 1082-8
47. Markowitz JC. Comorbidity of dysthymia. Psychiatr Ann 1993; 23: 617-24
48. Pilkonis PA, Frank E. Personality pathology in recurrent depression: nature, prevalence, and relationship to treatment response. Am J Psychiatry 1988; 145: 435-41
49. Greden JF. Antidepressant maintenance medications: when to discontinue and how to stop. J Clin Psychiatry 1993; 54 Suppl. 8: 39-45
50. Akiskal HS. Dysthymic and cyclothymic depressions: therapeutic considerations. J Clin Psychiatry 1994; 55 Suppl. 4: 46-52
51. Johnston JA, Lineberry CG, Ascher JA, et al. A 102-center prospective study of seizures in association with bupropion. J Clin Psychiatry 1991; 52: 450-6
52. Quitkin FM, Stewart JW, McGrath PJ, et al. Columbia atypical depression. A subgroup of depressives with better response to MAOI than to tricyclic antidepressants or placebo. Br J Psychiatry 1993; 21 Suppl.: 30-4
53. Fyer AJ, Mannuzza S, Coplan JD. Panic disorders and agoraphobia. In: Kaplan HI, Sadock BJ, editors. Comprehensive textbook of psychiatry. 6th ed. Baltimore: Williams and Wilkins, 1995: 1201-2
54. Rasmussen SA, Eisen JL, Pato MT. Current issues in the pharmacologic management of obsessive compulsive disorder. J Clin Psychiatry 1993; 54 Suppl.: 4-9
55. Schweizer E, Weise C, Calry C, et al. Placebo-controlled trial of venlafaxine for the treatment of major depression. J Clin Psychopharmacol 1991; 11: 233-6
56. Schweizer E, Feighner J, Mandos L, et al. Comparison of venlafaxine and imipramine in the acute treatment of major depression in outpatients. J Clin Psychiatry 1994; 55: 104-8
57. Nemeroff CB. Evolutionary trends in the pharmacotherapeutic management of depression. J Clin Psychiatry 1994; 55 Suppl. 12: 3-15
58. Deleo D, Magni G. Sexual side effects of antidepressant drugs. Psychosomatics 1983; 24: 1076-82
59. McElroy SL, Keck Jr PE, Friedman LM. Minimizing and managing antidepressant side effects. J Clin Psychiatry 1995; 56 Suppl. 2: 49-55
60. Fawcett J. Compliance: definition and key issues. J Clin Psychiatry 1995; 56 Suppl.: 4-8
61. Nierenberg AA. Treatment-resistant depression in the age of serotonin. Psychiatr Ann 1994; 24: 217-9
62. Haykal RF. Dysthymia comorbidity and predictors of response [paper session]. American Psychiatric Association Annual Meeting: 1993 May 22-27; San Francisco (CA), 182-3
63. Thase ME, Howland RH. Refractory depression: relevance of psychosocial factors and therapies. Psychiatr Ann 1994; 24: 232-40
64. Markowitz JC. Psychotherapy of dysthymia. Am J Psychiatry 1994; 151: 1114-21
65. Fava M, Rappe SM, Pava JA, et al. Relapse in patients on long-term fluoxetine treatment: response to increased fluoxetine dose. J Clin Psychiatry 1995: 56: 52-5
66. Nelsen MR, Dunner DL. Treatment resistance in unipolar depression and other disorders: diagnostic concerns and treatment responsibilities. Psychiatr Clin North Am 1993; 16: 541-66
67. Markowitz JC. Psychotherapy of the post-dysthymic patient. J Psychother Pract Res 1993; 2: 157-63

Correspondence: Dr *David J. Hellerstein*, Psychiatric Outpatient Services, Beth Israel Medical Center, 1st Avenue and 16th St, New York, NY 10003, USA.

Psychotic Depression
A Review of Clinical Features and Guide to Drug Choice

Erik B. Nelson and *Susan L. McElroy*

Biological Psychiatry Program, Department of Psychiatry, University of Cincinnati
College of Medicine, Cincinnati, Ohio, USA

It has long been recognised that patients who display depressive symptoms may also exhibit psychotic symptoms. For example, in 1907 Kraepelin[1] observed that delusions could arise out of altered mood states and be limited to the duration of these states. With the introduction of electroconvulsive therapy (ECT) as a somatic treatment for depression, the distinction between depression with and without delusions became less relevant, as depressed patients with psychotic symptoms responded as well as patients with depression alone (i.e. nonpsychotic depression) to this treatment.[2,3] Soon after tricyclic antidepressants (TCAs) became available, however, it was shown that patients with psychotic depression responded less favourably to these medications than depressed patients without psychosis.[2,3] Major depression with psychotic features was therefore added as a subtype of major depression to DSM-III[4] in 1980.

Since the inclusion of psychotic depression in the DSM, several other important differences between psychotic and nonpsychotic major depression have been reported in the literature, leading some researchers to recommend that psychotic depression be considered a disorder distinct from major depression without psychosis.[2-36] However, much is still unknown about the relationship between psychotic versus nonpsychotic unipolar depression, and between unipolar versus bipolar psychotic depression. Table I summarises the proposed differences between psychotic depression and depression without psychotic features.

1. Clinical Characteristics

Psychotic depression may be broadly defined as a major depressive episode accompanied by psychotic symptoms. In DSM-IV,[37] psychotic depression is defined as a major depressive episode, not due to a medical condition or induced by a substance, that is accompanied by delusions or hallucinations. Importantly, DSM-IV further specifies that psychotic depression may be due to a major depressive disorder or to a bipolar disorder. DSM-IV also specifies that the associated psychotic features may be mood congruent or incongruent. Mood congruent psychotic features are defined as being 'consistent with the typical depressive themes of personal inadequacy, guilt, disease, death, nihilism, or deserved punishment'. Mood incongruent psychotic features include all other types of delusions or hallucinations, such as persecutory, grandiose and bizarre delusions, thought insertion, thought broadcasting and delusions of

Table I. Summary of differences between psychotic depression and depression without psychotic features

Feature	Psychotic depression is associated with:
Epidemiology	Lower lifetime prevalence
	Higher proportion of women[a]
	Higher number of patients in lower SEC[a]
Phenomenology	Greater severity of overall depressive symptoms
	Greater psychomotor disturbance
	Greater severity of guilt and depressed mood[b]
	Greater suicide risk[b]
Course of illness	Worse short term outcome
	Higher risk of psychosis in future episodes
	Long term outcome similar to that for major depression
	Short term outcome better than that for schizoaffective disorder, depressed type
Comorbidity	Higher rates of comorbid OCD, somatisation disorder and phobias[a]
	Higher overall comorbidity at time of first break
Family history	Higher rates of bipolar disorder, major depression, psychotic depression and schizophrenia[b]
Biology	Greater incidence and magnitude of dexamethasone nonsuppression
	Higher urinary and plasma cortisol levels
	Higher levels of DA metabolites in blood and CSF
	Higher levels of DA in blood
	Higher levels of platelet 5-HT reuptake and 5-HT metabolites in CSF
	Higher ventricle to brain ratio and brain atrophy

a   According to the Epidemiological Catchment Area study.[20]
b   Difference only observed in some studies.
DA = dopamine; **5-HT** = 5-hydroxytryptamine (serotonin); **OCD** = obsessive-compulsive disorder; **SEC** = socioeconomic class.

control. Of note, DSM-IV defines formal thought disorder and catatonia as types of psychotic symptoms, both of which may occur in major depression. Although DSM-IV specifies that a major depressive episode may be classified as having catatonic features, it does not indicate whether major depression with catatonia or formal thought disorder is related to psychotic depression.

1.1 Epidemiology

In the Epidemiologic Catchment Area (ECA) study conducted in the US,[20] the lifetime incidence of psychotic depression in the general population was found to be 0.6% as opposed to 3.8% for major depression without psychotic features. Among samples of psychiatric patients, the prevalence rates of psychotic depression have been found to be as low as 14% among community-based depressed patients[20] and as high as 25% among depressed patients in inpatient settings.[34] Studies looking at sex ratios in psychotic depression have found the typical 2:1 female to male ratio[13,16] that has been described in major depression. An exception to these data are those of the ECA study. These data showed psychotic depression to occur in a significantly larger proportion of women as compared to nonpsychotic depression.[20] The ECA data also showed a larger proportion of psychotic depressed persons to be in the lower socioeconomic classes compared with nonpsychotic depressed persons.[20]

1.2 Phenomenology

Studies comparing depressive signs and symptoms in psychotic versus nonpsychotic depression have found important differences. The most consistent finding is increased psychomotor disturbance in psychotic depression. Compared with nonpsychotic depression, psychotic depression has been reported to be associated with greater psychomotor agitation,[7,13,38,39] psychomotor retardation[15,22,38] and psychomotor disturbance in general when scores for both retardation and agitation are combined.[27] Parker et al. reported a strong association between psychotic depression and the symptoms of severe psychomotor disturbance[30,40] and lack of diurnal mood variation.[30] Moreover, two studies have shown patients with psychotic depression to have increased cognitive impairment compared with patients with nonpsychotic depression.[41,42]

Many studies have found psychotic depression to be associated with more severe overall depressive symptoms compared with nonpsychotic depression.[13,16,22,28,38] Some studies have also found significantly higher ratings of guilt[7,13,39] and greater severity of depressed mood[16,22] in psychotic versus nonpsychotic depression. Suicidal ideation has been found to be greater in psychotic depression than in nonpsychotic depression in some studies.[28,39] One study showed that hospitalised psychotic depressed patients were five times more likely to commit suicide than hospitalised nonpsychotic depressed patients.[43]

1.3 Course and Outcome

The average age of onset reported in studies of psychotic depression has ranged from 29 to 53 years, which is not significantly different from that of nonpsychotic depression.[7,13,16,20,27]

Studies have shown poorer short term outcome and increased rates of relapse for psychotic versus nonpsychotic depression.[9,20,44,45] Available data also suggest that psychotic depressed patients are much more likely than nonpsychotic depressed patients to be psychotic in subsequent depressive episodes.[23,46] However, three long term follow-up studies showed no difference between psychotic and nonpsychotic depressed patients on various measures including level of psychiatric symptoms, psychosocial functioning, death by suicide and frequency of relapses after 2 years,[9] 6 years[23] and 40 years.[44] Also, psychotic depression has been shown to have a better short term outcome than schizoaffective disorder, depressed type.[10,47]

1.4 Comorbidity

Available epidemiological and clinical data suggest that patients with psychotic depression have higher rates of some comorbid Axis I disorders than nonpsychotic depressed patients. For example, in the ECA study, persons with psychotic depression had higher rates of comorbid obsessive-compulsive disorder (OCD), somatisation disorder and simple phobia than did nonpsychotic depressed persons.[20] Also, in their study of Axis I psychiatric comorbidity in inpatients with first-episode psychosis, Strakowski et al.[48] found that patients with psychotic depression had a higher rate of overall Axis I comorbidity (86%) than patients with schizophrenia (44%) or mania (74%), with substance abuse and post-traumatic stress disorder being the most frequent comorbid diagnoses.

1.5 Family History

Results of studies evaluating the family history of psychiatric disorders in patients with psychotic depression are mixed. Some studies show higher rates of mood disorders in the first-degree relatives of psychotic depressed patients than in those of nonpsychotic depressed patients. For example, a significantly higher rate of unipolar major depression was reported in relatives of psychotic depressed patients compared with those of nonpsychotic depressed patients.[28] In contrast, Weissman et al.,[49] using direct family interviews, found that first-degree relatives of psychotic depressed patients had a 6-fold higher risk of having bipolar disorder, but no significant increase in the rate of unipolar major depression compared with first-degree relatives of nonpsychotic depressed patients. In a more recent study, first-degree relatives of psychotic depressed patients displayed only a trend toward statistically higher rates of both unipolar depression and bipolar disorder than relatives of nonpsychotic depressed patients.[50] Moreover, one study found that 37% of first-degree relatives of psychotic depressed patients exhibited a psychotic depression when they had a depressive episode, which is considerably higher than the 16 to 25% of depressed patients in general with this subtype, suggesting that there may be a genetic predisposition specifically for psychotic depression.[51]

However, other studies have found no differences between the first-degree relatives of psychotic and nonpsychotic depressed patients in the prevalence rates of major depression,[32,46,52] bipolar disorder,[32,46] schizophrenia,[24] nonaffective psychosis,[32] affective illness in general,[14,53] and mental illness in general.[14] Studies looking for differences in the rates of schizophrenia between families of psychotic and nonpsychotic depressed patients have also given mixed results.[24,46] Of note, many of these studies did not use direct interviews to diagnose psychiatric disorders in the family members of psychotic depressed patients.

1.6 Biology

Several important biological differences have been found between patients with psychotic and those with nonpsychotic depression. Specifically, in approximately 50% of patients with major depression, the administration of dexamethasone does not suppress cortisol levels. This nonsuppression response has been shown to be more common and more pronounced in patients with psychotic depression.[54] In fact, a recent meta-analysis of 14 studies using the dexamethasone suppression test revealed that 64% of psychotic depressed patients versus 41% of nonpsychotic depressed patients exhibited nonsuppression of cortisol, a highly significant difference.[55] Also, higher urinary free cortisol levels[56] and plasma cortisol levels[57] have been found in patients with psychotic depression compared with patients with depression alone. These findings suggest that psychotic depression may be more often associated with hyperactivity of the hypothalamic-pituitary-adrenocortical system than nonpsychotic depression. Other neuroendocrine findings include differences in growth hormone responses to the α_2-adrenergic receptor agonist clonidine and growth hormone–releasing hormone between psychotic depressed patients and patients with depression alone.[58,59]

Findings of increased levels of dopamine metabolites in CSF[60] and plasma,[61] and of increased plasma dopamine levels,[57] in psychotic versus nonpsychotic depressed patients suggest that dopamine activity may be increased in psychotic depression. Serotonin (5-hydroxytryptamine; 5-HT) activity also seems to distinguish psychotic from nonpsychotic depression as evidenced by findings of increased platelet serotonin uptake[62] and increased CSF levels of the serotonin metabolite 5-hydroxyindoleacetic acid (5-HIAA)[60] in psychotic versus nonpsychotic depressed patients. Moreover, a neuroanatomical study comparing computed tomography scans of the brains of psychotic and nonpsychotic depressed patients showed greater ventricle to brain ratios and increased atrophy in psychotic patients.[63]

2. Evaluation and Differential Diagnosis of Psychotic Depression

The first and most important step in successfully treating psychotic depression is early recognition. Although many patients present with clear-cut depressive and psychotic symptoms, some present primarily with depressive symptoms, and others primarily with psychotic symptoms. Thus, clearly depressed patients may conceal their psychotic symptoms due to guardedness,[2] or fail to verbalise them due to severe psychomotor retardation or catatonia.[30]

Indeed, Parker et al.[30] have proposed that there is a subset of depressed patients with 'masked psychosis' who display severe psychomotor disturbance and lack of diurnal mood variation without apparent delusions or hallucinations. As noted in section 1.2, their data show a strong association between these symptoms and psychosis in depression, and suggest that the presence of these two symptoms is sufficient to predict psychosis in a depressive episode, even when psychotic symptoms are not observable.

By contrast, in patients with obvious psychosis, mood symptoms may be subtle or difficult to detect or the patient may be unable to articulate them adequately due to formal thought disorder. Such patients may therefore not appear to meet full DSM-IV criteria for a major depressive episode and may be misdiagnosed with schizophrenia.[35] It is also possible that psychosis in psychotic depression may present exclusively as formal thought disorder without delusions or hallucinations (unpublished observations).

2.1 Bipolar and Schizoaffective Disorders

It is extremely important to differentiate psychotic major depression from the psychotic depressive, manic and mixed states that occur in bipolar disorder or schizoaffective disorder, bipolar type. Patients with the latter diagnoses typically respond better when a mood stabiliser is included in their treatment regimen.[64] Also, patients with bipolar psychotic depression may become manic in response to antidepressant treatment.[65]

Indeed, there are considerable data that suggest that psychotic depression and bipolar disorder are related.[3,49] Prospective follow-up studies have found that adolescents and adults with psychotic depression, when compared with age-matched nonpsychotic depressed patients, have a significantly greater risk of developing a subsequent manic episode.[66-69] Conversely, patients presenting with a psychotic depressive episode have been found to be more likely than nonpsychotic depressed patients to have a past history of one or more manic episodes.[46]

Psychotic depression must also be distinguished from schizoaffective disorder, depressed type. Although both disorders probably respond best over the short term to antidepressant-antipsychotic combinations, the long term outcome of psychotic depression more closely resembles that of nonpsychotic depression, whereas the long term outcome of schizoaffective disorder, depressed type, more closely resembles that of schizophrenia.[10,47] Thus, long term maintenance treatment with antipsychotics may be required less often for psychotic depression than for schizoaffective disorder, depressed type.

2.2 Schizophrenia, Schizophreniform Disorder and Delusional Disorder

It is extremely important to differentiate psychotic depression from schizophrenia, schizophreniform disorder, delusional disorder and other nonaffective psychotic disorders. As discussed in section 3.4, antipsychotic monotherapy is often inadequate for psychotic depression. Indeed, some patients with delusions and subtle mood symptoms may respond more favourably to antidepressants than to antipsychotics. For example, Akiskal et al.[70] described a series of 5 patients whose clinical presentations were characterised by paranoid delusions with little or no depressive symptomatology and who responded to antidepressants after failing to respond to antipsychotics. Moreover, patients with mood disorders may be at higher risk for developing tardive dyskinesia upon antipsychotic exposure than are patients with schizophrenia.

2.3 Obsessive-Compulsive Disorder

OCD with comorbid major depression may present in such a manner as to be confused with psychotic depression. Obsessions may resemble or even transform into delusions as patients lose the ability to see that their obsessive thoughts are excessive or unreasonable.[71] This is defined by DSM-IV as OCD with poor insight, and termed elsewhere as obsessive psychosis[72] or OCD with psychotic features.[71]

Thus, patients with OCD who have poor insight and comorbid depression may be diagnosed as having psychotic depression if the obsessive part of their illness is unrecognised. There are no controlled psychopharmacological treatment studies of obsessive psychosis. Available open data, though mixed, suggest that some of these patients respond better to serotonin reuptake inhibitors (SRIs) than to antipsychotics, and to higher rather than lower SRI dosages.[73] Therefore, misdiagnosis of a patient with OCD who has poor insight and depression as having psychotic depression may preclude them from receiving SRIs and may expose them unnecessarily to antipsychotics. By contrast, patients with psychotic depression have been shown to have high rates of comorbid OCD. This suggests that psychotic depression may go undetected if mood and psychotic symptoms were subtle in a patient presenting with prominent obsessive symptoms. Such patients might be deprived of potential benefits of treatment with antidepressant-antipsychotic combinations (see section 3.5).

3. Initial Treatment

Although inconsistencies exist, substantial data suggest that psychotic depression may differ from nonpsychotic depression in terms of response to somatic treatment.

3.1 Tricyclic Antidepressants (TCAs)

Soon after the development of TCAs, researchers reported that psychotic depression appeared less responsive to these medications than did nonpsychotic depression.[15,74] Moreover, Glassman et al.[15] reported that the inferior response of psychotic depression to TCAs (imipramine) remained significant after controlling for greater severity of depression in the group with psychosis. Many subsequent studies have similarly found a significant lack of response to TCAs in patients with psychotic depression.[6,13,22,28] A meta-analysis of many of the treatment studies involving 325 patients with psychotic depression receiving various treatments showed a response rate of only 34% in those receiving TCA monotherapy.[36] This lack of response has led some researchers to recommend that patients with psychotic depression not be treated with TCAs alone.[15]

By contrast, one retrospective study and two prospective, controlled studies have found a comparable or superior response to TCAs in psychotic versus nonpsychotic depressed patients.[19,24,33] In two of these studies the authors attributed their findings to the use of higher dosages and longer periods of treatment.[19,33] Moreover, another controlled study found that psychotic and nonpsychotic depressed patients had a significantly greater response to amitriptyline than to placebo.[75] In this study, no patients with psychotic depression responded to placebo, raising the possibility that diminished response to TCAs in psychotic depression may be a result of a lower placebo response in these patients.[12,75]

3.2 Monoamine Oxidase Inhibitors

There are no controlled studies of monoamine oxidase inhibitors (MAOIs) in psychotic depression. In an open-label study of phenelzine, only 6 (29%) of 21 patients with psychotic depression appeared to respond, compared with 21 (68%) of 31 patients with nonpsychotic depression.[76] However, there is a report of 4 patients with psychotic depression responding to monotherapy with MAOIs.[77]

3.3 Serotonin Selective Reuptake Inhibitors (SSRIs)

Several studies suggest that selective SRIs (SSRIs) alone may be effective in psychotic depression. Bellini et al.[78] randomised 48 psychotic depressed patients (36 with unipolar and 12 with bipolar depression) to treatment with either fluvoxamine plus placebo, desipramine plus placebo, fluvoxamine plus

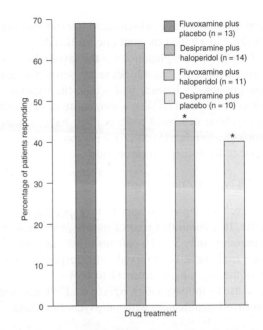

Fig. 1. Response to various drug combinations in 48 patients with psychotic depression.[78]
* indicates p < 0.05 versus fluvoxamine plus placebo.

haloperidol or desipramine plus haloperidol. They found that patients receiving fluvoxamine alone responded as well as those receiving desipramine plus haloperidol and significantly better than those receiving either desipramine alone or fluvoxamine plus haloperidol (see fig. 1). Unfortunately, the sample size in this study was small, thus limiting further interpretation of these findings.

In an open-label, 6-week trial of fluvoxamine in 59 inpatients with DSM-III-R–diagnosed[79] major depression with psychotic features, 48 patients (81%) responded, displaying significant reductions in both depressive and delusional symptoms.[80] The authors concluded that the response rate of delusional depression to fluvoxamine was comparable to an antidepressant-antipsychotic combination and ECT (see sections 3.5 and 3.7). In a recent follow-up study, all 25 patients with psychotic depression who had initially responded to fluvoxamine monotherapy avoided relapse for 6 months while 20 of 25 (80%) patients remained free from depression during the entire 30-month follow-up.[81] In a separate double-blind, controlled study, 28 of 35 (80%) psychotic depressed patients responded to fluvoxamine plus placebo and 29 of 36 (81%) patients responded to fluvoxamine plus pindolol.[82] Moreover, the group receiving pindolol showed a significantly greater response than the placebo group at 3 and 4 weeks of treatment.

In a double-blind, randomised comparison of paroxetine and sertraline monotherapy in patients who had unipolar or bipolar depression with psychotic features, 18 of 24 patients (75%) responded to sertraline while 6 (46%) of 13 patients responded to paroxetine (p = 0.16).[83] An intent-to-treat analysis in this study showed a significantly greater overall responseto sertraline, which the authors attributed to the titration of paroxetine being too rapid resulting in a higher dropout rate for this drug.

One possible explanation for the favourable response of psychotic depression to SSRIs in these studies is that blockade of serotonin reuptake down-regulates dopamine neuro-transmission.[80] Indeed, in 1 study, fluvoxamine was shown to decrease plasma levels of homovanillic acid (HVA), a metabolite of dopamine.[84] Another possibility is that delusions in psychotic depressed patients often have a ruminative or obsessive quality and may be aetiologically related to obsessive psychosis.[73] This may respond more favourably to drugs that enhance serotonergic transmission.

3.4 Typical Antipsychotics

Psychotic depression appears to respond as poorly to antipsychotics alone as it does to TCAs alone. In a controlled trial of psychopharmacological treatments in patients with psychotic depression, only 3 of 16 patients (19%) responded to antipsychotics alone.[36] The results of open trials have been mixed, with response rates of psychotic depression to antipsychotic monotherapy ranging from 31 to 66%.[7,21,25,26] In a review of five open studies examining response to antipsychotics, Spiker et al.[36] reported that 48% of psychotic depressed patients improved significantly with antipsychotics alone.

3.5 Combined Antidepressant-Antipsychotic Therapy

3.5.1 TCAs with Antipsychotics
Although preliminary, there is a growing body of data suggesting that psychotic depression may respond better to the combination of a TCA and an antipsychotic than to a TCA alone or an antipsychotic alone.

In a double-blind study comparing an antidepressant alone with an antidepressant-antipsychotic combination in 51 patients with psychotic depression (9 of whom had bipolar disorder), Spiker et al.[36] found that 14 of 18 patients (78%) responded to the combination of amitriptyline and perphenazine, whereas only 7 of 17 (41%) responded to amitriptyline alone. Open studies have found combination therapy to be an effective treatment for psychotic depression, and those that have directly compared antidepressant-antipsychotic combinations with TCAs alone have found the combination treatment to be superior.[7,8,13,21,25,26]

In the review by Spiker et al.[36] of 13 studies comparing the response of psychotic depression to TCA monotherapy, antipsychotic monotherapy, or TCA-antipsychotic combination therapy, the combination was more effective than either monotherapy. Specifically, 81% of patients responded to the combination, 48% to antipsychotics alone and 34% to TCAs alone. Parker et al.,[31] using a meta-analysis, analysed the combined results of these studies and found that response to the combination was statistically significantly superior to monotherapy with either class of psychotropic drug. However, in a second meta-analysis of 44 studies, Parker et al.[31] found only a trend for combination therapy being superior to TCAs alone. Moreover, a nonrandomised prospective study showed no difference in response between psychotic depressed patients treated with combination therapy versus TCAs alone.[22]

3.5.2 SSRIs with Antipsychotics
Two open trials have examined the efficacy of SSRIs combined with antipsychotics in patients who had psychotic depression, with encouraging results. In the first, Rothschild et

al.[85] treated 30 psychotic depressed patients with fluoxetine in combination with perphenazine for 5 weeks. 18 of the 23 (78%) unipolar patients and 4 of the 7 (57%) bipolar patients responded favourably. Also, the severity and frequency of adverse effects was less than that generally seen with TCAs in combination with antipsychotics. In the second trial, Wolfersdorf et al.[86] reported that 8 of 14 patients (57%) with psychotic depression responded favourably to paroxetine in combination with haloperidol and/or zotepine. Of note, response was evaluated after only 3 weeks. Again, the frequency of adverse effects was less than that found with TCA-antipsychotic combinations.

Conversely, in the previously mentioned double-blind study by Bellini et al.,[78] patients receiving fluvoxamine with haloperidol had a significantly lower response than patients receiving fluvoxamine alone or desipramine plus haloperidol. A possible complication which may arise with SSRI-antipsychotic combinations is the pharmacokinetic interaction whereby the SSRI, through inhibition of the cytochrome P450 metabolic pathway, may increase the plasma concentration of the antipsychotic. This could result in an increase in problematic antipsychotic-induced adverse effects such as extrapyramidal symptoms (EPS).[87]

3.6 Amoxapine

Amoxapine, a TCA with some antipsychotic properties, has been reported to be effective in psychotic depression in open trials[88,89] and in a 4-week, double-blind trial in which it was compared with the combination of amitriptyline and perphenazine.[90] In the latter study, both treatments were well tolerated, but amoxapine was associated with significantly fewer EPS. Although these studies suggest that amoxapine may be an effective and well tolerated monotherapy for psychotic depression, it is generally reserved for patients who do not respond to combination antidepressant-psychotic treatment, or who refuse to take polytherapy.

3.7 Electroconvulsive Therapy

The only controlled study of ECT in psychotic versus nonpsychotic depression showed a significant difference between real and sham ECT in patients with delusional depression and in patients with significant psychomotor retardation but not in patients with nonpsychotic depression.[91] However, there were only 8 patients in the nonpsychotic group which makes the results difficult to interpret. Also, an earlier uncontrolled study found ECT to be equally effective in psychotic and nonpsychotic depression.[17]

There are no controlled studies comparing ECT with antidepressants alone, antipsychotics alone, or the combination of an antidepressant and antipsychotic in patients with psychotic depression. Available uncontrolled studies suggest that ECT may be superior to treatment with antidepressants alone,[7,22,25,26,92] and equivalent or superior to antidepressant-antipsychotic combinations. For example, a nonrandomised, prospective study by Lykouras et al.[22] comparing a TCA alone, a TCA-antipsychotic combination and ECT in 13 patients with psychotic depression showed no difference between the three treatments. However, there was a trend for patients who did not respond to pharmacotherapy to respond to ECT. Specifically, 6 patients who did not respond to TCA alone and 2 who showed only a partial response to the combination subsequently responded to ECT.

In a retrospective analysis of 26 psychotic depressed patients treated with ECT (n = 14) or combination drug therapy (n = 12), Perry et al.[93] found that ECT was associated with a significantly higher and faster response rate. Specifically, 11 (79%) of the ECT-treated patients responded compared with only 5 (42%) of the patients receiving combination treatment. Also, ECT-treated patients displayed a significant reduction of symptoms an average of 2 weeks earlier than combination-treated patients. The authors noted, however, that the low response rate seen in those who received the combination treatment may have been due in part to the significantly shorter duration of antipsychotic treatment in nonresponders as compared with responders in this group. Indeed, in their updated meta-analysis, Parker et al.[31] did not find a significant difference between ECT and combination TCA-antipsychotic treatment, although they did find a trend towards ECT being more effective. Moreover, although ECT was significantly more effective than TCA monotherapy, there was only a trend for combination drug therapy being superior to TCA monotherapy in this meta-analysis.

By contrast, in a retrospective study, Minter and Mandel[25] reported that 15 of 16 psychotic depressed patients (94%) responded to combination drug therapy compared with 9 of 11 (82%) who responded to ECT. In another retrospective study, Charney and Nelson[7] found 25 of 37 patients (68%) with psychotic depression responded to a TCA-antipsychotic combination, compared with 9 of 11 (82%) who responded to ECT, a nonsignificant difference. Of the 12 patients who did not respond to combination drug treatment who subsequently received ECT, 8 (67%) responded.

Charney and Nelson[7] suggested that combination drug therapy should be used as first-line treatment for psychotic depression because the successful acute treatment regimen may be used as continuation and maintenance treatment, whereas maintenance drug therapy must be established after completion of ECT. (Of note, this view does not account for findings that suggest that maintenance ECT is an effective prophylactic treatment in psychotic depression – see section 4.3). Spiker et al.[36] recommended the use of ECT as a second-line treatment in patients with psychotic depression that was refractory to combination drug treatment based on their analysis of five studies that showed an overall response rate of 81% with the use of a TCA and an antipsychotic. They stated that there was not sufficient evidence to support the assertion that ECT is significantly superior to combination drug therapy to warrant it being used as first-line treatment.

3.8 Atypical Antipsychotics

Reports from open studies suggest that atypical antipsychotics may be effective in some patients with psychotic mood disorders, including some patients with psychotic depression.[94-97] Most of these reports have focused on the use of clozapine in patients with psychotic bipolar disorder or schizoaffective disorder that is refractory to other treatments, and have generally found that clozapine is more effective in psychotic mania than in psychotic depression. For example, in a retrospective review comparing response to clozapine in various mood disorders, Banov et al.[94] found that 46% of psychotic depressed patients responded compared with 73% of psychotic manic patients. Moreover, in a recent meta-analysis of studies that examined response of various mood and psychotic disorders to clozapine, the presence of manic symptoms, but not depressive symptoms, during psychosis predicted favourable response.[97]

Although there is less experience with other atypical antipsychotics in psychotic depression, preliminary reports suggest that some of these agents may have antidepressant as well as antipsychotic properties.[98,99] Of patients with psychotic depression (n = 7) or schizoaffective disorder, depressed type (n = 3) treated in an open-label study of risperidone, four of the patients with psychotic depression and all three of those with schizoaffective disorder showed significant improvement in both depressive and psychotic symptoms.[100] However, in a randomised, controlled trial of risperidone versus haloperidol and amitriptyline in psychotic patients, a subgroup of patients with psychotic depression showed signficantly greater improvement with the haloperidol/amitriptyline combination.[101] In a double-blind, randomised, controlled trial, Tollefson et al.[102] found olanzapine to be more effective than haloperidol for both psychotic and depressive symptoms in schizoaffective patients. However, the superiority of olanzapine over haloperidol was more robust in patients with the bipolar rather than the depressed subtype of schizoaffective disorder. In a retrospective review of olanzapine response in psychotic depression, 10 of 15 (67%) psychotic depressed patients were rated as much improved with olanzapine compared with 4 of 15 (27%) with other antipsychotics.[103] Two of 3 patients who received olanzapine without concomitant antidrepessant therapy responded.

Although the use of atypical antipsychotics in psychotic depression requires further study, these agents may be useful – either alone or in combination with an antidepressant – in patients who have an illness that is refractory to or who are unable to tolerate typical antipsychotics.

3.9 Lithium Augmentation

Although lithium augments the antidepressant effects of TCAs and other antidepressants in unipolar nonpsychotic depression – and unipolar psychotic depression may be related to bipolar disorder – there are no controlled studies of lithium monotherapy, combined lithium-antidepressant therapy, combined lithium-antipsychotic therapy, or lithium augmentation of combined antidepressant-antipsychotic therapy in psychotic depression. However, in one open, prospective trial in 6 patients with psychotic depression (5 with unipolar and 1 with bipolar depression) that had not responded to the combination of a TCA and an antipsychotic, 5 showed a good response when lithium was added to the TCA-antipsychotic combination.[104] Also, in a case series, 5 patients with psychotic depression responded when lithium was added to TCA monotherapy.[105] This report did not mention whether any of these patients had bipolar disorder. However, a retrospective study of lithium augmentation of combination antidepressant-antipsychotic therapy in psychotic depression showed a lower response, with only 3 of 12 unipolar patients responding.[106] A somewhat higher response rate was seen in bipolar psychotic depression in this study, with 8 of 9 patients (89%) exhibiting a significant response.

3.10 Amfebutamone (Bupropion)

Several case reports describe favourable outcomes with the use of amfebutamone (bupropion) in patients with psychotic depression – both alone and in combination with an antipsychotic.[107,108] However, amfebutamone has also been reported to induce psychosis in previously non-psychotic depressed patients.[109,110] In a 4-week trial of amfebutamone in 20 patients with schizoaffective disorder, depressed type,[111] 9 of 11 patients (82%) receiving amfebutamone in combination with haloperidol displayed moderate or marked improvement, whereas only 1 of 9 patients (11%) receiving amfebutamone alone displayed moderate improvement. Three patients (33%) in the group receiving only amfebutamone exhibited an exacerbation of psychotic symptoms. It has been hypothesised that the latter phenomenon may be due to the effects of amfebutamone on dopamine neurotransmission. Additional studies are needed to further assess the safety and effectiveness of amfebutamone alone and in combination with an antipsychotic in psychotic depression.

3.11 Other Agents

Other agents reported to be effective in isolated cases of psychotic depression include carbamazepine[112] and verapamil.[113]

4. Maintenance Therapy

4.1 Psychopharmacological Maintenance After Initial Medication Treatment

As mentioned in section 1.3, psychotic depression is associated with a high rate of relapse.[10,114] Although controlled data are lacking, open studies suggest that maintenance psychopharmacological treatment reduces recurrent mood episodes once the patient has recovered from an acute episode. For example, in a retrospective study of 8 patients followed for an average of 11 months after recovery from a psychotic depressive episode treated with an antidepressant-antipsychotic combination, Clower[8] reported a lower rate of relapse for patients who were maintained on the combination treatment compared with patients who discontinued medications or were tapered off antipsychotics following the acute episode. Also, in a 32-month naturalistic follow-up study of 52 patients with unipolar or bipolar psychotic depression who had recovered after receiving various treatments, the highest percentage of first year relapses (35%) occurred in patients who were not receiving maintenance medication.[114] The second highest percentage of relapses (29%) occurred in patients continued on antidepressants alone or shortly after an antipsychotic was tapered from a combination antidepressant-antipsychotic regimen. A 6-year follow-up study reported similar results.[23]

These results suggest that it may be necessary to continue an antipsychotic along with an antidepressant for at least 1 year after resolution of the acute episode. Further study is needed to clarify the appropriate point at which to taper an antipsychotic from the maintenance regimen after response to combination antidepressant-antipsychotic treatment.

4.2 Maintenance Psychopharmacological Treatment After ECT

Clinical data suggest that maintenance psychopharmacological treatment after ECT is often inadequate, with approximately 50% of patients relapsing within the first year after ECT.[115] However, patients who receive ECT are more likely to be severely ill, have recurrent illness, and/or to have not responded to prior combination antidepressant-antipsychotic treatment.[116] For example, Aronson et al.[117] reported a 95% relapse rate in a group of 21 psychotic depressed patients followed for a mean of 3.5 years after initial ECT treatment (total number of courses of ECT for the group was 47), compared with an 80% relapse rate during the maintenance phase after initial treatment with medications. Maintenance drug therapy was used after all but four of the acute ECT treatments. The authors note, however, that there was a selection bias towards patients with more severe and more recurrent illness receiving ECT. Moreover, after most of the acute ECT treatments, the patients (n = 23) received maintenance therapy with TCAs alone while 5 patients received combination antidepressant-antipsychotic therapy. Similar to reports with maintenance drug therapy following initial drug treatment (see section 4.1), relapse in this study was more likely to occur when a TCA was the sole mainte-

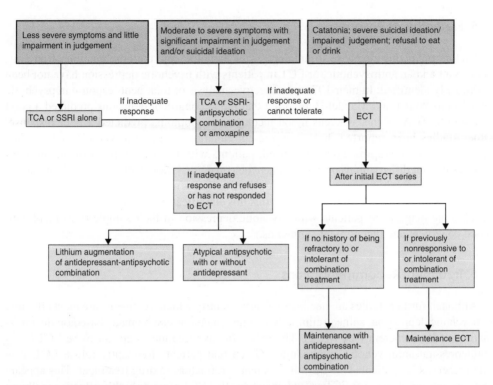

Fig. 2. A decision tree for the treatment of a patient with psychotic depression.
ECT = electroconvulsive therapy; **SSRI** = selective serotonin (5-hydroxytryptamine; 5-HT) reuptake inhibitor;
TCA = tricyclic antidepressant.

nance treatment, and when an antipsychotic was tapered from an antidepressant-antipsychotic combination.

Further study is needed to determine the efficacy of maintenance combination drug therapy after acute treatment with medications or ECT in patients who are randomly assigned to either treatment.

4.3 Continuation and Maintenance ECT

Several open studies suggest that continuation and maintenance ECT is effective in reducing recurrences in patients with psychotic depression that is initially treated with ECT.[118-120] The frequency and total number of maintenance ECT treatments in these studies varied from weekly ECT for 1 to 5 months to monthly treatments for 4 or more months. For example, in a retrospective study of continuation ECT for an average of 10 weeks (mean intertreatment interval = 10.1 days), Petrides et al.[119] reported a 42% relapse rate in 11 psychotic depressed patients. They compared this with the 95% relapse rate found by Aronson et al.[114] in patients receiving medication maintenance after ECT. However, as noted, only 5 of the 21 patients in the naturalistic study by Aronson et al.[117] received combination drug therapy as their maintenance treatment after ECT.

5. Predictors of Response

Factors predicting response to antidepressant monotherapy, the combination of an antidepressant and an antipsychotic, or ECT in patients with psychotic depression have not been definitively identified. In their 1979 retrospective analysis of treatment response in psychotic depression, Minter and Mandel[25] reported that mood congruent delusions predicted a good response to TCAs alone, whereas mood incongruent symptoms predicted a poor response. Other studies have reported that when the combination of an antipsychotic and an antidepressant, or amoxapine alone, was used, patients with mood congruent or incongruent features did not differ with respect to treatment outcome.[5,121] Moreover, although Kendler[122] concluded that mood-incongruent psychotic affective illness may be a distinct subtype of mood disorder, work by Burch et al.[123] suggests that this classification may be less clinically useful because the majority of patients with psychotic depression in their sample (58%) had both mood congruent and incongruent symptoms.

6. Treatment Recommendations

Although further studies are needed to clearly identify which treatments are most effective in psychotic depression, some preliminary recommendations can be made based on the information reviewed herein (see fig. 2). The most effective treatments appear to be ECT or an antidepressant-antipsychotic combination. Given that patients frequently refuse ECT, it is often reserved for patients who have illness that is refractory to drug treatment. This appears to be an appropriate role for ECT as studies suggest that ECT remains highly effective in illness that is refractory to treatment with medications. However, in patients who are catatonic, who refuse to eat or drink, or are severely suicidal, it is important to seriously consider using ECT as a first-line treatment.

When deciding which medications to use, one may consider starting with an antidepressant alone in patients who are not at immediate risk of serious harm. This is because some patients respond to antidepressant monotherapy and so can be spared the risk of potentially serious adverse effects associated with antipsychotics. However, in patients who display significant impairment of judgment, who report suicidal ideation, or who have not responded to previous trials with antidepressant monotherapy, an antidepressant-antipsychotic combination should be used. Although only TCA-antipsychotic combinations have been shown in a controlled trial to be superior to antidepressant monotherapy (see section 3.5.1), recent evidence from open trials suggests that SSRI-antipsychotic combinations are effective and probably better tolerated (see section 3.5.1). Recent studies of SSRI monotherapy also suggest efficacy and tolerability for these medications in psychotic depression when used alone (see section 3.5.2). Amoxapine is a viable alternative in patients who prefer taking only one medication, and may also be associated with decreased adverse effects.

There are some promising treatments which may benefit patients who have psychotic depression that is refractory to antidepressant-antipsychotic combinations and ECT or who are intolerant of these treatments. Atypical antipsychotics alone or in combination with antidepressants are effective in some patients, and generally cause less EPS than typical antipsychotics. Lithium augmentation provides additional benefit in some patients, particularly those with bipolar psychotic depression.

The available data on maintenance treatment after the resolution of the acute psychotic depressive episode point to the importance of continuing treatment with both an antipsychotic and an antidepressant for at least 1 year after successful treatment with either an antidepressant-antipsychotic combination or ECT. Maintenance ECT should be considered after initial ECT treatment in those patients already shown to have illness that is refractory to or who are unable to tolerate treatment with an antidepressant-antipsychotic combination.

7. Conclusion

Patients with psychotic depression are often a challenge for the psychiatrist to diagnose and treat. It is extremely important to consider this diagnosis in any patient who presents with either depressive symptoms, psychotic symptoms, or both. It is equally important to consider alternative diagnoses such as bipolar depression with psychosis, chronic psychotic disorders (such as schizoaffective disorder and schizophrenia) and OCD with poor insight when a patient presents with depressive and psychotic symptoms.

The challenge in treating patients with psychotic depression stems from the relative refractoriness of this illness to standard antidepressant treatments when compared with nonpsychotic depression. Although some patients do respond to antidepressant monotherapy, many may require antidepressant-antipsychotic combinations or ECT to obtain full resolution of the acute episode. Monotherapy with SSRIs or atypical antipsychotics, as well as lithium augmentation of antidepressants, are promising alternative treatments but require further study.

Recommendations for maintenance treatment are severely limited by the lack of available data. However, existing studies suggest a wait of at least 1 year before tapering the antipsychotic medication when an antidepressant-antipsychotic combination is used. Maintenance ECT may be an effective treatment in patients who are successfully treated with ECT in the acute episode and who have not responded to prior medication trials. Clearly, more studies need to be conducted to help clarify some of the unresolved questions about the treatment of this disorder.

References

1. Kraeplin E. Clinical psychiatry: a textbook for students and physicians. 2nd ed. New York: The Macmillan Co., 1907
2. Rothschild AJ. Delusional depression: a review of the literature and current perspectives. McLean Hosp J 1985; 10: 68-84
3. Schatzberg AF, Rothschild AJ. Psychotic (delusional) depression: should it be included as a distinct syndrome in DSM-IV? Am J Psychiatry 1992; 149: 733-45
4. American Psychiatric Association. Diagnostic and statistical manual of mental disorders. 3rd ed. Washington, DC: American Psychiatric Association, 1980
5. Brown RP, Frances A, Kocsis JH, et al. Psychotic *vs* nonpsychotic depression: comparison of treatment response. J Nerv Ment Dis 1982; 170: 635-7
6. Chan CH, Janicak PG, Davis JM, et al. Response of psychotic and nonpsychotic depressed patients to tricyclic antidepressants. J Clin Psychiatry 1987; 48: 197-200
7. Charney DS, Nelson JC. Delusional and nondelusional unipolar depression: further evidence for distinct subtypes. Am J Psychiatry 1981; 138: 328-33
8. Clower CG. Recurrent psychotic unipolar depression. J Clin Psychiatry 1983; 44: 216-8
9. Coryell W, Endicott J, Keller M. The importance of psychotic features to major depression: course and outcome during a 2-year follow-up. Acta Psychiatr Scand 1987; 75 (1): 78-85
10. Coryell W, Keller M, Lavori P, et al. Affective syndromes, psychotic features and prognosis: I. Depression. Arch Gen Psychiatry 1990; 47: 651-7
11. Coryell W. Psychotic depression. J Clin Psychiatry 1996; 57 Suppl. 3: 27-31
12. Dubovsky SL, Thomas M. Psychotic depression: advances in conceptualization and treatment. Hosp Community Psychiatry 1992; 43 (12): 1189-98
13. Frances A, Brown RP, Kocsis JH, et al. Psychotic depression: a separate entity? Am J Psychiatry 1981; 138: 831-3
14. Frangos E, Athanassenas G, Tsitourides S, et al. Psychotic depressive disorder: a separate entity? J Affect Disord 1983; 5: 259-65
15. Glassman AH, Kantor SJ, Shostak M. Depression, delusions and drug response. Am J Psychiatry 1975; 132: 716-9
16. Glassman AH, Roose SP. Delusional depression: a distinct clinical entity? Arch Gen Psychiatry 1981; 38: 424-7
17. Hobson R. Prognostic factors in electric convulsive therapy. J Neurol Neurosurg Psychiatry 1953; 16: 275-81

18. Hordern A, Holt NF, Burt CG, et al. Amitriptyline in depressive states: phenomenology and prognostic considerations. Br J Psychiatry 1963; 109: 815-25
19. Howarth BG, Grace MGA. Depression, drugs and delusions. Arch Gen Psychiatry 1985; 42: 1145-7
20. Johnson J, Horwath E, Weissman MM. The validity of major depression with psychotic features based on a community study. Arch Gen Psychiatry 1991; 48: 1075-81
21. Kaskey G, Nasr S, Meltzer HY. Drug treatment in delusional depression. Psychiatry Res 1980; 1: 267-77
22. Lykouras EP, Malliaras D, Christodoulou GN, et al. Delusional depression: phenomenology and response to treatment. Acta Psychiatr Scand 1986; 73: 324-9
23. Lykouras L, Christodoulou GN, Malliaras D, et al. The prognostic importance of delusions in depression: a 6-year prospective follow-up study. J Affect Disord 1994; 32: 233-8
24. Maj M, Pirozzi M, DiCaprio E. Major depression with mood-congruent features: a distinct clinical entity or a more severe form of depression? Acta Psychiatr Scand 1990; 82: 439-44
25. Minter RE, Mandel MR. A prospective study of the treatment of psychotic depression. Am J Psychiatry 1979; 136: 1470-2
26. Minter RE, Mandel MR. The treatment of psychotic major depressive disorder with drugs and ECT. J Nerv Mental Dis 1979; 167: 726-33
27. Nelson JC, Bowers MB. Delusional unipolar depression: description and drug response. Arch Gen Psychiatry 1978; 35: 1321-8
28. Nelson WH, Khan A, Orr WW. Delusional depression: phenomenology, neuroendocrine function, and tricyclic antidepressant response. J Affect Disord 1984; 6: 297-306
29. Parker G, Hadzi-Pavlovic D, Hickie I, et al. Psychotic depression: a review and clinical experience. Aust NZ J Psychiatry 1991; 25 (2): 169-80
30. Parker G, Hadzi-Pavlovic D, Hickie I, et al. Distinguishing psychotic and nonpsychotic melancholia. J Affect Disord 1991; 22 (3): 135-48
31. Parker G, Roy K, Hadzi-Pavlovic D, et al. Psychotic (delusional) depression: a meta-analysis of physical treatments. J Affect Disord 1992; 24 (1): 17-24
32. Price L, Nelson J, Charney D, et al. Family history in delusional depression. J Affect Disord 1984; 6: 109-14
33. Quitkin F, Rifkin A, Klein DF. Imipramine response in deluded depressive patients. Am J Psychiatry 1978; 135: 806-11
34. Roose S, Glassman A. Delusional depression. In: Georgotas A, Cancro R, editors. Depression and mania. New York: Elsevier Science Publishing Co., Inc., 1988: 76-85
35. Rothschild AJ. Management of psychotic, treatment-resistant depression. Psychiatr Clin North Am 1996; 19 (2): 237-52
36. Spiker DG, Weiss JC, Dealy RS, et al. The pharmacological treatment of delusional depression. Am J Psychiatry 1985; 142: 430-6
37. American Psychiatric Association. Diagnostic and statistical manual of mental disorders. 4th ed. Washington, DC: American Psychiatric Association, 1994
38. Coryell W, Endicott J, Keller M, et al. Phenomenology and family history in DSM-III psychotic depression. J Affect Disord 1985; 9 (1): 13-8
39. Thakur M, Hays J, Krishnan KRR. Clinical, demographic and social characteristics of psychotic depression. Psychiatry Res 1999; 86: 99-106
40. Parker G, Roussos J, Mitchell P, et al. Distinguishing psychotic depression from melancholia. J Affective Disorders 1997; 42: 155-67
41. Nelson E, Sax K, Strakowski S. Attentional performance in patients with psychotic depression, nonpsychotic depression and schizophrenia. Am J Psychiatry 1998; 155: 137-9
42. Jeste D, Heaton S, Paulsen J, et al. Clinical and neuropsychological comparison of psychotic depression with nonpsychotic depression and schizophrenia. Am J Psychiatry 1996; 153: 490-6
43. Roose S, Glassman A, Walsh B, et al. Depression, delusions and suicide. Am J Psychiatry 1983; 140: 1159-62
44. Coryell W, Tsuang M. Primary unipolar depression and the prognostic importance of delusions. Arch Gen Psychiatry 1982; 39: 1181-4
45. Robinson DG, Spiker DG. Delusional depression: a one-year follow-up. J Affect Disord 1985; 9: 79-83
46. Coryell W, Pfohl B, Zimmerman M. The clinical and neuroendocrine features of psychotic depression. J Nerv Ment Dis 1984; 172 (9): 521-8
47. Tsuang D, Coryell WC. An 8-year follow-up of patients with DSM-III-R psychotic depression, schizoaffective disorder, and schizophrenia. Am J Psychiatry 1993; 150 (8): 1182-8
48. Strakowski SM, Keck PE, McElroy SL, et al. Chronology of comorbid and principal syndromes in first-episode psychosis. Compr Psychiatry 1995; 36 (2): 106-12
49. Weissman MM, Prusoff BA, Merikangas KR. Is delusional depression related to bipolar disorder? Am J Psychiatry 1984; 141: 892-3
50. Goldstein R, Horwath E, Wickramartne P, et al. Familial aggregation of delusional depression: re-examination in a recent family study. Depression Anxiety 1998; 8: 160-5
51. Leckman JF, Weissman MM, Prusoff BA, et al. Subtypes of depression: family study perspective. Arch Gen Psychiatry 1984; 41: 833-8
52. Bond R, Rothschild A, Lerbinger J, et al. Delusional depression, family history and DST response: a pilot study. Biol Psychiatry 1986; 21: 1239-46
53. Maj M, Starace F, Pirozzi R. A family study of DSM-III-R schizoaffective disorder, depressive type, compared with schizophrenia and psychotic and nonpsychotic major depression. Am J Psychiatry 1991; 148 (5): 612-6
54. Schatzberg AF, Rothschild AJ. The roles of glucocorticoid and dopaminergic systems in delusional (psychotic) depression. Ann NY Acad Sci 1988; 537: 462-71
55. Nelson J, Davis J. DST studies in psychotic depression: a meta-analysis. Am J Psychiatry 1997; 154: 1497-1503
56. Anton Jr RF. Urinary free cortisol in psychotic depression. Biol Psychiatry 1987; 22 (1): 24-34
57. Rothschild AJ, Schatzberg AF, Langlais PJ, et al. Psychotic and nonpsychotic depression: comparison of plasma catecholamines and cortisol measures. Psychiatry Res 1987; 20: 143-53
58. Contreras F, Navarro MA, Menchon JM. Growth hormone response to growth hormone releasing hormone in non-delusional and delusional depression and healthy controls. Psychol Med 1996; 26: 301-7
59. Lykouras L, Markianos M, Hatzmanolis J, et al. Hormonal responses to clonidine and urinary MHPG in delusional and nondelusional melancholic patients: a placebo-controlled study. Eur Arch Psychiatry Clin Neurosci 1991; 241: 77-81
60. Åberg-Wistedt A, Wistedt B, Bertilsson L. Higher CSF levels of HVA and 5-HIAA in delusional compared to nondelusional depression [letter]. Arch Gen Psychiatry 1985; 42: 925-6

61. Devanand DP, Bowers MB, Hoffman FJ, et al. Elevated homovanillic acid in depressed females with melancholia and psychosis. Psychiatry Res 1985; 15: 1-4
62. Healy D, O'Hallorhan A, Carney PA, et al. Platelet 5-HT uptake in delusional and nondelusional depressions. J Affect Disord 1986; 10: 233-9
63. Rothschild AJ, Benes F, Hebben N, et al. Relationships between brain CT scan findings and cortisol in psychotic and nonpsychotic depressed patients. Biol Psychiatry 1989; 26: 565-75
64. Goodwin FK, Jamison KR. Manic-depressive illness. New York: Oxford University Press, 1990: 603-22
65. Prien RF, Klett CJ, Caffey Jr EM. Lithium carbonate and imipramine in prevention of affective episodes: a comparison in recurrent affective illness. Arch Gen Psychiatry 1973; 29: 420-5
66. Akiskal HS, Walker P, Puzantian VR, et al. Bipolar outcome in the course of depressive illness: phenomenologic, familial and pharmacologic predictors. J Affect Disord 1983; 5: 115-28
67. Akiskal HS, Maser JD, Zeller PJ, et al. Switching from 'unipolar' to bipolar II: an 11-year prospective study of clinical and temperamental predictors in 559 patients. Arch Gen Psychiatry 1995; 52 (2): 114-23
68. Strober M, Carlson G. Bipolar illness in adolescents with major depression: clinical, genetic and psychopharmacologic predictors in three- to four-year prospective follow-up investigation. Arch Gen Psychiarty 1982; 39: 549-55
69. Strober M, Lampert C, Schmidt S, et al. The course of major depressive illness in adolescents: I. Recovery and risk of manic switching in a follow-up of psychotic and nonpsychotic subtypes. J Am Acad Child Adol Psychiatry 1993; 32: 34-42
70. Akiskal HS, Arana G, Baldessarini R, et al. A clinical report of thymoleptic-responsive atypical paranoid psychoses. Am J Psychiatry 1983; 140: 1187-90
71. Insel TR, Akiskal HS. Obsessive-compulsive disorder with psychotic features: a phenomenological analysis. Am J Psychiatry 1986; 143: 1527-33
72. Solyom L, DiNicola VF, Phil M, et al. Is there an obsessive psychosis? Aetiological and prognostic factors of an atypical form of obsessive-compulsive neurosis. Can J Psychiatry 1985; 30: 372-80
73. McElroy SL, Phillips K. Obsessive compulsive spectrum disorder. J Clin Psychiatry 1994; 55 Suppl.: 33-51
74. Simpson GM, Lee JH, Cuculic Z, et al. Two dosages of imipramine in hospitalized endogenous and neurotic depressives. Arch Gen Psychiatry 1976; 33: 1093-103
75. Spiker DG, Kupfer DJ. Placebo response rates in psychotic and nonpsychotic depression. J Affect Disord 1988; 14: 21-3
76. Janicak P, Pandey G, Davis J, et al. Response of psychotic and nonpsychotic depression to phenelzine. Am J Psychiatry 1988; 145: 93-5
77. Lieb J, Collins C. Treatment of delusional depression with tranylcypromine. J Nerv Ment Dis 1978; 166: 805-8
78. Bellini L, Gasperini M, Gatti F, et al. A double-blind study with desipramine combined with placebo or haloperidol in delusional depression. In: Laeger SZ, Brunello N, Mendlewicz J, editors. Critical issues in the treatment of affective disorders. International Academy of Biomedical Drug Research; vol 9. Basel: Karger, 1994: 32-36
79. American Psychiatric Association. Diagnostic and statistical manual of mental disorders. 3rd ed. rev. Washington, DC: American Psychiatric Association, 1987
80. Gatti F, Bellini L, Gasperini M. Fluvoxamine alone in the treatment of delusional depression. Am J Psychiatry 1996; 153 (3): 414-6
81. Zanardi R, Franchini L, Gasperini M, et al. Long-term treatment of psychotic (delusional) depression with fluvoxamine: an open pilot study. Intern Clin Psychopharmacol 1997; 12: 195-7
82. Zanardi R, Franchini L, Gasperini M, et al. Faster onset of action of fluvoxamine in combination with pindolol in the treatment of delusional depression: a controlled study. J Clin Psychopharm 1998; 18: 441-6
83. Zanardi R, Franchini l, Gasperini M, et al. Double-blind controlled trial of sertraline versus paroxetine in the treatment of delusional depression. Am J Psychiatry 1996; 153: 1631-3
84. Salzman C, Jimerson D, Vasile R. Response to SSRI antidepressants correlates with reduction in plasma HVA: pilot study. Biol Psychiatry 1993; 34: 569-71
85. Rothschild AJ, Samson JA, Bessette MP, et al. Efficacy of the combination of fluoxetine and perphenazine in the treatment of psychotic depression. J Clin Psychiatry 1993; 54 (9): 338-42
86. Wolfersdorf M, Barg T, Konig F, et al. Paroxetine as antidepressant in combined antidepressant-neuroleptic therapy in delusional depression: observation of clinical use. Pharmacopsychiatry 1995; 28: 56-60
87. Taylor D, Lader M. Cytochromes and psychotropic drug interactions. Br J Psychiatry 1996; 168: 529-32
88. Anton Jr RF, Sexauer JD. Efficacy of amoxapine in psychotic depression. Am J Psychiatry 1983; 140 (10): 1344-7
89. Falk WE, Gelenberg AJ, Wojcik JD. Amoxapine for the treatment of psychotically depressed subjects: a pilot study. J Nerv Ment Dis 1985; 173 (2): 90-3
90. Anton Jr RF, Burch Jr EA. Amoxapine versus amitriptyline combined with perphenazine in the treatment of psychotic depression. Am J Psychiatry 1990; 147 (9): 1203-8
91. Brandon S, Cowley P, McDonald C, et al. Electroconvulsive therapy: results in depressive illness from the Leicestershire trial. BMJ 1984; 288: 22-5
92. Avery D, Lubrano A. Depression treated with imipramine and ECT: the DeCarolis study reconsidered. Am J Psychiatry 1979; 136: 559-62
93. Perry P, Morgan D, Smith R, et al. Treatment of unipolar depression accompanied by delusions: ECT vs TCA-antipsychotic combinations. J Affect Disord 1982; 4: 195-200
94. Banov MD, Zarate Jr CA, Tohen M, et al. Clozapine therapy in refractory affective disorders: polarity predicts response in long-term follow-up. J Clin Psychiatry 1994; 55: 295-300
95. Dassa D, Kaladjian A, Azorin JM, et al. Clozapine in the treatment of psychotic refractory depression. Br J Psychiatry 1993; 163: 822-4
96. Ranjan R, Meltzer HY. Acute and long-term effectiveness of clozapine in treatment-resistant psychotic depression. Biol Psychiatry 1996; 40: 253-8
97. Zarate CA, Tohen M, Baldessarini RJ. Clozapine in severe mood disorders. J Clin Psychiatry 1995; 56: 422-7
98. Dwight M, Keck P, Stanton S. Antidepressant activity and mania associated with risperidone treatment of schizoaffective disorder. Lancet 1994; 344: 554-5
99. McElroy S, Keck P, Strakowski S. Mania, psychosis, and antipsychotics. J Clin Psychiatry 1996; 57: 14-26
100. Hillert A, Maier W, Wetzel H, et al. Risperidone in the treatment of disorders with a combined psychotic and depressive syndrome: a functional approach. Pharmacopsychiatry 1992; 25: 213-7
101. Muller-Siecheneder F, Muller M, Hillert A, et al. Risperidone versus haloperidol and amitriptyline in the treatment of patients with a combined psychotic and depressive syndrome. J Clin Psychopharm 1998; 18: 111-20
102. Tollefson GD, Beasley Jr CM, Tran PV, et al. Olanzapine versus haloperidol in the treatment of schizophrenia and schizophreniform disorders: results of an international collaborative trial. Am J Psychiatry 1997; 154: 457-65

103. Rothschild A, Bates K, Boehringer K, et al. Olanzapine response in psychotic depression. J Clin Psychiatry 1999; 60: 116-8
104. Price LH, Conwell Y, Nelson JC. Lithium augmentation of combined neuroleptic-tricyclic treatment in delusional depression. Am J Psychiatry 1983; 140: 318-22
105. Pai M, White AC, Dean AG. Lithium augmentation in the treatment of delusional depression. Br J Psychiatry 1986; 148: 736-8
106. Nelson JC, Mazure CM. Lithium augmentation in psychotic depression refractory to combined drug treatment. Am J Psychiatry 1986; 143 (3): 363-6
107. Schenck CH, Mandell M, Lewis GM. A case of monthly unipolar psychotic depression with suicide attempt by self-burning: selective response to bupropion treatment. Compr Psychiatry 1992; 33 (5): 353-6
108. Manberg PJ, Carter RG. Bupropion in the treatment of psychotic depression: two case reports. J Clin Psychiatry 1984; 45 (5): 230-1
109. Jackson C, Head L, Kellner C. Catatonia associated with bupropion treatment [letter]. J Clin Psychiatry 1992; 53: 210
110. Golden RN. Psychoses associated with bupropion treatment. Am J Psychiatry 1985; 142: 1459-62
111. Goode D, Manning A. Comparison of bupropion alone and with haloperidol in schizoaffective disorder, depressed type. J Clin Psychiatry 1983; 44: 253-5
112. Schaffer C, Mungas D, Rockwell E. Successful treatment of psychotic depression with carbamazepine. J Clin Psychopharmacol 1985; 5: 233-5
113. Jacques RM, Cox SJ. Verapamil in major (psychotic) depression. Br J Psychiatry 1991; 158: 124-5
114. Aronson TA, Shukla S, Gujavarty K, et al. Relapse in delusional depression: a retrospective study of the course of treatment. Compr Psychiatry 1988; 29: 12-21
115. Spiker DG, Stein J, Rich CL. Delusional depression and electroconvulsive therapy: one year later. Convuls Ther 1985; 1: 167-72
116. Monroe RR. Maintenance electroconvulsive therapy. Psychiatr Clin North Am 1991; 14 (4): 947-60
117. Aronson TA, Shukla S, Hoff A. Continuation therapy after ECT for delusional depression: a naturalistic study of prophylactic treatments and relapse. Convuls Ther 1987; 3: 251-9
118. Grunhaus L, Panda AC, Haskett R. Full and abbreviated courses of maintenance electroconvulsive therapy. Convuls Ther 1990; 6: 130-8
119. Petrides G, Dhossche D, Fink M, et al. Continuation ECT: relapse prevention in affective disorders. Convuls Ther 1994; 10: 189-94
120. Thornton JE, Mulsant BH, Dealy R, et al. A retrospective study of maintenance electroconvulsive therapy in a university-based psychiatric practice. Convuls Ther 1990; 6: 121-9
121. Anton Jr RF, Burch Jr EA. Response of psychotic depression subtypes to pharmacotherapy. J Affect Disord 1993; 28 (2): 125-31
122. Kendler KS. Mood-incongruent psychotic affective illness. Arch Gen Psychiatry 1991; 48: 362-9
123. Burch Jr EA, Anton Jr R, Carson WH. Mood congruent and incongruent psychotic depressions: are they the same? J Affect Disord 1994; 31 (4): 275-80

Correspondence: Dr *Erik B. Nelson*, Biological Psychiatry Program, PO Box 670559, University of Cincinnati, College of Medicine, 231 Bethesda Avenue, Cincinnati, OH 45267-0559, USA.

Diagnosis and Treatment of Geriatric Depression

Robert Lasser,[1] *Erika Siegel,*[2] *Ruth Dukoff*[1] and *Trey Sunderland*[1]

1 Geriatric Psychiatry Branch, National Institute of Mental Health, Bethesda, Maryland, USA
2 Department of Psychology, The Catholic University of America, Washington, DC, USA

During the twentieth century, the life expectancy of individuals in most industrialised nations has skyrocketed from about 47 to nearly 80 years.[1,2] The enormous challenge this development presents to clinicians involves recognising and treating illnesses in an increasingly older population. Elderly individuals often present their psychiatric symptoms differently and require different therapeutic strategies compared with their younger counterparts. This is particularly true of depression, the most common psychiatric disorder in the elderly.

This review focuses on the variety of presentations and aetiologies of late-life depression and its impact on functionality, morbidity and mortality in older patients. Treatment strategies, both somatic and psychotherapeutic, will also be addressed, with attention paid to the pharmacodynamic changes resulting from advanced age and polypharmacy. Special consideration will be given to the topics of bereavement and suicide in the geriatric population.

1. Diagnostic Issues

1.1 Prevalence of Geriatric Depression

Controversy has surrounded estimates of the rate of depression among the elderly. Clinical impressions suggest that depressive symptoms are more common in geriatric populations than in younger age groups. In contrast, community-based epidemiological surveys indicate declining rates of depressive disorders with advancing age.[3-6] In addition, rates of depressive disorders in long term care facilities range from 20 to 50%;[7,8] however, when the institutionalised elderly are included in epidemiological samples, the 1-year incidence of major depression in the elderly increases to over 50%.[9] As somatic complaints present as depressive 'equivalents' in many older patients, the exclusion of physical illness–related complaints from many depression rating scales may lead to an underestimation of the prevalence of geriatric depression. When the percentage of somatic items on rating scales nears 30%, the prevalence of depression is approximately equivalent across age groups.[10]

Beyond the issue of somatisation, attributing symptoms of depression to physical illness may reflect a heuristic strategy used by the elderly when confronted with the complex questioning of epidemiological surveys.[11] By focusing on syndromes rather than symptoms, epidemiological surveys may be ill-equipped to identify the presence of less intense, yet chronic and disabling, depressive subsyndromes experienced by the elderly. Furthermore, recognising the full spectrum of geriatric depressive disorders has been hampered by the pervasive attitudes of both patients and physicians that persistent affective distress is a 'normal' consequence of aging or medical illness.[10,12,13]

1.2 Depressive-Spectrum Disorders in the Elderly

Depressive-spectrum disorders, which include minor depression, dysthymia, mixed anxiety/depression and bereavement-related depression, are much more common than major depression among the elderly,[14-17] reaching rates of 20% in community-dwelling samples and up to 50% in the institutionalised elderly.[17-19] These disorders cause clinically significant dysfunction, have abnormal biological markers[20] and may respond to both psychotherapy and pharmacotherapy.[12,17,21] Although some investigators report that at least 25% of the elderly who have subclinical depression may go on to develop major depression within 2 years,[22] no clear predictive markers exist to indicate which patients will become more severely depressed.

Older individuals may be particularly prone to subsyndromal depression because they may have greater difficulty expressing their affective experience (alexithymia) and lack knowledge concerning the symptoms of geriatric depression.[12,17] Therefore, the symptom threshold that indicates that treatment is required should perhaps be lower in depressed geriatric patients than in other patient groups.[15,23] Evaluating the elderly for depression should include family reports on the patient's functioning and symptomatology. When gathering such information, basic psychoeducation can help address fears, provide validation and offer hope to patients and their families.

Dysthymia among the elderly is clinically different from that in younger patients. Elderly individuals with dysthymia maintain an equal gender distribution, demonstrate a later age of onset, generally have lower rates of double depression and show a reduced comorbidity with anxiety or personality disorders compared with younger patients with dysthymia.[14] Elderly patients with dysthymia may also display a better long term prognosis compared with elderly patients with major depression.[24]

Anxiety is commonly a comorbid feature of geriatric depression. However, it is often misdiagnosed as an anxiety disorder and treated symptomatically with anti-anxiety agents, such as benzodiazepines. The most appropriate treatment for such mixed anxiety-depression is antidepressants.[12,15]

Given the discrepancy between the incidence of major mood disorders and that of subclinical disorders such as dysphoria, anxiety and depression-related disability among the elderly, studies to validate the various forms of depressive disorders in the elderly as diagnostically-reliable events are needed.

Often, the symptoms of geriatric depression are unrecognised by both the patient and the physician in the context of multiple physical illnesses and somatic complaints.[13,25] Depressed mood or sadness may be replaced by irritability, anxiety and a pronounced somatic focus without underlying medical abnormalities. As in younger patients, however, psychological symptoms, including a loss of enjoyment or interest in usual activities, hopelessness, helplessness or a wish to die, remain important markers of geriatric depression. The elderly have a higher rate of psychotic depression, particularly with somatic delusions, which is often clinically subtle.[26]

Substance abuse, especially alcohol (ethanol) abuse, among the elderly is an overlooked and understudied problem that can both cause and be a symptom of depression.[26,27]

Regardless of presentation, changes in cognition or personality which disrupt normal functioning are never a part of 'normal' aging, and deserve appropriate diagnostic attention and treatment.

1.3 Early- versus Late-Onset Depression

The clinical distinction between early-onset (first episode before age 50 years) and late-onset (first episode after age 50 years) depression is important. This is because late-onset depression appears to be more biologically heterogeneous, with hereditary factors and personality disorder comorbidity being less prevalent.[28-30] As such, late-onset depression has been associated with neurological and cerebrovascular disease,[31-34] neuroradiological abnormalities including ventriculomegaly and increased white matter hyperintensities on T_2-weighted magnetic resonance images[35-38] and possibly a higher frequency of the apolipoprotein E ε4 allele.[39]

Overall, patients with late-onset depression show greater cognitive impairment than those with early-onset depression,[38] with the cognitively impaired subgroup developing dementia at a higher rate.[40-42] In fact, evidence suggests that a significant number of those with late-onset depression are in the early stages of progressive dementing illness.[43] While neurological signs in elderly patients with depression may often be absent, clinicians should remain vigilant for the expression of more classic signs of particular neurological disorders given that these are possible harbingers of late-onset depression.

Depression-related cognitive impairment ('pseudodementia') in the elderly is distinguishable from primary dementing illness. For instance, older patients with depression commonly maintain a more rapid onset and progression of cognitive impairment with a greater awareness of their deficits than individuals with dementia. Additionally, equal impairment of both recent and remote memory in the setting of dysphoria is more consistent with geriatric depression.[12,42] Among individuals with mild-to-moderate depression, advanced age does not correlate with greater incidence or severity of depression-related cognitive impairment.[44]

1.4 Disability and Mortality Associated with Geriatric Depression

Elderly patients with depressive-spectrum disorders or major depression display more physical and social dysfunction than medically ill individuals without depression, i.e. the functional burden of depression is greater than that of medical illness.[45-47] Importantly, both subsyndromal and major depression can amplify the disability associated with long term medical illness,[15,22,48] leading to more cognitive impairment and premature institutionalisation[7,8,19,49] where even greater mortality rates are reported.[7,49]

More severe depression, as well as the specific symptoms of anxiety, depressive ideation, psychomotor retardation and bodyweight loss, have been associated with greater disability among elderly patients with depression.[50] Such direct and indirect morbidity and mortality persists despite the fact that, given adequate antidepressant therapy, the outcome for the elderly with depression does not differ from that of younger individuals.[48,51-53]

1.5 Medical Illness and Medications

Medical illness can cause or masquerade as late-life depression. Diseases of the cardiac and endocrine systems, as well as rheumatological disorders and cerebral disorders such as

Table I. Medical conditions commonly associated with the symptoms of depression[12,25]

Cardiovascular/respiratory
Congestive heart failure
Myocardial infarction
Chronic hypoxaemia

Endocrinological
Thyroid disease
Parathyroid dysfunction
Diabetes mellitus
Cushing's syndrome
Addison's disease

Neurological
Cerebrovascular accident
Subdural haematoma
Multiple sclerosis
Huntington's disease
Parkinson's disease
Erythematosus
Alzheimer's disease
Chronic pain syndrome
Sleep apnoea

Rheumatological
Fibromyalgia
Rheumatoid arthritis
Systemic lupus

Neoplastic
Pancreatic cancer
CNS tumours (primary/secondary)

Metabolic
Electrolyte disturbances
Malnutrition
Cyanocobalamin (vitamin B$_{12}$) deficiency
Folate deficiency

Parkinson's disease, Alzheimer's disease and stroke, can all present with overt depression (see table I).[12,25] Indeed, clinicians should expect 30 to 40% of patients with degenerative brain disease to exhibit symptoms of depression at some point during the course of their illness.[31,33] Among the medically ill, delirium may also be misdiagnosed as depression.[54]

Treatment of the underlying condition that is producing the symptoms of depression (illness-related lethargy and sleep disturbance) or cognitive impairment (medication or infection-related cognitive slowing and attentional difficulties) should be undertaken before, but not necessarily instead of, initiating antidepressant therapy. Indeed, the presence of psychological signs such as dysphoria, excessive guilt, anhedonia, hopelessness and helplessness are often reliable indicators of a depressive disorder in the setting of often confusing medical comorbidity. Regardless of aetiology, however, medical illness–related depression usually remains responsive to antidepressant pharmacotherapy.

The polypharmacy experienced by the elderly[55,56] also makes drug-induced depression, anxiety and cognitive impairment a common clinical entity. Depressive complaints have been associated with the use of corticosteroids and analgesics, as well as antihypertensives that have central adrenergic activity. Over-the-counter medications with antihistaminergic (diphenhydramine and cimetidine) and stimulant properties (phenylpropanolamine) can also produce mood and cognitive changes. Generally, however, drug-related symptoms will be temporally related (in the order of weeks or months) to the initiation of the medication.

2. Treatment of Geriatric Depression

In selecting any pharmacological agent, attention should focus initially on an individual patient's symptom profile, the potential adverse effects from the medication and the pharmacodynamic issues of both aging and polypharmacy. Selecting an antidepressant may also be guided by a personal or family history of response to a particular drug. However,

Table II. Factors affecting serum concentrations of psychotropic drugs in the elderly

Factors increasing concentrations	Factors decreasing concentrations
Age/physiological	
Reduced hepatic clearance	Decreased absorption
Reduced renal clearance	Increased body fat[a]
Reduced serum albumin level	
Comorbid illness/organ damage	
Decreased volume of distribution	
Pharmacological	
Polypharmacy/drug-drug interactions	Anticholinergic medications
Drug competition/protein binding	

a   This factor is offset by the decrease in volume of distribution, with the net effect being an increase in drug concentration.

treatment standardisation in the elderly is limited by the paucity of well-designed, double-blind studies in geriatric patients, especially those including the medically ill or individuals over 70 years of age.[57]

2.1 Pharmacological Options

2.1.1 Pharmacodynamics and Polypharmacy

Aging is accompanied by physiological changes that produce higher concentrations of pharmacologically active drug than would be achieved with the same dose in a younger individual (see table II). These factors, combined with the effect of age on neurotransmitter systems, suggest psychotropic agents in the elderly should be started at a dosage that is 25 to 50% of that which would be considered the standard adult dosage, with a more gradual dose titration using smaller increments.

With the growing appreciation of the influence of antidepressants on hepatic metabolic pathways, polypharmacy creates another layer of pharmacodynamic complexity. As the number of medications used for nonpsychiatric disorders is likely to be greater in the elderly, clinicians treating these patients will need to juggle the expected effects of a particular medication, its suspected adverse effects and the often unexpected impact of drug interactions secondary to polypharmacy. Table III provides a summary of the effect of antidepressants on the cytochrome P450 (CYP) enzyme system.

2.1.2 Selective Serotonin Reuptake Inhibitors

The selective serotonin (5-hydroxytryptamine; 5-HT) reuptake inhibitors (SSRIs) have revolutionised the treatment of geriatric depression.

SSRIs have little impact on cognition[63,64] and have a generally mild adverse effect profile of gastrointestinal events (diarrhoea and nausea) and sexual dysfunction (anorgasmia, ejaculatory delay and diminished libido). However, older patients may more commonly experience 'activating' effects (anxiety, psychomotor agitation and insomnia) and physiological disturbances [syndrome of inappropriate antidiuretic hormone secretion (SIADH), bradycardia and anorexia/bodyweight loss] when taking SSRIs. In addition, SSRI-associated extrapyramidal symptoms are likely to be experienced at higher rates by elderly than younger patients.[65]

In general, the SSRIs produce negligible anticholinergic effects. Paroxetine possesses the greatest *in vitro* anticholinergic potency,[47,66,67] with *in vitro* data showing it to be equipotent

Table III. Major cytochrome P450 (CYP) complexes, and their substrates and inhibitors (antidepressants are shown in bold)[58-62]

CYP complex	Inhibitor	Substrate	
		psychoactive agents	others
1A2	**Fluvoxamine, moclobemide,** fluoroquinolones, naringenin (grapefruit)	**TCAs (3° amines),** caffeine, clozapine (major), tacrine	Paracetamol (acetaminophen), phenacetin, propranolol, theophylline
2C9/10	**Fluvoxamine,** amiodarone, propoxyphene, fluconazole		NSAIDs, phenytoin (major), tolbutamide, warfarin
2C19[a]	**Fluoxetine, imipramine, moclobemide,** cimetidine, diazepam, felbamate, omeprazole	**Moclobemide, TCAs (3° amines),** citalopram, diazepam	Omeprazole, phenytoin (minor)
2D6[a]	**Fluoxetine, norfluoxetine, paroxetine, moclobemide, sertraline** (weak), **cimetidine, quinidine**	**Fluoxetine, paroxetine, TCAs (2°, 3° amines), venlafaxine,** clozapine (minor), haloperidol, perphenazine, risperidone, thioridazine	Codeine, dextromethorphan, flecainide, metoprolol, propafenone, propranolol, timolol
3A3/4	**Fluoxetine, fluvoxamine, nefazodone, norfluoxetine,** cimetidine, diltiazem, erythromycin, ketoconazole, verapamil	**Nefazodone, sertraline, TCAs (3° amines),** alprazolam, clonazepam, diazepam, midazolam, triazolam	Astemizole, carbamazepine, cisapride, erythromycin, felodipine, nifedipine, omeprazole, tamoxifen, terfenadine, quinidine, verapamil

a   Clinically significant polymorphisms reported.

NSAIDs = nonsteroidal anti-inflammatory drugs; **TCAs** = tricyclic antidepressants.

with nortriptyline as an antimuscarinic.[68] However, this appears to generate less serum anticholinergic activity than the TCAs.[66,67] The lack of anticholinergic activity with the SSRIs increases tolerability and reduces rates of premature discontinuation secondary to adverse effects during treatment.[25] Compared with older agents, the SSRIs are much safer in overdose and are better tolerated by patients with cardiac disease.[69]

Because the individual SSRIs have similar efficacy and adverse effect profiles, pharmacokinetic and pharmacodynamic differences in these drugs can help guide the clinician in deciding which one to prescribe.[58-62,70] For example, all the SSRIs, with the exception of fluvoxamine (77%), are extensively protein bound (>95%) and may elevate the serum concentrations of coadministered agents by displacing other protein bound medications.[47] The long elimination half-life of fluoxetine (5 days) and its active metabolite norfluoxetine (7 to 15 days) can complicate care in the case of an adverse event (as it will take some time for the drug to be removed from the body) or can assist with noncompliance (since a missed dose will not result in a clinically relevant decrease in plasma concentrations). Both paroxetine and sertraline have short elimination half-lives (1 day) and essentially inactive metabolites. *In vitro* data predict that sertraline will have less impact on hepatic drug metabolism compared with other SSRIs. However, coadministration of tricyclic antidepressants (TCAs) with sertraline has led to an increase in plasma TCA concentrations at higher dosages of sertraline, suggesting a possible dose-dependent effect of the SSRI on hepatic metabolism.[58] Because the

SSRIs can inhibit their own metabolism, dosage increases can produce relatively greater increases in the concentration of pharmacologically active drug.[69]

2.1.3 Tricyclic/Heterocyclic Agents

The TCAs have been available for over 3 decades. Despite the breadth of experience with these drugs, their use in treating older patients has remained clinically challenging, given their multiple physiological effects. They are cardiotoxic and often fatal in overdose, and interact with a variety of brain systems via their affinity for α_1-adrenergic, H_1 histaminergic and muscarinic-cholinergic receptors. These interactions produce sedation, orthostatic hypotension, constipation, urinary retention, impaired cognition and even delirium.[63]

The use of the secondary amines (nortriptyline and desipramine) is recommended to minimise anticholinergic adverse effects. However, these agents still have greater anticholinergic effects than any of the SSRIs (see section 2.1.2). Low doses of trazodone (25 to 100mg) can be used as a soporific with relatively few anticholinergic effects, offering an alternative to the benzodiazepines which can cause confusion, delirium and falls in older patients.[69]

Obtaining a therapeutic dosage of a TCA can be assisted by blood monitoring, providing a reliable measure of adequate dosage. However, it should be noted that the majority of the original serum concentration–drug dosage data were obtained from younger populations.[71] Careful, repeated dosage titration is required when using blood concentrations to determine dosage in the elderly, given the pharmacodynamic changes associated with aging.

The comparable efficacy of TCAs and SSRIs in relation to depressive subtypes remains a topic of clinical debate. While these antidepressant classes appear equally efficacious among groups of younger and older medically well individuals with depression,[72-78] the effectiveness of SSRIs compared with TCAs in the more severely depressed, medically compromised elderly has been questioned.[79,80]

2.1.4 Atypical Antidepressants

Amfebutamone (Bupropion)

Amfebutamone (bupropion) is an aminoketone that is theorised to act via noradrenergic and dopaminergic mechanisms. At present, it appears to be underutilised in treating elderly patients with depression. The drug has reliable activating effects and so can be especially helpful in treating patients who have retarded depression, without producing anticholinergic or hypotensive effects. At higher dosages (>500 mg/day), amfebutamone has been associated with an increase in seizure risk compared with other antidepressants.[81]

Venlafaxine

Venlafaxine is the first agent specifically designed to produce antidepressant activity by blocking the reuptake of both serotonin and noradrenaline (norepinephrine). Advanced age does not substantially alter its pharmacokinetics, nor its primarily serotonergic adverse effect profile.[82] The short elimination half-life of venlafaxine (3 to 5 hours), and that of its active metabolite O-demethyl-venlafaxine (9 to 11 hours), necessitates multiple daily administration.[25]

Nefazodone

Nefazodone is a selective serotonin 5-HT$_2$ receptor antagonist that is chemically related to trazodone. It has not been well studied in geriatric populations. The adverse effect profile of nefazodone includes sedation, dizziness, nausea and dry mouth.[25] The coadministration of nefazodone (or fluvoxamine) with terfenadine, astemizole or cisapride is contraindicated due to the inhibition of CYP3A3/4 by the antidepressant and the resultant risk of cardiac arrhythmias arising from increased concentrations of terfenadine, astemizole or cisapride.

Mirtazapine

Mirtazapine is a newly introduced antidepressant that is primarily an α_2-adrenoreceptor antagonist. The drug was designed to enhance the firing of both serotonergic and noradrenergic neurons through complex pre- and post-synaptic regulatory mechanisms. Mirtazapine has been shown to be efficacious in the elderly.[83] It can cause dry mouth, dizziness and sedation, but appears to be associated with a lower incidence of gastrointestinal adverse effects compared with the SSRIs and venlafaxine.[84]

Stimulants

Stimulants, such as dexamphetamine (dextroamphetamine) and methylphenidate, have also been advanced as both an adjunctive treatment for retarded depression and as primary antidepressants in the elderly.[85,86]

2.1.5 Monoamine Oxidase Inhibitors

The irreversible monoamine oxidase (MAO) inhibitors (MAOIs), such as phenelzine and tranylcypromine, have been used since the 1950s to treat depression. However, more recently, they have been relegated to use primarily in cases of treatment-resistant depression, although they are effective as both acute and maintenance pharmacotherapy in elderly individuals with depression.[87-89] The reason for the reduction in the usage of these drugs is that, while they produce minimal cognitive impairments[63] and cardiotoxicity, they frequently cause orthostatic hypotension. In addition, the interaction between irreversible MAOIs and foodstuffs containing tyramine and certain over-the-counter medications (e.g. phenylpropanolamine and pseudoephedrine) can have serious consequences. This necessitates the adherence to a low tyramine diet and the avoidance of the above-mentioned medications.

In recent years, MAOIs that have specificity for one of the two different types of MAO and that have reversible effects on these enzymes have been developed. Selegiline (deprenyl), a MAO-B inhibitor which loses specificity at higher dosages, has shown antidepressant activity in elderly individuals who have treatment-resistant depression.[90] A newly introduced reversible MAO-A inhibitor, moclobemide, is free from significant anticholinergic and orthostatic effects, as well as dietary restrictions.[91]

2.2 Electroconvulsive Therapy

Elderly individuals with depression receive electroconvulsive therapy (ECT) more often than those in the younger age groups,[92] although persistent physician and patient misconceptions of the procedure result in its underutilisation. While the elderly may have a higher risk of post-ECT confusion, ECT represents a well tolerated and effective option for depression complicated by treatment-resistance, psychosis, refusal of oral intake or active suicidality.

Although short term efficacy rates for ECT exceed those of pharmacotherapy,[93] maintenance medication issues must be revisited after ECT has been used effectively; studies on maintenance ECT remain sparse, particularly in the elderly.

2.3 Nonsomatic Therapy

A growing body of evidence demonstrates the effectiveness of verbal treatments for depression. In a milestone study, more than half of geriatric patients assigned to brief psychodynamic, cognitive or behavioural therapy conditions attained remission in symptomatology; 70% showed marked improvement overall.[94] Much research has been devoted to short term treatments, usually of a cognitive or behavioural nature, with such treatments being found effective for older adults with mild or moderate levels of depression.[95] Group models of therapy for the elderly have also been found to reduce the symptoms of depression.[96]

While a specific mode of psychosocial treatment cannot yet be recommended as superior, it seems clear that psychotherapy addresses a range of issues faced by elderly individuals with depression.[97] In light of these findings, some have suggested that psychotherapy be considered highly effective in treating elderly individuals with depression, rather than just moderately efficacious.[98]

Nevertheless, presuming that a single treatment will affect change in a disorder as complex as depression in older adults may be overly simplistic.[99] Along these lines, long term, as well as short term, psychotherapy may be considered an ally of biological approaches in treating depression.[99] Indeed, the complexity of elderly patients' profiles may necessitate continuing treatments that begin with an acute, symptom-based focus but expand to include structural issues.[97] While no firm conclusions can yet be drawn, some preliminary investigations have been encouraging in demonstrating improvement in the symptoms of depression as a result of combined somatic and verbal treatments.[100,101]

2.4 Response and Relapse

2.4.1 Response

Elderly individuals with depression may show slower resolution of symptoms and have higher relapse rates than younger individuals with depression,[102-104] although if treated within the first 2 weeks of relapse, older patients respond to the index antidepressant as well as younger patients.[104] Furthermore, when appropriate antidepressant dosages and duration of treatment are employed, older patients do not display higher rates of treatment-resistance compared with younger individuals.[27]

2.4.2 Relapse

Once an older patient responds to pharmacotherapy, medication should be continued, utilising full dosages, for at least 1 year post-remission. Indeed, clinicians must expand their focus to encompass long term strategies, both pharmacological and psychotherapeutic, aimed at maintaining remission and preventing relapse. Poor compliance remains the major obstacle to successful long term antidepressant therapy; a 'family approach' involving social supports to monitor symptoms and medication use can help improve compliance rates.[105] For patients with more than two episodes of relapse, life-long therapy is indicated.

2.4.3 Treatment Resistance

Partial response to pharmacotherapy presents a growing challenge. The few studies of augmentation strategies in geriatric depression have reported mixed results, particularly concerning the effectiveness and neurotoxicity of lithium.[106,107] Given the increasing number of relatively well tolerated agents and the recognition of the involvement of multiple receptor systems in depression, dual antidepressant therapy is also a growing therapeutic option for patients with treatment-resistant depression.[108,109] Careful monitoring of adverse effects and blood antidepressant concentrations is necessary when using more than one antidepressant. Regardless of the augmentation strategy, adjunctive medication should be continued into the maintenance phase of treatment to reduce the risk of relapse.[110]

Prior to declaring treatment failure, depressed elderly individuals should receive 8 to 12 weeks of the maximally tolerated dosage of a particular agent (or adequate blood TCA concentration). Following this, if the patient appears to have treatment-resistant psychotic depression, the diagnosis should be revisited, either by the addition of an antipsychotic to the medication regimen or the use of ECT to attempt to achieve a response.

After the failure of monotherapy, standard practice has been to switch to an antidepressant from another class. Within-class switching with TCAs provides no clinical benefit (e.g. substituting desipramine for nortriptyline),[81] while the benefit gained from within-class switching with SSRIs remains undetermined.

Patients with treatment-resistant depression may benefit from the use of an older irreversible MAOI or the more recently introduced selegiline or moclobemide.[90] When moving from an SSRI to MAOI treatment, a drug wash-out period of at least 2 weeks is required.

In geriatric individuals with depression that is treatment-resistant and partially responsive and who have been exposed to only pharmacological treatment, adding a psychotherapeutic component should be a first-line consideration.

3. Special Considerations

3.1 Bereavement

An aging individual's skills to adapt and cope with stress may be overwhelmed when faced with tremendous loss, such as from professional and financial changes, the death of life-partners and close friends, or physical disability from medical illness.

Although personality structure and prior life experience can shape the response of an individual to repeated loss, identifying who will progress to subsyndromal or clinical depression remains understudied. The loss of social relationships and the subjective sense of diminished support, however, can both predict future depression and limit recovery.[111,112] Also, individuals with the greatest number of initial symptoms tend to have the poorest long term outcome.[111]

Interestingly, while antidepressant therapy is effective against bereavement-related depression,[113,114] grief-related symptoms, including searching, yearning and preoccupation with thoughts of the deceased, may be relatively unresponsive to pharmacotherapy.[113,115] Some have suggested classifying these less responsive symptoms as a unique disorder termed 'complicated grief',[116,117] which often coexists with more routine depressive disorders. While individual and cultural differences blur the distinction between pathology and 'normal grief', DSM-IV[118] does allow for a diagnosis of major depression within 2 months of a significant loss. Decisions concerning diagnosis should be guided by a patient's symptoms and dysfunction, rather than attribution of the symptoms to environment or circumstance. This will allow treatment decisions to be unencumbered by unintended bias.

3.2 Suicide

In the US, the rate of suicide among the elderly has been found to be consistently higher than that of any other age group,[119] particularly among the 80- to 84-year-old age group.[120] The fact that suicide completion rates increase with age and are highest among White men aged 65 years and older also argues against the suggested decrease of depressive disorders with increasing age (see section 1.1).[111,120] Men (divorced or widowed), Caucasians and the very aged are at highest risk of suicide.[121] Older adults appear to demonstrate more serious intent in their attempts to kill themselves than do younger individuals; they use more lethal means and require fewer attempts to achieve their end.[122-124]

Suicidality is also an important matter in inpatient settings, although the acknowledgment of suicidal ideation is reportedly lower among elderly than younger individuals with depression who are in hospital.[125] In one sample of elderly individuals hospitalised for major depression, 8.7% attempted suicide within 1 year of admission; this group was also 6-times more likely to have attempted suicide before their current episode.[126] There is also an association between suicide attempts and late-onset depression among inpatients.[123]

Although the biology of suicide is not well understood, evidence suggests that CSF levels of 5-hydroxyindoleacetic acid (5-HIAA) and homovanillic acid (HVA) are significantly lower in groups of suicide attempters compared with nonattempters and healthy individuals.[127] In addition, low CSF levels of 5-HIAA in patients with mood disorders who are hospitalised after attempting suicide may predict suicide risk within the first year after the attempt.[128]

Covert acts of deliberate self-harm, such as intentional noncompliance with medication regimens, cessation of eating and drinking, and experiencing fatal 'accidents', may in fact be instances of suicidality.[124,129] While depression itself is considered a primary risk factor for suicide among elderly individuals,[122,130] it is more often one of many factors involved.[131] Thus, researchers have turned to additional variables, such as hopelessness, to uncover the link between depression and suicide. While the linking of depression and suicide through hopelessness across all age groups has been well described,[132,133] it is less commonly explored in elderly populations. However, in a study of elderly patients with depression, previous suicide attempters had significantly higher hopelessness scores than nonattempters; in addition, a relationship between persistent high levels of hopelessness (post-symptom remission) and a history of suicidality emerged.[134]

Recommendations for the prevention of suicide in the elderly are the same as those in younger individuals (for a review, see Schifano[135]).

4. Perspectives

Increases in life expectancy during this century combined with the post-war population expansion have created a large cohort of adults now passing through mid-life. The World Health Organization estimates that during the period from 1990 to 2020, the worldwide population of those over 65 years of age will more than double.[136]

With these individuals entering late-life early in the next century, the number of elderly individuals who have or may develop psychiatric symptoms will grow considerably. By 2020, unipolar major depression is expected to become the second leading cause of disability worldwide.[136] The diagnosis and treatment of geriatric depression will, therefore, become a much larger issue in psychiatric medicine and beyond. Furthermore, the treatment of depressive disorders in the setting of degenerative brain disease, as well as long term medical illness and repeated loss, will also become commonplace. As a result, the cohort of clinicians equipped to recognise and treat these symptoms will need to be expanded.

To lessen the impact of depression-related comorbidity on recovery from medical illness, reduce the loss of life from elder suicide and lighten the economic burden associated with long term undertreated depression, more focused studies are needed to examine depression in the geriatric population. While there is tremendous overlap with depression in young and middle-aged adults, geriatric depression has its own unique epidemiological profile, diagnostic complexities, sociological pressures and therapeutic sensitivities, all of which require special attention.

References

1. United Nations Statistical Office. Demographic yearbook. New York: Department of Economic and Social Affairs, United Nations, 1993: 142-53
2. United States, Bureau of the Census. Statistical abstract of the United States. 115th ed. Washington, DC: US Department of Commerce, 1995: 88-9
3. Bland RC, Newman SC, Orn H. Period prevalence of psychiatric disorders in Edmonton. Acta Psychiatr Scand 1988; 77: 43-9
4. Robins LN, Regier DA. Psychiatric disorders in America: the Epidemiological Catchment Area study. New York: The Free Press, MacMillan Inc, 1991
5. Henderson AS, Jorm AF, Mackinnon A, et al. The prevalence of depressive disorders and the distribution of depressive symptoms in later life: a survey using Draft ICD-10 and DSM-III-R. Psychol Med 1993; 23 (3): 719-29
6. Slater SL, Katz IR. Prevalence of depression in the aged: formal calculations versus clinical facts. J Am Geriatr Soc 1995; 43: 78-9
7. Rovner BW, German PS, Brant LJ, et al. Depression and mortality in nursing homes. JAMA 1991 Feb 27; 265 (8): 993-6
8. Parmelee PA, Katz IR, Lawton MP. Incidence of depression long-term care settings. J Gerontol 1992; 47 (6): M189-96
9. Blazer D. The epidemiology of depression in late life. J Geriatr Psychiatry 1989; 22: 35-52
10. Ernst C, Angst J. Depression in old age: is there a real decrease in prevalence? A review. Eur Arch Psychiatry Clin Neurosci 1995; 245: 272-87
11. Knäuper B, Wittchen HU. Diagnosing major depression in the elderly: evidence for response bias in standardized diagnostic interviews? J Psychiatr Res 1994; 28 (2): 147-64
12. Martin LM, Fleming KC, Evans JM. Recognition and management of anxiety and depression in elderly patients. Mayo Clin Proc 1995; 70: 999-1006
13. Richardson JP, Gallo JJ. Geriatrics for the clinician: treatment of depression in the elderly. Md Med J 1996 Jul; 45 (7): 553-6
14. Devanand DP, Nobler MS, Singer T, et al. Is dysthymia a different disorder in the elderly? Am J Psychiatry 1994 Nov; 151 (11): 1592-9
15. Kennedy GJ. The geriatric syndrome of late-life depression. Psychiatr Serv 1995 Jan; 46 (1): 43-8
16. Lebowitz BD, Martinez RA, Niederehe G, et al. Treatment of depression in late life: NIMH/MacArthur Foundation Workshop report. Psychopharmacol Bull 1995; 31 (1): 185-202
17. Tannock C, Katona C. Minor depression in the aged. Drugs Aging 1995; 6 (4): 278-92
18. Blazer D, Hughes DC, George LK. The epidemiology of depression in an elderly community sample. Gerontologist 1987; 27: 281-7
19. Katz IR, Lesher E, Kleban M, et al. Clinical features of depression in the nursing home. Int Psychogeriatr 1989; 1 (1): 5-15
20. Howland RH, Thase ME. Biological studies of dysthymia. Biol Psychiatry 1991 Aug 1; 30 (3): 283-304
21. Hellerstein DJ, Yanowitch P, Rosenthal J, et al. A randomized double-blind study of fluoxetine versus placebo in the treatment of dysthymia. Am J Psychiatry 1993; 150: 1169-75
22. Wells KB, Burnam MA, Rogers W, et al. The course of depression in adult outpatients: results from the medical outcomes study. Arch Gen Psychiatry 1992 Oct; 49: 788-94
23. Koenig HG, Blazer DG III. Minor depression in late-life. Am J Geriatr Psychiatry 1996; 4 Suppl. 1: S14-21
24. Kivelä SL. Long-term prognosis of major depression in old-age: a comparison with prognosis of dysthymic disorder. Int Psychogeriatr 1995; 7: 69-82
25. Rothschild AJ. The diagnosis and treatment of late-life depression. J Clin Psychiatry 1996; 57 Suppl. 5: 5-11
26. Brodaty H. Think of depression: atypical presentations in the elderly. Aust Fam Physician 1993 Jul; 22 (7): 1195-203
27. Bonner D, Howard R. Treatment-resistant depression in the elderly. Int Psychogeriatr 1995; 7: 83-94
28. Baron M, Mendlewicz J, Klotz J. Age-of-onset and genetic transmission of affective disorders. Acta Psychiatr Scand 1981; 64: 373-80
29. Fava M, Alpert JE, Borus JS, et al. Patterns of personality disorder comorbidity in early-onset versus late-onset major depression. Am J Psychiatry 1996 Oct; 153 (10): 1308-12
30. Ranga Rama Krishnan K, Gadde KM. The pathophysiologic basis for late-life depression. Am J Geriatr Psychiatry 1996; 4 Suppl. 1: S22-33
31. Folstein SE, Peyser CE, Starkstein SE, et al. Subcortical triad of Huntington's disease: a model for a neuropathology of depression, dementia, and dyskinesia. In: Carroll BJ, Barrett JE, editors. Psychopathology and the brain. New York: Raven Press, 1991: 65-75
32. Coffey CE, Figiel GS. Neuropsychiatric significance of subcortical encephalomalacia. In: Carroll BJ, Barrett JE, editors. Psychopathology and the brain. New York: Raven Press, 1992: 243-64
33. Cummings J. Depression and Parkinson's disease: a review. Am J Psychiatry 1992; 149: 443-54

34. Ranga Rama Krishnan K. Neuroanatomic substrates of depression in the elderly. J Geriatr Psychiatry Neurol 1993 Jan-Mar; 6: 39-58
35. Figiel GS, Rama Ranga Krishnan K, Doraiswamy PM, et al. Subcortical hyperintensities on brain MRI: a comparison between late age onset and early onset elderly depressed subjects. Neurobiol Aging 1991; 26: 245-7
36. Alexopoulos GS, Young RC, Shindledecker R. Brain computed tomography in geriatric depression and primary degenerative dementia. Biol Psychiatry 1992; 31: 591-9
37. Lesser IM, Boone KB, Mehringer CM, et al. Cognition and white matter hyperintensities in older depressed patients. Am J Psychiatry 1996; 153: 1280-7
38. Salloway S, Malloy P, Kohn R, et al. MRI and neuropsychological differences in early- and late-onset geriatric depression. Neurology 1996 Jun; 46: 1567-74
39. Ranga Rama Krishnan K, Turpler LA, Ritchie JC, et al. Apolipoprotein E-e4 frequency in geriatric depression. Biol Psychiatry 1996; 40: 69-71
40. Reding M, Haycox J, Blass J. Depression in patients referred to a dementia clinic: a three-year prospective study. Arch Neurol 1986; 42: 894-6
41. Kral VA, Emery OB. Long-term follow-up of depressed pseudodementia of the aged. Can J Psychiatry 1988 Jun; 34 (5): 445-6
42. Alexopoulos GS, Meyers BS, Young RC, et al. The course of geriatric depression with 'reversible dementia': a controlled study. Am J Psychiatry 1993 Nov; 150 (11): 1693-9
43. Alexopoulos GS, Young RC, Meyers BS. Geriatric depression: age of onset and dementia. Biol Psychiatry 1993; 34: 141-5
44. Boone KB, Lesser I, Miller B, et al. Cognitive functioning in a mildly to moderately depressed geriatric sample: relationship to chronological age. J Neuropsychiatry 1994 Summer; 6 (3): 267-72
45. Wells KB, Stewart A, Hays RD, et al. The functioning and well-being of depressed patients: results from the medical outcomes study. JAMA 1989; 262: 914-9
46. Caine ED, Lyness JM, Conwell Y. Diagnosis of late-life depression. Am J Geriatr Psychiatry 1996; 4 Suppl. 1: S45-50
47. Newhouse P. Use of serotonin selective reuptake inhibitors in geriatric depression. J Clin Psychiatry 1996; 57 Suppl. 5: 12-22
48. Conwell Y. Outcomes of depression. Am J Geriatr Psychiatry 1996; 4 Suppl. 1: S34-44
49. Rovner BW. Depression and increased risk of mortality in the nursing home patient. Am J Med 1993 May 24; 94 Suppl. 5A: 19S-22S
50. Alexopoulos GS, Vrontou C, Kakuma T, et al. Disability in geriatric depression. Am J Psychiatry 1996 Jul; 153 (7): 877-85
51. Brodaty H, Harris L, Peters K, et al. Prognosis of depression in the elderly. Br J Psychiatry 1993; 163: 589-96
52. Alexopoulos GS, Meyers BS, Young RC, et al. Recovery in geriatric depression. Arch Gen Psychiatry 1996 Apr; 53: 305-12
53. Reynolds III CF, Frank E, Kupfer DJ, et al. Treatment outcome in recurrent major depression: a post hoc comparison of elderly ('young old') and midlife patients. Am J Psychiatry 1996; 153: 1288-92
54. Farrell KR, Ganzini L. Misdiagnosing delirium as depression in medically ill elderly patients. Arch Intern Med 1995 Dec 11; 155: 2459-64
55. Kalchthler T, Coccaro E, Lichtiger S. Incidence of polypharmacy in a long-term care facility. J Am Geriatr Soc 1977; 25: 308-13
56. Everitt DE, Avorn J. Drug prescribing for the elderly. Arch Intern Med 1986; 146: 2393-6
57. Katz IR. Drug treatment of depression in the frail elderly: discussion of the NIH consensus development conference on the diagnosis and treatment of depression in late life. Psychopharmacol Bull 1993; 29 (1): 101-8
58. Kerremans AL. Cytochrome P450 isoenzymes: importance for the internist. Neth J Med 1996; 48: 237-43
59. Nemeroff CB, DeVane CL, Pollock BG. Newer antidepressants and the cytochrome P450 system. Am J Psychiatry 1996 Mar; 153 (3): 311-20
60. Ereshefsky L, Riesenman C, Lam YW. Antidepressant drug interactions and the cytochrome P450 system: the role of cytochrome P450 2D6. Clin Pharmacokinet 1995; 29 Suppl. 1: 10-9
61. Brøsen K. Are pharmacokinetic drug interactions with the SSRIs an issue? Int Clin Psychopharmacol 1996; 11 Suppl. 1: 23-7
62. Ketter TA, Flockhart DA, Post RM, et al. The emerging role of cytochrome P450 3A in psychopharmacology. J Clin Psychopharmacol 1995; 15: 387-98
63. Knegtering H, Eijck M, Huijsman A. Effects of antidepressants on cognitive functioning of elderly patients: a review. Drugs Aging 1994 Sep; 5 (3): 192-9
64. Oxman TE. Antidepressants and cognitive impairment in the elderly. J Clin Psychiatry 1996; 57 Suppl. 5: 38-44
65. Leo R. Movement disorders associated with the serotonin-selective reuptake inhibitors. J Clin Psychiatry 1996; 57: 449-54
66. Richelson E. The pharmacology of antidepressants at the synapse: focus on newer compounds. J Clin Psychiatry 1994 Sep; 55 Suppl. A: 34-9
67. Cusack B, Nelson A, Richelson E. Binding of antidepressants to human brain receptors: focus on the newer generation compounds. Psychopharmacology 1994 May; 114 (4): 559-65
68. Laghrissithode F, Pollock BG, Miller MC, et al. Double-blind comparison of paroxetine and nortriptyline on the postural stability of late-life depressed patients. Psychopharmacol Bull 1995; 31 (4): 659-63
69. Preskorn SH. Recent pharmacologic advances in antidepressant treatment for the elderly. Am J Med 1993 May 24; 94 Suppl. 5A: 2-12S
70. Rosenbaum J. Managing selective serotonin reuptake inhibitor-drug interactions in clinical practice. Clin Pharmacokinet 1995; 29 Suppl. 1: 53-9
71. Amsterdam J, Brunswick D, Mendels J. The clinical application of tricyclic antidepressant pharmacokinetics and plasma levels. Am J Psychiatry 1980 Jun; 137 (6): 653-62
72. Feighner JP, Cohn JB. Double-blind comparative trials of fluoxetine and doxepin in geriatric patients with major depressive disorder. J Clin Psychiatry 1985 Mar; 46 (3): 20-5
73. Falk WE, Rosenbaum JF, Otto MW, et al. Fluoxetine versus trazodone in depressed geriatric patients. J Geriatr Psychiatry Neurol 1989; 2 (4): 208-14
74. Guillibert E, Pelcier Y, Archambault JC, et al. A double-blind multicenter study of paroxetine versus clomipramine in depressed elderly subjects. Acta Psychiatr Scand 1989; 80 Suppl. 350: 132-4
75. Cohn CK, Shirvastava R, Mendels J, et al. Double-blind, multicenter comparison of sertraline and amitriptyline in elderly depressed patients. J Clin Psychiatry 1990 Dec; 51 Suppl. 12B: 28-33
76. Claghorn JL, Feighner JP. A double-blind comparison of paroxetine with imipramine in the long-term treatment of depression. J Clin Psychopharmacol 1993 Dec; 13 (6): 23S-7S

77. Geretsegger C, Stuppaeck CH, Mair M, et al. Multicenter double blind study of paroxetine and amitriptyline in elderly depressed inpatients. Psychopharmacology 1995; 119: 277-81
78. Miller FT, Freilicher J. Comparison of TCAs and SSRIs in the treatment of major depression in hospitalized geriatric patients. J Geriatr Psychiatry Neurol 1995 Jul; 8: 173-6
79. Glassman A, Ballenger J, Stokes P, et al. Tricyclic antidepressants: advantages and limitations. Geriatrics 1993 Nov; 48 Suppl. 2: 6-8
80. Roose SP, Glassman AH, Attia E, et al. Comparative efficacy of selective serotonin reuptake inhibitors in the treatment of melancholia. Am J Psychiatry 1994 Dec; 151 (12): 1735-9
81. Baldessarini RJ. Drugs and the treatment psychiatric disorders, depression and mania. In: Molinoff P, Ruddon R, editors. Goodman and Gilman's the pharmacologic basis of therapeutics. 9th ed. New York: McGraw Hill, 1996: 431-59
82. Drevets WC. Geriatric depression: brain imaging correlates and pharmacologic considerations. J Clin Psychiatry 1994 Sep; 55 Suppl. 9a: 71-81
83. Halikas JA. Org 3770 (mirtazapine) versus trazodone: a placebo-controlled trial in depressed elderly patients. Hum Psychopharmacol 1995; 10: S125-33
84. Frazer A. Pharmacology of antidepressants. J Clin Psychopharmacol 1997; 2 Suppl. 1: 2-18S
85. Gurian B, Rosowsky E. Low-dose methylphenidate in the very old. J Geriatr Psychiatry Neurol 1990 Jul-Sep; 3 (3): 152-4
86. Wallace AE, Kofoed LL, West AN. Double-blind, placebo-controlled trial of methylphenidate in older, depressed, medically ill patients. Am J Psychiatry 1995 Jun; 152 (6): 929-31
87. Georgotas A, McCue RE, Friedman E, et al. Response of depressive symptoms to nortriptyline, phenelzine and placebo. Br J Psychiatry 1987; 151: 102-6
88. Georgotas A, McCue RE, Cooper TB, et al. How effective and safe is continuation therapy in elderly depressed patients? Arch Gen Psychiatry 1988; 45: 929-33
89. Georgotas A, McCue RE, Cooper TB. A placebo-controlled comparison of nortriptyline and phenelzine in maintenance therapy of elderly depressed patients. Arch Gen Psychiatry 1989 Sep; 46: 783-6
90. Sunderland T, Cohen RM, Molchan S, et al. High-dose selegiline in treatment-resistant older depressive patients. Arch Gen Psychiatry 1994 Aug; 51 (8): 607-15
91. Nair NP, Ahmed SK, Ng Ying Kin NM, et al. Reversible and selective inhibitors of monoamine oxidase A in the treatment of depressed elderly patients. Acta Psychiatr Scand 1995; 91 Suppl. 386: 28-35
92. Reynolds III CF, Lebowitz BD, Schneider LS. The NIH consensus development conference on the diagnosis and treatment of depression in late life. Psychopharmacol Bull 1993; 29 (1): 83-95
93. Philibert RA, Richards L, Lynch CF, et al. Effect of ECT on mortality and clinical outcome in geriatric unipolar depression. J Clin Psychiatry 1995 Sep; 56 (9): 390-4
94. Thompson LW, Gallagher D, Steinmetz-Breckenridge J. Comparative effectiveness of psychotherapies for depressed elders. J Consult Clin Psychology 1987; 55: 385-90
95. Thompson LW. Cognitive-behavioral therapy and treatment for late-life depression. J Clin Psychiatry 1996; 57 Suppl. 5: 29-37
96. Steuer JL, Mintz J, Hammen CL, et al. Cognitive-behavioral and psychodynamic group psychotherapy in the treatment of geriatric depression. J Consult Clin Psychology 1984; 52: 80-9
97. Sadavoy J. Integrated psychotherapy for the elderly. Can J Psychiatry 1994; 39: S19-26
98. Scogin F, McElreath L. Efficacy of psychosocial treatments for geriatric depression: a quantitative review. J Consult Clin Psychology 1994; 62: 69-74
99. Reynolds III CF. Treatment of depression in late life. Am J Med 1994; 97: 39S-46S
100. Reynolds III CF, Frank E, Perel JM, et al. Combined pharmacotherapy and psychotherapy in the acute and continuation treatment of elderly patients with recurrent major depression: a preliminary report. Am J Psychiatry 1992; 149: 1687-92
101. Reynolds III CF, Frank E, Perel JM, et al. Maintenance therapies for late-life recurrent major depression: research and review circa 1995. Int Psychogeriatr 1995; 7: 27-39
102. Hinrichsen GA, Hernandez NA. Factors associated with recovery from and relapse into major depressive disorder in the elderly. Am J Psychiatry 1993 Dec; 150 (12): 1820-5
103. Kamath M, Finkel SI, Moran MB. A retrospective chart review of antidepressant use, effectiveness, and adverse effects in adults age 70 and older. Am J Geriatr Psychiatry 1996; 4: 167-72
104. Reynolds III CF, Frank E, Perel JM, et al. Treatment of consecutive episodes of major depression in the elderly. Am J Psychiatry 1994 Dec; 151 (12): 1740-3
105. Reynolds III CF. Recognition and differentiation of elderly depression in the clinical setting. Geriatrics 1995 Oct; 50 Suppl. 1: S6-15
106. Kushnir SL. Lithium-antidepressant combination in the treatment of depressed, physically ill geriatric patients. Am J Psychiatry 1986; 143: 378-9
107. Flint AJ, Rifat SL. A prospective study of lithium augmentation in antidepressant-resistant geriatric depression. J Clin Psychopharmacol 1994 Oct; 14 (5): 353-6
108. Weilburg JB, Rosenbaum JF, Biederman J, et al. Fluoxetine added to non-MAOI antidepressants converts nonresponders to responders: a preliminary report. J Clin Psychiatry 1989; 50: 447-9
109. Seth R, Jennings AL, Bindman J, et al. Combination treatment with noradrenaline and serotonin reuptake inhibitors in treatment resistant depression. Br J Psychiatry 1992; 161: 562-5
110. Reynolds III CF, Frank E, Perel JM, et al. High relapse rate after discontinuation of adjunctive medication for elderly patients with recurrent major depression. Am J Psychiatry 1996 Nov; 153 (11): 1418-22
111. Jorm AF. The epidemiology of depressive states in the elderly: implications for recognition, intervention and prevention. Soc Psychiatr Epidemiol 1995; 30: 53-9
112. Lebowitz B. Diagnosis and treatment of depression in late life. Am J Geriatr Psychiatry 1996; 4 Suppl. 1: S3-6
113. Pasternak RE, Reynolds III CF, Schlernitzauer M, et al. Acute open-trial of nortriptyline therapy of bereavement related depression in late life. J Clin Psychiatry 1991; 52: 307-10
114. Pasternak RE, Reynolds III CF, Frank E, et al. The temporal course of depressive symptoms and grief intensity in late-life spousal bereavement. Depression 1993; 1: 45-9
115. Jacobs SC, Nelson JC, Zisook S. Treating depressions of bereavement with antidepressants: a pilot study. Psychiatr Clin North Am 1987; 10: 501-10
116. Prigerson HG, Frank E, Kasl SV, et al. Complicated grief and bereavement-related depression as distinct disorders: preliminary empirical validation in elderly bereaved spouses. Am J Psychiatry 1995 Jan; 152 (1): 22-30
117. Prigerson HG, Bierhals AJ, Kasl SV, et al. Complicated grief as a disorder distinct from bereavement-related depression and anxiety: a replication study. Am J Psychiatry 1996 Nov; 153 (11): 1484-6

118. American Psychiatric Association. Diagnostic and statistical manual of mental disorders. 4th ed. Washington, DC: American Psychiatric Association, 1994

119. Blazer DG, Bachar JR, Manton KG. Suicide in late life: review and commentary. J Am Geriatr Soc 1986; 34: 519-25

120. Kanowski S. Age-dependent epidemiology of depression. Gerontology 1994; 40 Suppl. 1: 1-4

121. Danto BL, Danto JM. Psychiatric treatment of the elderly suicidal patient. In: Lester D, Tallmer M, editors. Now I lay me down: suicide in the elderly. Philadelphia: Charles Press, 1994: 43-55

122. Conwell Y, Rotenberg M, Caine ED. Completed suicide at age 50 and over. J Am Geriatr Soc 1990; 38: 640-4

123. Lyness JM, Conwell Y, Nelson JC. Suicide attempts in elderly psychiatric inpatients. J Am Geriatr Soc 1992; 40: 320-4

124. Szanto K, Reynolds III CF, Frank E, et al. Suicide in elderly depressed patients: is active *vs* passive suicidal ideation a clinically valid distinction? Am J Geriatr Psychiatry 1996; 4: 197-207

125. Blazer D, Bachar JR, Hughes DC. Major depression with melancholia: a comparison of middle-aged and elderly adults. J Am Geriatr Soc 1987; 35: 927-32

126. Zweig RA, Hinrichsen GA. Factors associated with suicide attempts by depressed older adults: a prospective study. Am J Psychiatry 1993; 150: 1687-92

127. Jones JS, Stanley B, Mann JJ, et al. CSF 5-HIAA and HVA concentrations in elderly depressed patients who attempted suicide. Am J Psychiatry 1990; 147: 1225-7

128. Nordström P, Samuelsson M, Åsberg M, et al. CSF 5-HIAA predicts suicide risk after attempted suicide. Suicide Life Threat Behav 1994; 24: 1-9

129. McIntosh JL, Santos JF, Hubbard RW, et al. Elder suicide: research, theory, and treatment. Washington, DC: American Psychological Association, 1994: 127-31

130. Meehan PJ, Saltzman LE, Sattin RW. Suicides among older United States residents: epidemiologic characteristics and trends. Am J Pub Health 1991; 81: 1198-200

131. Tallmer M. Symptoms and assessment of suicide in the elderly patient. In: Lester D, Tallmer M, editors. Now I lay me down: suicide in the elderly. Philadelphia: Charles Press, 1994: 17-30

132. Beck AT, Kovacs M, Weissman A. Assessment of suicidal intention: the scale for suicide ideation. J Consult Clin Psychology 1979; 47: 343-52

133. Beck AT, Steer RA, Kovacs M, et al. Hopelessness and eventual suicide: a 10-year prospective study of patients hospitalized with suicidal ideation. Am J Psychiatry 1985; 142: 559-63

134. Rifai AH, George CJ, Stack JA, et al. Hopelessness in suicide attempters after acute treatment of major depression in late life. Am J Psychiatry 1994; 151: 1687-90

135. Schifano F. Pharmacological strategies for preventing suicidal behaviour. CNS Drugs 1994; 1 (1): 16-25

136. Murray C, Lopez AD, editors. The global burden of disease. Cambridge (MA): Harvard University Press, 1996: 375-85

Correspondence: Dr *Robert A. Lasser,* Bldg 10, Rm 3D41, NIMH, NIH, Clinical Center, 10 Center Drive, MSC 1264, Bethesda, MD 20892-1264, USA.

A Risk-Benefit Assessment of Pharmacotherapies for Clinical Depression in Children and Adolescents

Johanne Renaud, David Axelson and *Boris Birmaher*

Department of Psychiatry, University of Pittsburgh, School of Medicine, Western Psychiatric Institute and Clinic, Pittsburgh, Pennsylvania, USA

Child and adolescent major depressive disorders are common and recurrent disorders. The prevalence of major depressive disorders is estimated to be approximately 2% in children and 4 to 8% in adolescents.[1-8] Major depressive disorders in children and adolescents are frequently accompanied by other psychiatric disorders, poor psychosocial outcome and a high risk of suicide and substance abuse, indicating the need for efficacious treatments and prevention. The use of antidepressants in the treatment of child and adolescent depression appears reasonable in light of the significant morbidity and mortality associated with this disorder, the multiple lines of evidence suggesting continuity from child and adolescent to adult depression and the well established efficacy of antidepressants in the treatment of adult depression.

While the goal of this article is to address the risk-benefit issues related to the pharmacological treatment of major depressive disorders in childhood and adolescence, all the studies in children have focused on major depressive disorders and none on dysthymic disorder. However, general principles for the pharmacological treatment of major depressive disorders may also be applied to the treatment of dysthymia.

Although it is beyond the scope of this review, it is important to mention that psychotherapeutic techniques, such as cognitive-behaviour therapy and interpersonal therapy have been found to be efficacious interventions in treating children and adolescents with mild to moderate depressive disorders.

1. Psychopharmacological Interventions

An acute phase medication trial usually lasts at least 6 to 12 weeks, during which patients are seen weekly or biweekly for monitoring of symptoms, adverse effects, dose adjustments and psychotherapy.

Most of the studies published in the child and adolescent literature to date have evaluated the effects of the tricyclic antidepressants (TCAs) and few have addressed the selective serotonin (5-hydroxytryptamine; 5-HT) reuptake inhibitors (SSRIs). Other antidepressants, including the heterocyclics (e.g. amoxapine, maprotiline), amfebutamone (bupropion), venlafaxine and nefazodone, have been found to be efficacious for the treatment of adults with depression,[9] but they have not been studied for the treatment of children and adolescents with depression.[10]

Factors to consider when selecting an antidepressant include the patient's subtype of depression, chronicity of symptoms and past treatment history, as well as the medication's likelihood of adverse effects, safety in overdose and cost.[11] Before using antidepressants, parents and patients should be informed about adverse effects, dose and the lag time before onset of therapeutic effects. Prior to starting medication treatment, it is advisable to assess the severity of the depressive symptoms using one of the available depression rating scales (e.g. Beck Depression Inventory),[12] and assess the existence of physical signs and symptoms that resemble medication adverse effects. Patients and parents should be informed about the danger of an overdose, in particular with TCAs. For patients at risk of suicide, we recommend that parents be responsible for storing and administering the medications, especially during the acute episode of depression and during the first 2 to 4 months after complete remission.

A medical history and examination are indicated before using antidepressants. Use of other medications that may interact with the antidepressants and history of allergies should be ascertained. Thus far, there has been no need for baseline laboratory testing before using SSRIs. As we will discuss in more detail in section 1.2, before starting one of the TCAs, a baseline electrocardiogram, resting blood pressure and heart rate (supine or sitting, standing) and body-weight should be obtained. No other tests are generally indicated in a healthy child before starting antidepressants.

1.1 Selective Serotonin Reuptake Inhibitors (SSRIs)

In children and adolescents, SSRIs are favoured as first-line medications for treatment of depression for a number of reasons. SSRIs are efficacious for the treatment of all ages with major depressive disorders.[11,13,14] SSRIs have a relatively acceptable adverse effect profile, very low lethality after an overdose and easy administration (generally once a day). In fact, despite the paucity of research with the SSRIs, the use of SSRIs for the treatment of depressed children and adolescents has increased rapidly over the past few years. IMS America noted an increase of 69% in the total number of prescriptions of SSRIs for children and adolescents from 1995 to 1996.[15]

The SSRIs have been shown to selectively block the presynaptic neuronal reuptake of serotonin with little or no affinity for the adrenergic, cholinergic or histaminic receptor.[13,16] SSRI relative potency to block serotonin reuptake has been reported to be: citalopram > paroxetine > fluvoxamine > sertraline > clomipramine > fluoxetine.[16] However, potency has not been shown to be correlated with clinical improvement.[16]

Noncomparative studies have reported that 70% to 90% of adolescents with major depressive disorders experienced an improvement in depressive symptomology with fluoxetine or sertraline.[16,17] A double-blind, placebo-controlled study in a very small sample of adolescents with major depressive disorders did not find significant differences between placebo and fluoxetine.[18] However, a recent 8-week, double-blind study involving a large sample of youths with major depressive disorders showed that a significantly greater number of children and adolescents experienced an improvement in depressive symptomology with fluoxetine than to placebo (58% *vs* 32%, as measured by the Clinical Global Improvement Scale).[14] Despite the significant response to fluoxetine, many patients had only partial improvement in their symptoms of depression and only 31% experienced a full remission. A possible explanation for many patients experiencing only a partial improvement is that effective treatment may involve variation in dose or length of treatment. Also, it is possible that the ideal treatment may involve a combination of pharmacological and psychosocial treatments.

A preliminary analysis of a multicentre study in outpatient adolescents comparing paroxetine, imipramine and placebo (n = 270) for the treatment of major depressive disorders also suggested that paroxetine was efficacious and well tolerated.[19]

1.1.1 Adverse Effects

The adverse effects of all SSRIs are similar, dose-dependent and may subside with time.[13] One of the main adverse effects is so-called 'behavioural activation', which manifests as agitation, impulsiveness, silliness and 'daring' behaviours. It needs to be differentiated from mania, given that, similar to other antidepressants, the SSRIs may trigger an episode of hypomania or mania in vulnerable patients. In addition, the SSRIs may induce gastrointestinal symptoms (e.g. nausea, diarrhoea), decreased appetite, decreased or increased bodyweight, headaches (and migraines in patients with family history), restlessness, tremor, jitteriness, insomnia or hypersomnia (in particular paroxetine and fluvoxamine), diaphoresis, vivid dreams, sexual dysfunction (delayed ejaculation, anorgasmia), disruption of sleep architecture, apathy and indifference.

The SSRIs may also induce extrapyramidal symptoms (e.g. akathisia), in particular when combined with antipsychotics.[20,21] In rare cases, SSRIs have been associated with hyponatraemia[22] and with ecchymoses.[23-25] Allergies have been reported but, as with any other medication, these need to be differentiated from allergies to the dyes contained in the medication preparation.

SSRIs, in particular fluoxetine, were initially thought to be associated with increased risk for suicide (perhaps linked to behavioural activation or akathisia).[26,27] However, while not ruling out such phenomena in a small number of cases, several studies and a recent meta-analysis suggest that SSRIs reduce the risk of suicide in depressed patients.[28] It is important to underline that most studies of SSRIs in children and adolescents have focused on acute adverse effects with no studies evaluating the long term adverse effects.

1.1.2 Prescribing SSRIs

We recommend starting with a lower dose of an SSRI and increasing it progressively. A slow, but steady approach may reduce the likelihood of inducing adverse effects (particularly in patients with comorbid panic disorder) which could jeopardise patient and parents' compliance with treatment. Fluoxetine takes a longer time to reach steady state plasma concentrations and may require longer trials. However, it appears that, in adults, steady state pharmacokinetics are not required for clinical efficacy.[29]

All SSRIs seem to be equally efficacious for the treatment of major depression and they have similar adverse effects. Currently, it appears that no recommendations can be made as to the choice of particular SSRI to use. However, they have some differences, including elimination half-lives, drug interactions and antidepressant activity of their metabolites.[13,16,30,31] Time to peak concentration after ingestion, plasma half-life, doses and metabolites, based on studies in adults, are outlined in table I. It is important to emphasise that individual patients may respond differently to some SSRIs.

The time course of improvement with the SSRIs appears to be similar to that of the TCAs (4 to 6 weeks). Therefore, guidelines to change dosages of TCAs described in section 1.2.3

Table I. Pharmacokinetic parameters and dosage recommendations for selective serotonin (5-hydroxytryptamine; 5-HT) reuptake inhibitors (based on studies in adults, except for Findling et al.[32])

| Drug | Time to peak plasma concentration (h) | Plasma half-life | | Inhibition of own metabolism | Active metabolites | Initial dosage (mg/day) | Dosage range (mg/day) |
		single dose	multiple dose				
Fluoxetine	6-8	2 days	6 days	Yes	Norfluoxetine (half-life 7-15 days; after treatment for 2-3 mo concentrations are 2-3 times higher than those of fluoxetine)	5-10	10-60
Sertraline	4-8	1 day	1 day	No[a]	Demethyl-sertraline (mildly active)	25-50	50-200
Paroxetine[32]	3-8	16h	1 day	Yes	Metabolites are active at higher doses	10-20	10-60
Fluvoxamine	2-8	16h	1 day	Yes (mildly)	Fluvoxamine acid (mildly active)	25-50	50-300
Citalopram	2-4	33h	33h	No[a]	Demethyl-citalopram and didemethyl-citalopram	10-20	10-60

a   Linear pharmacokinetics.

may be applied for the SSRIs. However, these guidelines need to be applied cautiously because it is not clear if longer trials with SSRIs will reveal an increase in the number of patients with late improvement.[33] Patients receiving standard dosages have similar probabilities of responding as those on higher dosages.[34,35] However, individual patients may need higher doses to achieve responses.

1.1.3 Pharmacokinetics and Blood Concentrations

A pharmacokinetic study in children and adolescents showed that after 8 weeks of treatment, concentrations of fluoxetine and its metabolite norfluoxetine had not reached steady state,[36] suggesting that clinical efficacy studies using this drug must last 12 weeks or more. This study exemplifies the importance of studying the pharmacokinetics of psychotropics in children and adolescents before embarking on clinical efficacy studies because, as in the case of medications with long half-lives, shorter studies may not find differences between the medication and placebo. Interestingly, however, preliminary analysis of a recent study suggested that the half-life of paroxetine may be shorter in children and adolescents than in adults.[32]

Overall, the SSRIs possess a relatively flat dose-response curve suggesting that maximal clinical response may be achieved at minimum effective dosages. Thus, allowing adequate time to reach a clinical response is preferable to increasing dosages repeatedly. In the absence of a serious concern about toxicity or unless checking for compliance, monitoring of plasma SSRIs concentration is not indicated.[13,30,31]

1.1.4 Discontinuation

SSRIs with shorter half-lives, e.g. paroxetine, may induce withdrawal symptoms when discontinued abruptly; these symptoms may mimic a relapse or recurrence of a depressive episode, e.g. tiredness, irritability.[37] Furthermore, there is preliminary evidence that rapid discontinuation of an antidepressant may induce a relapse or recurrence of depression. Therefore, if these medications need to be discontinued, they should be tapered over time.

1.1.5 Interactions with Other Medications

All SSRIs inhibit, in various degrees, the metabolism of many medications that are metabolised by the hepatic cytochrome P450 (CYP) isoenzymes. Some well known medications that interact with SSRIs include: the TCAs, antipsychotics, antiarrhythmics, some anticonvulsants, some β-blockers and calcium antagonists, cisapride, benzodiazepines, carbamazepine, theophylline, warfarin, terfenadine and astemizole.[13,16] This is not an exhaustive list and new interactions are frequently discovered. The reader is urged to consult additional sources and stay abreast of new information about interactions. When using SSRIs in combination with other medications, we recommend being cautious with dosage administration, paying close attention to any symptoms which could indicate toxicity, and monitoring of blood concentrations of medications with low therapeutic indices.

Interactions with other serotonergic medications, e.g. monoamine oxidase inhibitors (MAOIs), may induce the serotonergic syndrome, characterised by agitation, confusion, hyperthermia, etc. It is important to emphasise that MAOIs should not be given within 5 weeks of stopping fluoxetine and within at least 2 weeks for other SSRIs. Also, the SSRIs should not be administered within 2 weeks of stopping MAOIs. Lithium is also a serotonergic compound and, while all possible interactions with SSRIs should be monitored carefully, this possible interaction has not been well studied.[38,39] The SSRIs also have a high rate of protein binding, which can lead to altered therapeutic or toxic effects of other highly protein-bound medications.

1.2 Tricyclic Antidepressants

Randomised controlled studies in adults with major depressive disorder have consistently confirmed the efficacy of TCAs, with 50 to 70% of patients receiving TCAs achieving an improvement in depressive symptoms and drug-placebo differences ranging from 20 to 40%.[9,40] In contrast, in children and adolescents with depression, 12 double-blind psychopharmacological trials showed that 50 to 60% of patients experienced an improvement in depressive symptoms with both TCAs (nortriptyline, desipramine, amitriptyline) and placebo.[41-43] Furthermore, a recent large multicentre study showed no differences between imipramine and placebo in a large group of adolescents with depression.[19]

These findings suggest that the TCAs are not useful in the treatment of children and adolescents with depression. However, TCAs may be indicated in certain individual cases, for example to augment the effects of SSRIs and for treatment of a child with major depressive disorder and attention deficit hyperactivity disorder (ADHD).

1.2.1 Adverse Effects

Most studies in children have focused on the short term adverse effects of TCAs, with few studies describing the long term adverse effects. TCA adverse effects are mainly caused by blockade of cholinergic, histaminic and adrenergic receptors.[44] Anticholinergic adverse effects include dry mouth (and as a consequence, dental cavities), impaired ability to focus vision at close range, constipation and urinary hesitation. Adrenergic blockade may cause orthostatic hypotension and fainting. TCAs may also induce sedation, bodyweight gain, dizziness, lowered seizure threshold, myoclonus or a confusional state. As with other antidepressants, the TCAs may trigger a switch to mania.[45] Patients and their families should be educated about the symptoms of mania or hypomania and instructed to call their clinicians if these symptoms appear. At therapeutic dosages it appears that the TCAs do not affect short term memory or cognitive functions,[46] but distinct cognitive disturbances have been reported with high concentrations of TCAs.[47]

The most common cardiovascular adverse effect of TCAs is sinus tachycardia, affecting approximately one-third of children and adolescents treated with these agents.[48] Although heart rates below 130 beats/minute in children and 120 beats/minute in adolescents are considered normal, the long term clinical or haemodynamic significance of mild tachycardia is not known.[49] Other cardiovascular adverse effects include high blood pressure, orthostatic hypotension, prolongation of the PR, QRS, QT and QTc intervals and, more rarely, cardiac arrhythmias.[48] Some of these adverse effects may be minimised by slowly increasing the dosage of the TCA or, if effects do occur, by reducing the dosage.

TCA treatment should be carefully considered and is sometimes contraindicated in the presence of significant conduction delays (e.g. atrioventricular delay or block, Wolff-Parkinson-White syndrome), cardiac structural abnormalities and significant rhythm disturbances. The use of TCAs should be considered with caution in persons with a personal or a family history of premature cardiac disease, sudden death, arrhythmias or syncope. In any of these circumstances, consultation with a paediatric cardiologist is advisable before starting a patient on a TCA.

1.2.2 Sudden Death and Tricyclic Antidepressants

In children, desipramine[50-54] and, possibly, imipramine[55,56] have been associated with sudden death. In adults, desipramine may have a higher risk of fatality after overdose than other TCAs.[57,58] These findings suggest that desipramine may be more toxic and associated with more cardiovascular adverse effects than other TCAs. In contrast, Wilens and colleagues[48] found that desipramine was not associated with a higher incidence of cardiovascular effects than other TCAs. Although controversial, a Task Force of the American Academy of Child and Adolescent Psychiatry[57] estimated that the relative risk of sudden death with desipramine in children was 2.5 times higher than the annual population base rate of 4.2 sudden deaths/million children in the US. In any case, if the TCAs are indeed associated with this phenomena, it is unclear whether close monitoring of cardiovascular parameters can reduce or prevent the risk of sudden death.

1.2.3 Prescribing Tricyclic Antidepressants

It is recommended that TCAs be started at low dosages to avoid the emergence of adverse effects and improve the adherence to treatment. Usually, the initial dosage is imipramine 10 to 25 mg/day or its equivalent. In adolescents, TCAs are generally administered once a day at bedtime to help with compliance and, when sedating TCAs are used, to help with sleep. Divided doses are used most commonly in children, as they metabolise TCAs more rapidly,[59] and in patients who experience adverse effects because of high blood peak concentrations. The dosage can be increased by 25mg every 5 to 7 days, as adverse effects allow. The final dosage chosen is that at which the patient has a therapeutic response without experiencing disturbing adverse effects. The maximum dosage for imipramine, desipramine and amitriptyline is 5 mg/kg/day (with a maximum dosage of 300 mg/day). Nortriptyline, being about twice as potent, has as its maximum dosage 2.5 mg/kg/day or a maximum of 150 mg/day.

Due to the fatality risk associated with TCAs in overdose, special caution should be taken in terms of the amount of medication prescribed at each appointment.

It is advisable to perform a baseline electrocardiogram and electrocardiogram rhythm strips after reaching dosages higher than 2.5 mg/kg/day for imipramine and desipramine and 1 mg/kg for nortriptyline. Thereafter, it is recommended that the rhythm strip be repeated after each dosage increase of 50 to 100 mg/day.

There have been as yet no studies in children and adolescents indicating the optimal time to increase the dosage or to change medications if the patient has not responded to treatment. A recent study in depressed adults[33] recommended that patients should be treated with adequate and tolerable doses of TCAs for at least 4 weeks. At 4 weeks, if there is not even minimal improvement in the patient's condition, e.g. a 25% reduction on the initial Hamilton Depression Rating Scale[60] or on the Beck Depression Inventory score,[12] then the patient's treatment should be modified (e.g. dosage increase, change medications). If the patient shows minimal improvement, they should continue the same dosage until completing at least 6 weeks of treatment. At this point, if no further improvement has been observed, other treatment strategies should be considered and the reader is referred to section 4 on treatment-resistant depression.

1.2.4 Pharmacokinetics and Blood Concentrations

Only a few studies have analysed the pharmacokinetics of TCAs in children and adolescents, e.g. Clein and Riddle,[59] Kye and Ryan.[43] The metabolism, distribution, half-life and protein binding of TCAs in children and adolescents appear to be different compared with in adults, underscoring the need to examine developmental differences in the pharmacokinetics of patients with early-onset mood disorders.[61] For example, children and adolescents display a more rapid metabolism of drugs, thereby requiring relatively larger doses for a given body-weight than adults.[62] Children also have more efficient hepatic metabolism of drugs than adults, resulting in rapid deamination of TCAs and they can convert initially serotonergic tertiary-amine TCAs into less serotonergic secondary-amine TCAs.[43,59]

At any given oral dose, studies across the lifespan have shown marked interindividual differences in tricyclic antidepressant steady-state blood concentrations.[43,59] No correlations between plasma concentrations and clinical response have been reported in adolescents with major depressive disorder.[43,59] In contrast, in depressed children, it appears that a combined plasma concentration of imipramine and desipramine of >150 µg/L are associated with better response;[63,64] however, these results need further replication. Given the above-noted pharmacokinetic results, routine measurement of TCA concentrations in children and adolescents is controversial. In adults, the recommended blood concentrations in adults for imipramine and desipramine range between 150 µg/L and 300 µg/L. In adults, an inverted U-curve relationship between nortriptyline plasma concentrations (50 µg/L and 150 µg/L) and response has been reported.

We believe that instead of frequent measurement of blood concentrations, clinical observation is still the best method to achieve maximal benefit without producing intolerable adverse effects. However, measurement of blood TCA concentrations may be useful to assess compliance, confirm rapid metabolism, which often may be induced by other substances, e.g. anticonvulsants or cigarette smoking, and to assess slow metabolism which is usually present in about 10% of the Caucasian population.[59] Blood concentrations should be assessed after the addition of agents that may interact pharmacokinetically with TCAs, e.g. SSRIs, and before terminating a medication trial. They also should be obtained when there is concern about lack of response or worsening symptoms, as TCA toxicity can at times be mistaken for worsening depression. Blood concentrations should be obtained 10 to 12 hours after administration of the last oral dose.

1.2.5 Discontinuation

To avoid withdrawal adverse effects, it is recommended that dosages of TCAs be tapered gradually. It is also important to mention that it appears that rapid discontinuation of treatment may be associated with increased relapse or recurrences of depression.[65,66] Therefore, unless a TCA must be stopped for a clinically urgent reason, e.g. the presence of conduct delays, manic symptoms, etc., it is advisable to discontinue the medications progressively, possibly over a period of 6 weeks. Further research in this area is necessary.

1.2.6 Interactions with Other Medications

It is important to be aware of possible interactions between TCAs and other medications and substances that may worsen sedation [e.g. antihistamines, alcohol (ethanol), antipsychotics], hypotension (e.g. clonidine, low potency antipsychotics), anticholinergic adverse effects (e.g. antihistamines, low potency antipsychotics) and potentiate cardiac adverse effects (e.g. terfenadine).

Also, concentrations of TCAs can be varied with the use of other medications or substances. TCA blood concentrations may increase with coadministration of SSRIs, stimulants, certain antimicrobial agents [e.g rifampicin (rifampin), fluconazole and related antifungals, erythromycin and other macrolides], certain antiarrhythmics (e.g. quinidine, propafenone), some calcium antagonists (e.g. verapamil), thiazides and cimetidine. Concentrations may decrease with long term use of alcohol, carbamazepine and with heavy cigarette smoking.

When MAOIs have been used and a switch to TCAs is wanted, discontinuation of the MAOIs 10 to 14 days before starting TCA treatment is required. Also, new pharmacokinetic interactions (via the CYP hepatic metabolism system) between TCAs and other medications are being continually discovered and thus the reader is encouraged to stay abreast of changes noted in the literature.

1.3 Other Antidepressants

Very few studies exist on the use of other antidepressants [e.g. amfebutamone (bupropion), venlafaxine, nefazodone and MAOIs] in the treatment of depressed children and adolescents and most are uncontrolled.[67-69] A recent controlled double-blind study comparing venlafaxine and placebo in a small sample of children and adolescents with depression (n = 30) using small doses of venlafaxine (up to 75 mg/day) showed no differences in outcome or adverse effects between venlafaxine and placebo.[70] Venlafaxine has been found to be beneficial for treating ADHD symptoms in adults,[71,72] but so far this has not been shown in children and adolescents.[73]

Amfebutamone is effective for treating ADHD in children and adolescents.[74,75] Amfebutamone can be considered an alternative treatment for adolescents with depression and comorbid ADHD. A recent study showed that the pharmacokinetics of nefazodone are similar among adults, adolescents and children.[67,76] However, efficacy data for nefazodone in adolescents with depression have not been published.

1.4 Pharmacological Treatments of Major Depressive Disorder Subtypes

Subtypes of major depressive disorders, such as atypical, seasonal or bipolar depression, may require alternative treatments. No studies on atypical depression in children and adolescents have been published, but adults with atypical depression respond better to treatment with

MAOIs, and possibly SSRIs, than to TCAs.[77-79] Studies in adults and one investigation in children and adolescents have shown that bright light therapy is efficacious in seasonal depression.[80-82]

Because the symptoms of unipolar and bipolar depression are similar, it is difficult to determine whether children and adolescents need only an antidepressant, or concomitant use of mood stabilisers. If clinical indicators of bipolar depression, e.g. psychosis, psychomotor retardation or a family history of bipolar disorder are present, the clinician should consider with the patient and family the pros and cons of initiating a prophylactic mood stabiliser. There are no pharmacological studies in adolescents with bipolar depression and few controlled studies in adults. However, it has been recommended that treatment be initiated with a mood stabiliser [lithium, valproic acid (sodium valproate) or carbamazepine], given that antidepressants may induce mania.[83] If no response is observed, an antidepressant should be added to the treatment. Amfebutamone, SSRIs and MAOIs seem to give a better response in bipolar depression than TCAs. This may be related to their possible lower risk of inducing a switch from depression to mania and rapid cycling.[84-86] For patients presenting with mixed states (depression plus mania), the use of valproic acid instead of lithium should be considered.[87]

When depression is accompanied by psychotic features, the rate of recovery is better if antidepressants are combined with an antipsychotic.[88-90] Given the potential risk of tardive dyskinesia associated with the long term use of antipsychotics, these agents should be tapered soon after the remission of depression. The 'atypical' antipsychotics (risperidone, olanzapine, clozapine) may represent an alternative to classic antipsychotics, but further research is needed. In adults, electroconvulsive therapy has been found to be particularly effective for psychotic depression.[91] In addition, in adults, the best response has been associated with higher blood concentrations of TCAs.[90,92] Finally, there has not been sufficient research to definitively determine if the new antidepressants, including the SSRIs, demonstrate the same efficacy as the TCAs for psychotic and severe depressions.

2. Continuation and Maintenance Treatments

There are very few continuation and no maintenance studies in adolescents with depression. Thus, anticipating future research, most of the following recommendations outlined are based on adult studies. Given the high rate of depressive relapse and recurrence, continuation therapy is recommended for all patients and maintenance therapy should be considered for some patients.

2.1 Continuation Therapy

Successful acute phase pharmacotherapy or psychotherapy should be followed for at least 6 months by continuation treatment. However, symptomatic breakthroughs may prolong the continuation phase for as long as 9 to 12 months. During the continuation phase, the patient and the patient's family should be taught to recognise early signs of relapse. In addition, antidepressants must be continued at the same dose used to attain remission of acute symptoms, providing that there are no significant adverse effects or dose-related negative effects on the patient's compliance.[9,40,93] In adults, pharmacotherapy treatment during this phase reduces the risk of relapse from 40 to 60% to 10 to 20%.[93,94] TCAs, SSRIs and lithium have been found to be significantly more effective in preventing relapses than placebo. In some adult studies, >50% of patients randomised to placebo relapsed during continuation trials, most within 3 months of antidepressant discontinuation.[93,95,96]

If maintenance therapy is not required, at the end of the continuation phase the antidepressant dosage should be decreased gradually over 6 weeks or more to avoid withdrawal effects, e.g. sleep disturbance, irritability, gastrointestinal symptoms. The clinician could potentially misinterpret withdrawal effects as the need for continued medication. Rapid discontinuation of antidepressants may also precipitate a relapse or recurrence of depression. In children and adolescents, extended vacations are a good time to gradually discontinue medications.

2.2 Maintenance Therapy

The main goal of the maintenance phase is to prevent recurrences. This treatment period may extend from 1 year to indefinitely and usually commences after the patient has been asymptomatic for a period of approximately 6 to 12 months (continuation phase).

2.2.1 Maintenance Psychopharmacological Studies

Despite differences in methodology, several controlled trials comparing TCAs or SSRIs with placebo have shown that these antidepressants diminish the risk of recurrences of major depressive episodes in adult patients with unipolar depression.[93,97-99] In fact, early studies which used reduced dosages of TCAs reported that the rate of recurrence for patients taking placebo was more than twice that for active medication.[65,66] In contrast, new studies, using 'full dose' TCA maintenance dosages found a 5-fold medication-placebo difference.[65,66,97,99] Nevertheless, medications are not always efficacious and up to 25% of patients have recurrences. Apparently all antidepressants are equally useful for maintenance treatment in unipolar depression.[65,66,96-103] Although there are no published long term randomised controlled trials of the SSRIs, amfebutamone, nefazodone or venlafaxine in children and adolescents, some studies in adults with depression showed 1-year recurrence prevention rates of 80 to 90% with these agents.[100-103] There is controversy as to whether lithium and other mood stabilisers are useful for maintenance treatment of patients with depression.[104]

2.2.2 Who Should Receive Maintenance Therapy?

The recommendation for maintenance therapy depends on several factors related to the severity of the latest depressive episode, e.g. suicidality, psychosis, functional impairment, number and severity of prior depressive episodes, chronicity, comorbid disorders, family psychopathology, presence of support, patient and family willingness to adhere to the treatment programme and any medical contraindications to continued medication treatment.

In adults, it has been recommended that patients who experience only a single uncomplicated episode of depression, mild episodes, or a lengthy interval between episodes, e.g. 5 years, probably should not start maintenance treatment.[93] Otherwise, patients with three or more episodes, those with chronic depression,[9,40] or those patients who have experienced two episodes and who have one or more of the following criteria: (i) a family history of bipolar disorder or recurrent depression; (ii) early-onset of the first depressive episode (before age 20); and (iii) both episodes were severe or life threatening and occurred during the past 3 years,[9] should receive maintenance treatment. Given that depression in adolescents has similar clinical presentations, sequelae and natural course compared with adults, the above-noted guidelines probably apply to adolescents with depression. Clinicians should also consider that comorbid psychiatric disorders (anxiety, substance abuse), conflictive environments and residual or subsyndromal symptomatology are associated with high risk for recurrences.

2.2.3 Duration of the Maintenance Phase

Considering what has appeared in the medical literature concerning adult patients with depression,[40,93] it is recommended that adolescents who experience second episodes of depression should be maintained for at least 1 to 3 years on the same dosage of the antidepressant that was used to achieve clinical remission during the acute treatment phase. Patients experiencing second episodes of depression accompanied by psychosis, severe impairment, severe suicidality and refractory treatment or patients who experience 3 or more episodes, should be considered for longer or lifelong treatment.

2.2.4 Which Treatment?

Practically, unless there is any contraindication, e.g. medication adverse effects, the treatment that was effective in treating the acute episode should be used for maintenance therapy. Instead of maintaining patients on medications only, multimodal treatments should be offered to help the patients to cope with the 'psychosocial scars' induced by the depression and/or with environments charged with stressful situations. In children and adolescents, there have been a few noncomparative investigations with small samples of adolescents with depression which suggest that psychotherapy may be useful to prevent recurrences of major depression.[105-107]

3. Treatment of Comorbid Conditions

In addition to the treatment of depressive symptoms, it is of prime importance to treat the comorbid conditions that frequently accompany major depressive disorder. Forty to 90% of adolescents with major depressive disorders have other psychiatric disorders, with at least 20 to 50% having two or more comorbid disorders.[108-120] Most frequent comorbid diagnoses are dysthymic and anxiety disorders (occurring in 30 to 80% of adolescents with major depressive disorders), disruptive disorders (10 to 80%) and substance use disorders (20 to 30%).

Specific treatment guidelines for each of the comorbid psychiatric disorders should be considered. If it is possible, choose the medication that optimises response for both the depression and comorbid disorder. For example, TCAs and SSRIs may help both anxiety disorders and major depressive disorders in adults and children;[121-123] TCAs, amfebutamone and venlafaxine appear to be useful in treating other disorders such ADHD in adults and children;[74,124,125] and SSRIs may help in the treatment of bulimia and major depressive disorders, clomipramine and the SSRIs can help both depression and obsessive-compulsive disorders and both TCAs and SSRIs may help dysthymia and major depressive disorders.[126,127] Nevertheless, at times, it is necessary to use two medications to treat the two conditions, e.g. SSRIs and stimulants.

4. Treatment-Resistant Depression

In adults, the term treatment-resistant depression is used when there is a lack of response to antidepressants in patients who are accurately diagnosed, compliant with treatment and assessed with valid outcome measures.[128] Patients must have had at least two trials with two different classes of antidepressants, administered at standard doses for at least 6 weeks each. In contrast with adults with depression, there is no clear definition of treatment-resistant depression in adolescents with major depressive disorders.[129]

When managing patients with treatment-resistant depression the following reasons for treatment failure should be considered: inadequate drug dosage, inadequate length of drug trial, comorbidity with other psychiatric disorders (anxiety, dysthymic, substance use and personality disorders), comorbid medical illnesses, undetected existence of bipolar depression, exposure to chronic or severe life events such as sexual abuse, and incorrect diagnoses.[128,130] All of these conditions may require different modalities of therapy other than simply antidepressant treatment. Clinical observation suggests that sometimes after a medication-free interval (4 to 6 weeks), patients may respond to previously unsuccessful antidepressant trials. In addition, psychotherapeutic interventions also appear to be beneficial for adult patients with treatment-resistant depressions.[131,132]

4.1 Psychopharmacological Strategies

Several psychopharmacological strategies have been recommended for adults with treatment-resistant depression: (i) optimisation (extending the initial medication trial and/or adjusting the dose); (ii) switching to another agent from the same or a different class of medications, or augmentation or combination therapy, e.g. lithium, thyroid hormone; and (iii) use of electroconvulsive therapy.[9,128,130] Each strategy requires implementation in a systematic fashion, education of the patient's family and support from clinicians to avoid the development of hopelessness in the patient and family.

Placebo-controlled studies of the efficacy of alternative treatments for patients with treatment-resistant depressions are difficult to pursue for pragmatic reasons, e.g. small sample sizes, as well as the dilemma of offering placebo to patients with treatment-resistant disorders. Consequently, there are very few randomised controlled treatment trials and few noncomparative studies in adults[128] and children and adolescents.

One noncomparative study in adolescents with treatment-resistant major depressive disorder showed significant improvement of depressive symptoms after augmentation of TCA treatment with lithium.[133] Nevertheless, another noncomparative study, using an historical control group, did not replicate this finding.[134] Two small nonblinded studies, one with fluoxetine[135] and a second with the MAOI phenelzine,[68] found these agents to be effective in the treatment of adolescents who did not respond to TCAs. Geller and colleagues,[136] in a group of adolescents with chronic and severe major depressive disorder, found that intravenous clomipramine was superior to placebo for adolescents with treatment-resistant depression.

Anecdotal reports have suggested that adolescents with treatment-resistant depression may respond to electroconvulsive therapy.[137-139] Interestingly, a recent randomised controlled trial comparing amitriptyline with placebo in a sample (n = 30) of 'treatment-resistant' depressed adolescents showed a 70% improvement for both treatments.[140]

5. Developmental Considerations and Compliance

5.1 Developmental Considerations

It is critical to consider key developmental factors such as age, gender and pubertal status and their impact on drug concentration and response. Age should be treated as a major variable in response and adverse effects. Also, puberty may affect the pharmacokinetics of medications, possibly via competition for hepatic drug-metabolising enzymes by gonadal hormones.[141] Because drugs are differentially distributed into body tissues depending on their solubility characteristics, estimation of the amount of fat or water in a given patient may be a key factor in understanding why that patient requires a certain amount of a given drug.

As an individual enters puberty, the amount of fat, water and lean body mass changes.[142-145] Because height is increased by approximately 25% and bodyweight is nearly doubled in adolescence, it is likely that drugs will be distributed in a different way than in childhood. Lean body mass, skeletal mass and body fat are equal per unit bodyweight in prepubertal boys and girls, but, by maturity, women have twice as much fat relative to total bodyweight as adult men. The peak lean body mass growth velocity in men occurs 2 years later than in women on average and coincides with peak height velocity.

Change in the volume of distribution (age-related decrease of total body water and extracellular water) of a drug is a predictable and important event and will affect the dose needed to achieve a certain concentration in children and adolescents. If the drug is distributed largely in body water, the dose for men may be higher than women after puberty, but similar before puberty. If the drug is fat soluble, mature women might require a higher dose than younger women or mature men.[146,147]

Finally, variables such as race, gender and variations in genetically determined polymorphisms of the CYP enzymes can influence the pharmacokinetics and pharmacodynamics of medications, in particular, in the paediatric population. However, few studies have systematically determined the exact timing or nature of the differences as related to children and adolescents.

5.2 Compliance

It has been stated that noncompliance may be among the most significant problems that medicine faces today.[148] Failure to comply with treatment may be devastating for the patient and may also affect the interpretation of clinical research and trials, and may increase healthcare costs.

There are several excellent literature reviews on adult patients' compliance with medication regimens.[149] In general, approximately 40% of adult patients who are receiving psychiatric medications are noncompliant. The limited experience from studies of long term TCA administration for affective disorders indicates that adult patients' compliance is a major factor for ensuring continued response. It has been estimated that 70% of depressed patients taking TCAs fail to take 25 to 50% of their prescribed dose.[149] About 40% of patients who are receiving what should be adequate dosages of oral TCAs have concentrations in plasma outside the therapeutic range.[149] Similar data with SSRIs have not been published. Objective compliance assessments have not yet been completed systematically with paediatric populations.

The assessment of compliance in pharmacological studies is critical as otherwise the value of a pharmacotherapeutic regimen cannot be assessed. For example, if the dose interval was correct but only half of each prescribed dose was taken, the response is likely to be 50% of that predicted with a much higher variability in clinical outcome. For oral dose administration, attenuation of effect as a result of imperfect compliance resembles the attenuation due to reduced bioavailability. In pharmacological terms, the dose-response curve is shifted to the right, just as though a competitive antagonist had been administered at the same time. Poor compliance in clinical research studies, though unlikely to occur consistently to this degree, could result in a new medicine being judged less potent than it really is and thus the recommended dose range would be too high. Furthermore, in comparative efficacy studies involving more than one1 drug per treatment arm, nonuniform and/or differential compliance among arms may increase the risk of a misinterpretation in findings.

6. Conclusions

In summary, in children with depression, the choice of the initial acute therapy depends on several factors including symptom severity, number of prior episodes, chronicity, subtype of depression (e.g. psychotic, bipolar, atypical), age of the patient, contextual issues (family conflict, academic problems, exposure to negative life events), patient compliance with treatment, previous response to treatment and patient and family motivation for treatment (e.g. adolescents may be reluctant to participate in family therapy, an anxious parent and patient may refuse medications as the first line of treatment, etc.) Also, clinician motivation and expertise to perform any specific therapy can affect the outcome of the treatment.[150,151]

Research into the pharmacological treatment of major depressive disorders in children and adolescents is relatively preliminary. Psychotherapy strategies (in particular cognitive-behavioural therapy) have been shown to be efficacious for the treatment of children and adolescents with mild to moderate depressions.[152] Thus, we would recommend initially at least an 8 to 12 week trial of psychotherapy. For patients whose depression does not respond, or who are not suitable for psychotherapy, and for patients with severe depression, psychosis, nonrapid cycling bipolar depression, a trial with an antidepressant is indicated. In this case, given their efficacy, benign adverse effect profile and low risk of death after an overdose, the SSRIs are the first choice of antidepressant.[10] However, TCAs or other medications such amfebutamone may be indicated in cases where comorbid ADHD is present.

Given the chronicity, recurrence and psychosocial consequences of childhood major depressive disorders and dysthymia, further research in child and adolescent continuation and maintenance treatments is needed. Also, studies on the treatment of comorbid conditions, subtypes of depression (e.g. bipolar, atypical, seasonal) and combinations of pharmacotherapy and psychotherapy are warranted. Finally, further studies in developmental considerations, prevention, pharmacokinetics, pharmacodynamics and antidepressant long term adverse effects in this population are also warranted.

References

1. Garrison CZ, Addy CL, Jackson KL, et al. Major depressive disorder and dysthymia in young adolescents. Am J Epidemiol 1992; 135 (7): 792-802
2. Garrison CZ, Waller JL, Cuffe SP, et al. Incidence of major depressive disorder and dysthymia in young adolescents. J Am Acad Child Adolesc Psychiatry 1997; 36 (4): 458-65
3. Kashani JH, Beck NC, Hoeper EW, et al. Psychiatric disorders in a community sample of adolescents. Am J Psychiatry 1987; 144: 584-9
4. Lewinsohn PM, Duncan EM, Stanton AK, et al. Age at onset for first unipolar depression. J Abnorm Psychol 1986; 95: 378-83
5. Lewinsohn PM, Hops H, Roberts RE, et al. Adolescent psychopathology: I. Prevalence and incidence of depression and other DSM-III-R disorders in high school students. J Abnorm Psychol 1993; 102: 133-44
6. Lewinsohn, PM. Psychosocial risk factors for future adolescent suicide attempts. J Consult Clin Psychol 1994; 62 (2): 297-305
7. Polaino-Lorente A, Domenech E. Prevalence of childhood depression: results of the first study in Spain. J Child Psychol Psychiatry 1993; 34 (6): 1007-17
8. Fleming JE, Offord DR. Epidemiology of childhood depressive disorders: a critical review. J Am Acad Child Adolesc Psychiatry 1990; 29 (4): 571-80
9. Thase ME, Kupfer DJ. Recent developments in the pharmacotherapy of mood disorders. J Consult Clin Psychol 1996; 64 (4): 646-59
10. Kutcher S. Practitioner review: the pharmacotherapy of adolescent depression. J Child Psychol Psychiatry 1997; 38: 755-67
11. Depression Guideline Panel (1993). Depression in primary care: vol. I: treatment of major depression. Clinical practice guideline. Rockville: US Department of health and human services, public health service, agency for health care policy and research, 1993
12. Beck AT, Steer RA, Garbin MG. Psychometric properties of the Beck depression inventory: twenty-five years of evaluation. Clin Psychol Rev 1988; 8: 77-100

13. Preskorn S. Targeted pharmacotherapy in depression management: comparative pharmacokinetics of fluoxetine, paroxetine and sertraline. Int Clin Psychopharmacol 1994; 9: 13-9
14. Emslie GJ, Rush J, Weinberg WA, et al. A double-blind, randomized, placebo-controlled trial of fluoxetine in children and adolescents with Depression. Arch Gen Psychiatry 1997; 54: 1031-7
15. IMS America. New prescriptions or recommendations by doctors for prescriptions for three of the most common antidepressants. In: Strauch B. Use of antidepression medicine for young patients has soared. New York Times 1997 Aug 10
16. Leonard HL, March J, Rickler KC, et al. Review of the pharmacology of the SSRI in children and adolescents. J Am Acad Child Adolesc Psychiatry 1997; 36 (6): 725-36
17. DeVane CL, Sallee FR. Serotonin selective reuptake inhibitors in child and adolescent psychopharmacology: a review of published experience. J Clin Psychiatry 1996; 57 (2): 55-66
18. Simeon J, Dinicola V, Ferguson H. Adolescent depression: a placebo-controlled fluoxetine treatment study and follow-up. Prog Neuropsychopharmacol Biol Psychiatry 1990; 14: 791-5
19. Wagner DK, Birmaher B, Carlson G, et al. A multi-center trial of paroxetine and imipramine in the treatment of adolescent depression [abstract]. 45th Annual Meeting of the Academy of the American Academy of Child and Adolescent Psychiatry: Oct 1998; Anaheim (CA)
20. Arya DK. Extrapyramidal symptoms with SSRI. Br J Psychiatry 1994; 165: 728-33
21. Jones-Fearing KB. SSRI and EPS with fluoxetine [letter]. J Am Acad Child Adolesc Psychiatry 1996; 35 (9): 1107-8
22. Liu BA, Mittmann N, Knowles SR. Hyponatremia and the syndrome of inappropriate secretion of antidiuretic hormone associated with the use of SSRI: a review of spontaneous reports. Can Med Assoc J 1996; 155 (5): 519-27
23. Aranth J, Lindberg C. Bleeding, a side effect of fluoxetine [letter]. Am J Psychiatry 1992; 149: 412
24. Calhoun J, Calhoun D. Prolonged bleeding time in a patient treated with sertraline [letter]. Am J Psychiatry 1996; 152: 143
25. Ottervanger JP, Sticker BH, Huls J. Bleeding attributed to the intake of paroxetine [letter]. Am J Psychiatry 1994; 151: 781-2
26. Teicher MH, Glod C, Cole JO. Emergence of intense suicidal preoccupation during fluoxetine treatment. Am J Psychiatry 1990; 147: 207-10
27. King RA, Riddle MA, Chappell PB. Emergence of self-destructive phenomena in children and adolescents during fluoxetine treatment. J Am Acad Child Adolesc Psychiatry 1991; 30 (2): 179-86
28. Beasley CM, Dornseif BE, Bosomworth JC, et al. Fluoxetine and suicide: a meta-analysis of controlled trials of treatment for depression. BMJ 1991; 303: 685-92
29. Tollefson GD, Holman SL. How long to onset of antidepressant action: a meta-analysis of patients treated with fluoxetine or placebo. Int Clin Psychopharmacol 1994; 9: 245-50
30. DeVane CL. Pharmacokinetics of the SSRI. J Clin Psychiatry 1992; 53: 13-20
31. Preskorn SH. Comparison of tolerability of bupropion, fluoxetine, imipramine, nefazodone, paroxetine, sertraline, and venlafaxine. J Clin Psychiatry 1995; 56: 12-21
32. Findling R, Fiala S, Myers C, et al. Putative determinants of paroxetine response in pediatric patients with major depression. Psychopharmacol Bull 1996; 32: 446-7
33. Quitkin FM, McGrath PJ, Stewart JW, et al. Chronological milestones to guide drug change. When should clinicians switch antidepressants? Arch Gen Psychiatry 1996; 53 (9): 785-92
34. Dunner DL, Dunbar GC. Optimal dose regime for paroxetine. J Clin Psychiatry 1992; 53 (Suppl.): 21-6
35. Fabre LF, Abbuzzahab FS, Amin M, et al. Sertraline safety and efficacy in major depression: a double-blind fixed dose comparison with placebo. Biol Psychiatry 1995; 38: 592-602
36. Travis G, Emslei GJ, Rush J, et al. Plasma fluoxetine levels in depressed children and adolescents. 40th Annual Meeting of the American Academy of Child and Adolescent Psychiatry: Oct 1993; San Antonio (TX)
37. Zajecka J, Tracy KA, Mitchell S. Discontinuation symptoms after treatment with serotonin reuptake inhibitors: a literature review. J Clin Psychiatry 1997; 58 (7): 291-7
38. Albukrek D, Moran DS, Epstein Y. A depressed workman with heatstroke. Lancet 1996; 347: 1016-7
39. Karle J, Bjorndal F. Serotonergic syndrome – in combination therapy with lithium and fluoxetine. Ugeskr Laeger 1995; 157 (9): 1204-5
40. American Psychiatric Association. Practice guidelines for major depressive disorders in adults. Am J Psychiatry 150; Suppl.: 1-26
41. Birmaher B, Ryan ND, Williamson DE. Childhood and adolescent depression: a review of the past 10 years – part II. J Am Acad Child Adolesc Psychiatry 1996; 35 (12): 1575-83
42. Birmaher B. Should we use antidepressant medications for children and adolescents with depressive disorders? Psychopharmacol Bull 1998; 34 (1): 35-9
43. Kye C, Ryan ND. Pharmacologic treatment of child and adolescent depression. Child Adolesc Psychiatr Clin North Am 1995; 4 (2): 261-81
44. Preskorn SH, Burke M. Somatic therapy for major depressive disorder: selection of an antidepressant. J Clin Psychiatry 1992; 53: 5-18
45. Geller B, Fox LW, Fletcher M. Effect of tricyclic antidepressants on switching to mania on the onset of bipolarity in depressed 6- to 12-year-olds. J Am Acad Child Adolesc Psychiatry 1993; 32 (1): 43-50
46. Aman MG. Psychotropic drugs and learning problems: a selective review. J Learn Disabil 1980; 13: 87-97
47. Preskorn SH, Weller E, Jerkovich G, et al. Depression in children: concentration dependent CNS toxicity of tricyclic antidepressants. Psychopharmacol Bull 1988; 24: 275-9
48. Wilens T, Biederman J, Baldessarini J, et al. The cardiovascular effects of tricyclic antidepressants in children and adolescents. J Am Acad Child Adolesc Psychiatry 1996; 35: 1491-501
49. Garson A, Bricker JT, McNamara DG, editors. The science and practice of pediatric cardiology: vols 1-3. Philadelphia: Lea & Febiger, 1990
50. Abramowicz M, editor. Sudden death in children treated with tricyclic antidepressant. Med Lett Drugs Ther 1990; 32: 53
51. Riddle MA, Nelson JC, Kleinman CS, et al. Case-study: sudden death in children receiving Norpramin: a review of three reported cases and commentary. J Am Acad Child Adolesc Psychiatry 1993; 32 (1): 104-8
52. Popper CW, Ziminitzky B. Sudden death putatively related to desipramine treatment in youth: a fifth case and a review of speculative mechanisms. J Child Adolesc Psychopharmacol 1995; 5: 283-300
53. Riddle MA, Geller B, Ryan N. Case study: another sudden death in a child treated with desipramine. J Am Acad Child Adolesc Psychiatry 1993; 32: 792-7
54. Ziminitzky B, Popper CW. A fifth case of sudden death in a child taking desipramine [abstract]. American Psychiatric Association Annual Meeting: May 25, 1994; Philadelphia
55. Saraf K, Klein D, Gittelman-Klein R, et al. Imipramine side effects in children. Psychopharmacologia 1974; 37: 265-74

56. Varley CK, McClellan J. Case study: two additional sudden deaths with tricyclic antidepressants. J Am Acad Child Adolesc Psychiatry 1997; 36 (3): 390-4
57. Biederman J, Thisted RA, Greenhill LL, et al. Estimation of the association between desipramine and the risk for sudden death in 5- to 14-year-old children. J Clin Psychiatry 1995; 56 (3): 87-93
58. Kapur S, Mieczkowski T, Mann J. Antidepressant medications and the relative risk of suicide attempt and suicide. JAMA 1992; 268: 3441-5
59. Clein PD, Riddle MA. Pharmacokinetics in children and adolescents. Child Adolesc Psychiatr Clin North Am 1995; 4 (1): 59-75
60. Hamilton M. A rating scale for depression. J Neurol Neurosurg Psychiatry 1960; 23: 56-61
61. Green WH. Child and adolescent clinical psychopharmacology. 2nd ed. Baltimore: Williams and Wilkins, 1995
62. Jatlow PI. Psychotropic drug disposition during development. In: Popper C, editor. Psychiatric pharmacoscience of children and adolescents. Washington DC: American Psychiatric Press, 1989: 29-44
63. Puig-Antich J, Perel J, Lupatkin W, et al. Imipramine in prepubertal major depressive disorders. Arch Gen Psychiatry 1987; 44: 81-9
64. Preskorn SH, Bupp SJ, Weller RA. Plasma levels of imipramine and metabolites in 68 hospitalized children. J Am Acad Child Adolesc Psychiatry 1989; 28: 373-5
65. Frank E, Kupfer DJ, Perel JM, et al. Comparison of full dose versus half dose pharmacotherapy in the maintenance treatment of recurrent depression. J Affect Disord 1993; 27: 139-45
66. Frank E, Karp JF, Rush AJ. Efficacy of treatments for major depression. Psychopharmacol Bull 1993; 29: 457-75
67. Findling RL, Magnus RD, Preskorn SH, et al. An open-label pharmacokinetic trial of nefazodone in depressed children and adolescents [abstract]. Annual Meeting Canadian and American Academies Child Adolescent Psychiatry; 1997 Oct; Toronto
68. Ryan N, Puig-Antich J, Rabinovich H, et al. MAOIs in adolescent major depression unresponsive to tricyclic antidepressant. J Am Acad Child Adolesc Psychiatry 1988; 27: 755-8
69. Wilens TE, Spencer TJ, Biederman J, et al. Case study: nefazodone for juvenile mood disorders. J Am Acad Child Adolesc Psychiatry 1997; 36 (4): 481-5
70. Mandoki MW, Tapia MR, Tapia M A, et al. Venlafaxine in the treatment of children and adolescents with major depression. Psychopharmacol Bull 1997; 33 (1): 149-54
71. Findling RL, Schwartz MA, Flannery DJ, et al. Venlafaxine in adults with attention-deficit/hyperactivity disorder: an open clinical trial. J Clin Psychiatry 1996; 57 (5): 184-9
72. Hedges D, Reimherr FW, Rogers A, et al. An open trial of venlafaxine in adult patients with attention deficit hyperactivity disorder. Psychopharmacol Bull 1995; 31 (4): 779-83
73. Olvera RL, Pliszka SR, Luh J, et al. An open trial of venlafaxine in the treatment of attention-deficit/hyperactivity disorder in children and adolescents. J Child Adolesc Psychopharmacol 1996; 6 (4): 241-50
74. Barrickman LL, Perry, PJ, Allen AJ, et al. Bupropion versus methylphenidate in the treatment of attention deficit hyperactivity disorder. J Am Acad Child Adolesc Psychiatry 1995; 35: 649-57
75. Conners CK, Casat CD, Gualtieri CT, et al. Bupropion hydrochloride in attention deficit disorder with hyperactivity. J Am Acad Child Adolesc Psychiatry 1996; 35 (10): 1314-21
76. Magnus R D, Findling R, Preskorn SH, et al. An open-label pharmacokinetic trial of nefazodone in depressed children and adolescents [abstract]. 37th Annual Meeting New Clinical Drug Evaluation Unit Program (NCDEU): 1997 May; Boca Raton (FL)
77. Stewart JW, McGrath PJ, Rabkin JG, et al. Atypical depression: a valid clinical entity? Psychiatr Clin North Am 1993; 16 (3): 479-94
78. Stewart JW, Tricamo E, McGrath PJ, et al. Prophylactic efficacy of phenelzine and imipramine in chronic atypical depression: likelihood of recurrence on discontinuation after 6 months' remission. Am J Psychiatry 1997; 154 (1): 31-6
79. Thase ME, Trivedi MH, Rush AJ. MAOIs in the contemporary treatment of depression. Neuropsychopharmacol 1995; 12: 185-219
80. Tam EM, Lam RW, Levitt AJ. Treatment of seasonal affective disorder: a review. Can J Psychiatry 1995; 40 (8): 457-66
81. Papatheodorou G, Kutcher S. The effect of light therapy on ameliorating breakthrough depressive symptoms in adolescent-onset bipolar disorder. J Psych Neuroscience 1995; 20: 226-32
82. Swedo S, Allen AJ, Gold CA, et al. A controlled trial of light therapy for the treatment of pediatric seasonal affective disorder. J Am Acad Child Adolesc Psychiatry 1997; 36: 816-21
83. American Psychiatric Association. Diagnostic and statistical manual of mental disorders: 4th ed. (DSM-IV). Washington, DC: American Psychiatric Association, 1994
84. Haykal RF, Akiskal HS. Bupropion as a promising approach to rapid cycling bipolar II patients. J Clin Psychopharmacol 1990; 51: 450-5
85. Himmelhoch J, Thase M, Mallinger A, et al. Tranylcypromine versus imipramine in anergic bipolar depression. Am J Psychiatry 1991; 148: 910-6
86. Simpson SC, DePaulo JR. Fluoxetine treatment of bipolar II depression. J Clin Psychopharmacol 1991; 11: 52-4
87. Swann AC, Bowden CL, Morris D, et al. Depression during mania. Arch Gen Psychiatry 1997; 54: 37-42
88. Anton RF, Burch EA. Response of psychotic depression subtypes to pharmacotherapy. J Affect Dis 1993; 28: 125-31
89. Spiker DG, Weiss JC, Dealy RS et al. The pharmacological treatment of delusional depression. Am J Psychiatry 1985; 142: 430-6
90. Spiker D, Kupfer D. Placebo response rates in psychotic and nonpsychotic depression. J Affect Dis 1988; 14: 21-3
91. Coryell W. Psychotic depression. J Clin Psychiatry 1996; 7: 27-31
92. Puig-Antich J, Perel J, Lupatkin W, et al. Plasma levels of imipramine (IMI) and desmethyl-imipramine (DMI) and clinical response to prepubertal major depressive disorder: a preliminary report. J Am Acad Child Psychiatry 1979; 18: 616-27
93. Prien RF, Kocsis JH. Long-term treatment of mood disorders. In: Bloom FE, Kupfer DJ, editors. Psychopharmacology: the fourth generation of progress. New York: Raven Press, 1995: 1067-79
94. Thase ME. Maintenance treatments of recurrent affective disorders. Curr Opin Psychiatry 1993; 6: 16-21
95. Keller MB, Lavori PW, Lewis CE, et al. Predictors of relapse in major depressive disorder. JAMA 1983; 250 (24): 3299-304
96. Keller MB, Lavori PW, Endicott J, et al. Double depression: two year follow-up. Am J Psychiatry 1983; 140: 689-94
97. Frank E, Kupfer D, Perel J, et al. Three-year outcomes for maintenance therapies in recurrent depression. Arch Gen Psychiatry 1990; 47: 1093-9
98. Kupfer D, Frank E, Perel J. Five-year outcome for maintenance therapies in recurrent depression. Arch Gen Psychiatry 1992; 49: 769-73

99. Reynolds CF, Frank E, Perel JM, et al. Maintenance therapies for late-life recurrent major depression: research and review. Int J Psychogeriatrics 1995 (7 Suppl.): 27-39

100. Claghorn JL, Feighner J P. A double-blind comparison of paroxetine with imipramine in the long-term treatment of depression. J Clin Psychopharmacol 1993; 13 (6 Suppl.): 23-7

101. Duboff EA. Long-term treatment of major depressive disorder with paroxetine. J Clin Psychopharmacol 1993; 13 (6 Suppl.): 28S-33S

102. Montgomery SA, Dufour H, Brion S, et al. The prophylactic efficacy of fluoxetine in unipolar depression. Br J Psychiatry 1988; 153: 69-76

103. Shrivastava RK, Cohn C, Crowder J, et al. Long-term safety and clinical acceptability of venlafaxine and imipramine in outpatients with major depression. J Clin Psychopharmacol 1994; 14: 322-9

104. Schou M. Forty years of lithium treatment. Arch Gen Psych 1997; 54: 9-13

105. Kroll L, Harrington R, Jayson D, et al. Pilot study of continuation cognitive-behavioral therapy for major depression in adolescent psychiatric patients. J Am Acad Child Adolesc Psychiatry 1996; 35 (9): 1156-61

106. Jayson D, Wood A, Kroll L, et al. Which depressed patients respond to cognitive-behavioral treatment? J Am Acad Child Adolesc Psychiatry 1998; 37 (1): 35-9

107. Mufson L, Fairbanks J. Interpersonal psychotherapy for depressed adolescents: a one-year naturalistic follow-up study. J Am Acad Child Adolesc Psychiatry 1996; 35 (9): 1145-55

108. Anderson JC, McGee R. Comorbidity of depression in children and adolescents. In: Reynolds WM, Johnson HF, editors. Handbook of depression in children and adolescents. New York: Plenum Press, 1994: 581-660

109. Angold A, Costello EJ. Depressive comorbidity in children and adolescents. Empirical, theoretical, and methodological issues. Am J Psychiatry 1993; 150: 1779-91

110. Biederman J, Faraone S, Mick E, et al. Psychiatric comorbidity among referred juveniles with major depression: fact or artifact? J Am Acad Child Adolesc Psychiatry 1995; 34 (5): 579-90

111. Bird HR, Canino G, Rubio-Stipec M, et al. Estimates of the prevalence of childhood maladjustment in a community survey in Puerto Rico: the use of combined measures. Arch Gen Psychiatry 1988; 45: 1120-6

112. Ferro T, Carlson GA, Grayson P, et al. Depressive disorders: distinctions in children. J Am Acad Child Adolesc Psychiatry 1994; 33 (5): 664-70

113. Goodyer IM, Herbert J, Secher S, et al. Short-term outcome of major depression: I: comorbidity and severity at presentation as predictors of persistent disorder. J Am Acad Child Adolesc Psychiatry 1997; 36 (2): 179-87

114. Kashani JH, Carlson GA, Beck NC, et al. Depression, depressive symptoms, and depressed mood among a community sample of adolescents. Am J Psychiatry 1987; 144: 931-4

115. Kovacs M. Presentation and course of major depressive disorder during childhood and later years of the life span. J Am Acad Child Adolesc Psychiatry 1996; 35 (6): 705-15

116. Kovacs M, Mukerji P, Iyengar S, et al. Psychiatric disorder and metabolic control among youths with IDDM. A longitudinal study. Diabetes Care 1996; 19 (4): 318-23

117. Kovacs M, Feinberg TL, Crouse-Novak M, et al. Depressive disorders in childhood: II: a longitudinal study of the risk for a subsequent major depression. Arch Gen Psychiatry 1984; 41: 643-9

118. Kovacs M, Feinberg TL, Crouse-Novak MA, et al. Depressive disorders in childhood: I: a longitudinal prospective study of characteristics and recovery. Arch Gen Psychiatry 1984; 41: 229-37

119. Rohde P, Lewinsohn PM, Seeley JR. Comorbidity of unipolar depression: II: comorbidity with other mental disorders in adolescents and adults. J Abnorm Psychiatry 1991; 100: 214-22

120. Ryan ND, Puig-Antich J, Ambrosini P, et al. The clinical picture of major depression in children and adolescents. Arch Gen Psychiatry 1987; 44: 854-61

121. Birmaher B, Waterman GS, Ryan N, et al. Fluoxetine for childhood anxiety disorders. J Am Acad Child Adolesc Psychiatry 1994; 33 (7): 993-9

122. Black B, Udhe TW. Treatment of elective mutism with fluoxetine: a double-blind, placebo-controlled study. J Am Acad Child Adolesc Psychiatry 1994; 33 (7): 1000-6

123. Rickels K, Downing R, Schweizer E, et al. Antidepressants for the treatment of generalized anxiety disorder: a placebo-controlled comparison of imipramine, trazodone, and diazepam. Arch Gen Psychiatry 1993; 50: 884-95

124. Derivan A, Aguiar I, Upton G, et al. A study of venlafaxine in children and adolescents with conduct disorder [abstract]. 42th Annual Meeting of the American Academy of Child and Adolescent Psychiatry: 1995; New Orleans (LA)

125. Spencer T, Biederman J, Wilens T, et al. Pharmacotherapy of attention-deficit hyperactivity disorder across the life cycle. J Am Acad Child Adolesc Psychiatry 1996; 35 (4): 409-32

126. Kocsis JH, Zisook S, Davidson J, et al. Double blind comparison of sertraline, imipramine and placebo in the treatment of dysthymia-psychosocial outcomes. Am J Psychiatry 1997; 154 (3) 390-5

127. Thase ME, Fava M, Halbreich U, et al. A placebo-controlled, randomized clinical trial comparing sertraline and imipramine for the treatment of dysthymia. Arch Gen Psychiatry 1996; 53 (9): 777-84

128. Thase ME, Rush AJ. Treatment-resistant depression. In: Bloom FE, Kupfer DJ, editors. Psychopharmacology: the fourth generation of progress. New York: Raven Press Ltd, 1995: 1081-97

129. Geller B, Todd RD, Luby J, et al. Treatment-resistant depression in children and adolescents. Psychiatr Clin North Am 1996; 19 (2): 253-67

130. Amsterdam JD, Hornig-Rohan M. Treatment algorithms in treatment-resistant depression. Psychiatr Clin North Am 1996; 19: 371-86

131. Fava GA, Savron G, Grandi S, et al. Cognitive-behavioral management of drug-resistant major depressive disorder. J Clin Psychiatry 1997; 58 (6): 278-82

132. Miller IW, Bishop SB, Norman WH, et al. Cognitive-behavioural therapy and pharmacotherapy with chronic, drug-refractory depressed inpatients: a note of optimism. Behav Psychother 1985; 13: 320-7

133. Ryan N, Meyer V, Dachille S, et al. Lithium antidepressant augmentation in TCA-refractory depression in adolescents. J Am Acad Child Adolesc Psychiatry 1988; 27: 371-6

134. Strober M, Freeman R, Rigali J, et al. The pharmacotherapy of depressive illness in adolescence: II: effects of lithium augmentation in nonresponders to imipramine. J Am Acad Child Adolesc Psychiatry 1992; 31: 16-20

135. Boulos C, Kutcher S, Gardner D, et al. An open naturalistic trial of fluoxetine in adolescents and young adults with treatment-resistant major depression. J Child Adolesc Psychopharmacol 1992; 2: 103-11

136. Geller B, Cooper T, Graham D, et al. Double-blind placebo-controlled study of nortriptyline in depressed adolescents using a 'fixed plasma level' design. Psychopharmacol Bull 1990; 26: 85-90

137. Ghaziuddin N, Kinc C, Naylor M, et al. Electroconvulsive therapy (ECT) in refractory adolescent depression. 42nd Annual Meeting of the American Academy of Child and Adolescent Psychiatry, New Orleans (LA): Oct 1995

138. Moise FN, Petrides G. Case study: electroconvulsive therapy in adolescents. J Am Acad Child Adolesc Psychiatry 1996; 35: 312-8

139. Rey JM, Walter G. Half a century of ECT use in young people. Am J Psychiatry 1997; 154: 595-602
140. Birmaher B, Watterman GS, Ryan ND et al. A randomized controlled trial of amitriptyline vs. placebo for adolescents with 'treatment-resistant' major depression. J Am Acad Child Adolesc Psychiatry 1998; 37: 527-35
141. Morselli PL, Pippenger CE. Drug disposition during development: an overview. In: Moyer TP, Boeck RL, editors. Applied therapeutic drug monitoring: vol. 1. New York, American Association for Clinical Chemistry, 1982
142. Marshall WA, Tanner JM. Variations in the pattern of pubertal changes in girls. Arch Dis Child 1970; 44: 291-303
143. Marshall WA, Tanner JM. Variations in the pattern of pubertal changes in boys. Arch Dis Child 1970; 45: 13-23
144. Parizkova J. Growth and growth velocity of lean body mass and fat in adolescent boys. Pediatr Res 1976; 10: 647-50
145. Wynne HA, Cope LH, Mutch E, et al. The effect of age upon liver volume and apparent liver blood flow in healthy men. Hepatology 1989; 9: 297-301
146. Aranda JV, Stern L. Clinical aspects of developmental pharmacology and toxicology. Pharmacol Ther 1983; 20: 1-51
147. Morselli PL, editor. Drug disposition during development. New York: SP Books Division of Spectrum Publications, 1977
148. Pullar T, Pumar S, Tindall H, et al. Time to stop counting the tablets? Clin Pharmacol Ther 1989; 46: 163-8
149. Loo H, Benyacoub AK, Rovei V, et al. Long-term monitoring of tricyclic antidepressant plasma concentrations. Br J Psychiatry 1980; 137: 444-51
150. Jacobson NS, Dobson KS, Truax PA, et al. A component analysis of cognitive-behavioral treatment for depression. J Consult Clin Psychol 1996; 64 (2): 295-304
151. Spanier C, Frank E, Mc Eachran AB, et al. The prophylaxis of depressive episodes in recurrent depression following discontinuation of drug therapy: integrating psychological and biological factors. Psychol Med 1996; 26: 461-75
152. Brent DA, Holder D, Kolko D, et al. A clinical psychotherapy trial for adolescent depression comparing cognitive, family, and supportive therapy. Arch Gen Psychiatry 1997; 54: 877-85

Correspondence: Dr *Boris Birmaher*, Western Psychiatric Institute and Clinic, University of Pittsburgh, School of Medicine, 3811 O'Hara Street, Pittsburgh, PA 15213, USA.
E-mail: birmaherb@msx.upmc.edu

Postpartum Psychiatric Disorders
Guidelines for Management

Anne Buist

Austin Repatriation Medical Centre, University of Melbourne, Melbourne, Victoria, Australia

Despite uncertainty about the definition and aetiology of postpartum psychiatric disorders, they have been the focus of increasing public and professional interest. Whilst some argue for the existence of distinct, separate syndromes in the postpartum period,[1] others believe that they do not differ from disorders at other times of life,[2] and diagnostic classification systems have tended to ignore them or include them only as a diagnosis of exclusion.[3]

Quite aside from whether the postpartum syndromes are distinct from the perspective of symptomatology, the fact that they may have a different, hormonal aetiology has ramifications for management. The presence of a dependent infant and the issue of breastfeeding, generally not considered in the management of psychiatric disorders at other times in the life cycle, are also significant.

Whilst any psychiatric disorder may occur coincidentally in the postpartum period (e.g. there is an increased risk of relapse of schizophrenia and bipolar disorder at this time), there is a marked increase in the occurrence of affective psychosis, generally referred to as puerperal psychosis, and major, or postpartum, depression.[4]

1. Definition

Puerperal psychosis occurs in 1 in 600 births[4] and is characterised by rapid onset, usually in the first week postpartum, of psychotic and affective symptoms. It is essentially indistinguishable from bipolar disorder, often with mood swings and an initial manic phase followed by depression.[5] There may also be confusion and disorientation, similar to a delirium.

Postpartum depression affects 14% of women.[6] Although the symptoms generally fit the DSM-IV criteria for major depression,[3] in clinical practice the depression may differ from depression at other times in the life cycle. There is frequently a very high level of anxiety, often with obsessive compulsive symptoms, and affected individuals may try hard to appear less severely affected than they really are.

A larger group of women, some 29%,[6] probably experience a milder adjustment disorder with depressed and/or anxious mood, relating to the marked psychosocial changes and pressures associated with becoming a mother. This group do not generally require medication and will not be dealt with in this review.

2. Aetiology

Despite considerable research interest in the aetiology of postpartum psychiatric disorders, studies have failed to show a conclusive link with any biological factors. Given the marked changes in hormone levels occurring through pregnancy, and then very dramatically at delivery, a hormonal aetiology has been attractive. This would link the findings of some studies that show premenstrual syndrome as a risk factor,[6] and the clinical experience that as depression in some of these women improves, their symptoms return or worsen premenstrually.

Although treatment with progesterone has been advocated by Dalton,[7] scientific evidence of the effectiveness of the hormone has not been forthcoming. Sichel and colleagues[8] used high dose oral estrogen in 11 women who had past histories of puerperal psychoses or depression, with all but 1 woman remaining well. However, this intervention required heparinisation, and the study involved small numbers of patients and lacked a control group. Work by Gregoire et al.[9] suggests that women using transdermal estrogen 'patches' have a more rapid response to therapy with psychotropic drugs than women receiving psychotropic drugs alone, but this finding needs to be replicated. At present, the use of estrogen in the treatment of postpartum disorders is advocated only in research, and clinical practitioners need to await further results.

Other work on thyroid hormone, showing an increased incidence of thyroid antibodies in women with postpartum psychiatric disorders,[10] has doubtful implications for aetiology in the majority of women. However, women with abnormal thyroid function tests 6 weeks after delivery should be assessed by an endocrinologist.

The only other factors that have been repeatedly shown to be associated with an increased risk of postpartum disorders are psychosocial factors: marital stress, excessive life stresses, inadequate social supports and difficulties in relationships with parents.[6,11] These factors have also been associated with depression at other times. It is interesting to note that according to the study of Brown and Harris,[12] having 3 young children was a high risk factor for depression in a general population, which raises the possibility that some of the women in this study actually had, at least initially, postpartum depression.

3. Long Term Sequelae

Research into postpartum disorders has highlighted some alarming probabilities:
- These disorders may not be short term; over half the women in the study by Uddenberg and Englesson[13] were depressed 4 years later.
- The partners may also be depressed, with potential effects on their work performance and marital relationship, increasing the likelihood of marital breakdown.[14]
- Maternal depression, probably in combination with other factors, may also have a long term negative impact on child cognitive and emotional development.[13,15]

These findings highlight the need for identification of puerperal disorders, aggressive treatment and follow up, and management studies as to which treatments are effective.

4. Management

The management of postpartum disorders depends particularly on a number of factors:

Accurate Diagnosis. Postpartum depression in particular presents a problem of under recognition. Traditional symptoms such as bodyweight loss, middle and late insomnia, psychomotor retardation and anhedonia, that have been viewed as indicators of a 'biological' depression and suggest that the illness is likely to be responsive to antidepressants, may not be evident in postpartum depression. When they are evident, they may be deemed to be normal. Because of stigma and taboo, these women frequently endeavour to 'put up a front', appearing to be coping considerably better than they are.

Severity and Resource Availability. Severity of symptoms (independent of any apparent or nonapparent aetiology) in conjunction with the wishes of the woman and her family, will dictate the need for hospitalisation, ECT or antidepressants versus psychological therapies alone or in conjunction with pharmacological treatments. Availability of resources such as mother-baby units and specialised community support services will also influence these decisions.

Table I. Psychotropic medication and breastfeeding

- All psychotropic medications pass into breastmilk
- Concentrations in breastmilk do not relate in a linear fashion to dose, with considerable interindividual variation, and variation over a 24h period
- Occasional case reports[16] document the possibility of accumulation in infants, with toxic symptoms
- Lithium and high dose benzodiazepines should be avoided
- Little is known about the long term effects of the newer antidepressants
- Premature infants are particularly at risk of toxic effects, and psychotropic medication should be used with caution and parental consent
- There is: (i) clear evidence of the benefits to the infant of breastmilk; (ii) a long term risk to the mother and the development of the child of untreated postpartum psychiatric disorders; and (iii) no evidence that psychotropic drugs cause long term harm to the infant. Therefore, psychotropic medications can be used in the mother where indicated, with careful initial observation of the infant and informed consent by the parents

The Infant. Unlike depression at other life stages, the welfare of the dependent infant must also be considered. This will be a clear consideration if the mother is expressing infanticidal thoughts, or is neglectful of or delusional about the baby. The infant must also be considered when prescribing drugs to the breastfeeding mother (see table I for a summary of psychotropic medication and breastfeeding), and in the short and long term management plan, as depression may affect the mother-infant interaction and affect the child's development.

4.1 Hospitalisation

Since mother-baby units were first proposed in 1948 by Thomas Main, there has been an increasing interest in their development in the UK and Australia.[17] A majority of women with psychosis will require hospitalisation, while only those with severe depression, or depression with compounding factors, require such facilities. The concept of a mother-baby unit is popular with women, preventing separation from the infant and allowing breastfeeding to continue. It is also justified on the grounds of aiding the woman's confidence in herself as a mother, diminishing guilt and providing support from women in similar positions. Evidence from attachment theory[18] and long term studies looking at the impact of maternal depression on the developing infant[13,15] show that the mother-infant relationship is crucial, and that where an inpatient stay is necessary, separation is not desirable. An exception to this is when the safety of the infant is in question.

Of course, in many instances a mother-baby unit bed is unavailable. In this situation, the safety of the woman must be considered. Where intensive mobile support teams are available this may be an option, but few services have the expertise and availability of nursing staff on a roster basis in the home that the more extensive teams (such as that proposed by Oates and colleagues[19]) provide.

4.2 Medication

In contrast to the many studies of the management of psychosis and depression, few studies have been conducted relating specifically to postpartum disorders.

4.2.1 Antipsychotics

The pharmacological treatment of puerperal psychosis is essentially the same as for other psychotic illnesses; early intervention with antipsychotics is usually required. Dosages range from as little as haloperidol 1 mg/day or equivalent, to high doses in more severely ill women with resistant and distressing symptoms.

The choice of antipsychotic depends on a number of factors; symptomatology, adverse effects, whether breastfeeding, past response, compliance, safety, and the physician's own experience and preferences.

Women with puerperal psychosis are frequently anxious and agitated.[5] Although they may want to be alert for their infant, the need to settle the symptoms may be more acute, particularly when, as an inpatient, the safety and some care of the infant can be assumed by staff. Agitation in the mother will be perceived and responded to by the infant; rapid resolution will free the woman to interact in a more positive manner. In this situation, thioridazine is an effective and generally well tolerated choice that is unlikely to result in extrapyramidal side effects (EPS). Chlorpromazine is an alternative, and published data, including a small follow up study of 7 women, suggests minimal risk to the breastfed infant.[20]

Women with more pronounced psychotic symptoms may be better treated with more efficacious antipsychotics such as haloperidol or trifluoperazine, often in low dosages which can then be adjusted according to response. EPS are common, however, and close monitoring is needed. Although many women will respond quickly and will not require prolonged treatment – 2 weeks may be adequate – a significant proportion will need higher dosages that require maintenance for some months. In these women, excessive sedation needs to be considered, and a less sedating alternative is appropriate. In addition, only isolated reports exist with respect to these antipsychotics in breastmilk. Like other drugs, they are excreted into breastmilk and are present at generally lower concentrations than those in the maternal plasma. Agitation and EPS in the infant have been expressed as possible risks on the basis of animal studies.[21]

Newer antipsychotics such as olanzapine and risperidone are being used increasingly because of their improved adverse effect profile. Risperidone has been found to be excreted in breastmilk;[22] our own early work on olanzapine has found that it appears to be excreted at about half the plasma level. No long term studies have been done, however, on these infants, so use of these drugs needs to be cautious. Dev and Krupp[23] reported on four women who breastfed while receiving clozapine; one infant was sedated and another developed a reversible agranulocytosis. With this limited but concerning information, the use of clozapine is not recommended in breastfeeding women.

4.2.2 Antidepressants

Antidepressants are indicated in women with a moderate to severe depressive illness postpartum. In addition, many women with puerperal psychosis require antidepressants after or concurrently with antipsychotics. Because mood swings are common in this group, the dosage and duration of antidepressants need to be carefully monitored.

Table II. Concentrations of dothiepin in plasma and breastmilk at five dosages[28]

Patient	Daily dose (mg)	Plasma concentration		Breastmilk concentration	
		dothiepin (μg/L)	northiaden (μg/L)	dothiepin (μg/L)	northiaden (μg/L)
1	75	60	ND	45	ND
2	75	65	41	115	58
3	125	55	24	50	22
4	200	85	20	95	20
5	225	38	28	63	37

ND = not detected.

Tricyclics and Related Compounds

Tricyclic antidepressants (TCAs) inhibit the reuptake of noradrenaline (norepinephrine) and serotonin (5-hydroxytryptamine; 5-HT) to varying extents via interference with the amine pump, as well as potentiating the response to the monoamines both peripherally and centrally.[24]

Clinical effects are not usually observed for 2 or more weeks; this is thought to be due to time dependent adaptive changes in receptor sensitivity.[25] TCAs are rapidly absorbed, take 7 to 21 days to reach steady-state and are highly protein bound. Both plasma and breastmilk concentrations show significant individual variation without a linear relationship to dose.[25,26]

Mianserin, a tetracyclic piperinoazepine, also blocks serotonin and noradrenaline uptake, although less effectively than the TCAs, and increases turnover of noradrenaline.

Until recently, with the development of selective serotonin uptake inhibitors (SSRIs), TCAs have been the treatment of choice in major depression.[25] Specialists in postpartum disorders still find them useful,[27] but they may be no longer the agents of first choice. The choice of TCA depends on factors similar to those described for antipsychotics. One of the strengths of TCAs is that they have been prescribed for some 40 years; clinicians are familiar with them and relatively confident of the risks associated with them.

Although there are occasional reports of TCAs accumulating in the infant and causing sedation,[16] these effects appear uncommon and reversible. From our study of dothiepin[28] we know that breastmilk concentrations show wide individual variation, to which dose is not an accurate guide (table II). The only follow up study of children exposed to antidepressants in breastmilk indicated that dothiepin had no negative effects. On the contrary, the children of the women receiving the highest doses of dothiepin appeared to be functioning at a higher cognitive level than those on lower doses or none at all.[29] Although this was a small study of only 15 women, it suggests not only that dothiepin is well tolerated, but that aggressive treatment is important.

For postpartum women, the most common and concerning adverse effects of TCAs are sedation, postural hypotension and bodyweight gain. In women who are at risk of suicide, the toxicity of these drugs in overdose is also an issue. For this reason, and because of its reduced sedative effect, lofepramine is more commonly used where available.

Women need to be alert to care for their infants. Although this may not be crucial initially if the woman is hospitalised, continuing sedation may impair her ability to be fully independent and may interfere with her relationship with her child. However, anxiety is a common feature of postpartum illness and as a result women are often able to tolerate the sedation induced by the TCA and indeed find that it provides symptomatic relief from anxiety. This obviates the need for minor tranquillisers. In this regard, short term dothiepin is often a good choice. Highly anxious women may gain more benefit from the more sedating TCAs such as amitriptyline.

However, sedation may be a problem with longer term use of these medications; nortriptyline and desipramine have a more favourable adverse effect profile.

Bodyweight gain often does not become apparent until after the depressive symptoms have significantly improved, which becomes a dilemma for the woman and her treating physician. Where there is a history of bodyweight gain or swings, the merits of TCAs versus alternatives need to be considered carefully. If the bodyweight gain is causing loss of self esteem, the risks of ceasing treatment versus the likelihood of relapse need to be discussed with the patient. Where the depression has been very severe, careful attention to diet and exercise for the time on antidepressants may be a better alternative than cessation.

Suicide is fortunately uncommon in postpartum depression,[30] but may be a significant risk in puerperal psychosis. Women with psychosis are likely to be in hospital in the acute phases, where supervision can minimise this risk.

Treatment with TCAs should be maintained for at least 6 months. Further pregnancies should be avoided until the child is 2 years old and the woman has been well and off medication for 1 year. Prophylactic antidepressants may also have a place in treatment, as suggested by the preventative effects of even low dosages (75 mg/day) of a TCA,[31] although later as yet unpublished data do not appear to support this.

Selective Serotonin Reuptake Inhibitors

Only relatively recently available, the SSRIs offer a real alternative to the TCAs, particularly for those women who find the adverse effects intolerable or in whom the antidepressant effects were inadequate.

SSRIs specifically block the parasynaptic reuptake of serotonin, with much more variance as a class than the TCAs. They are 90% absorbed with a half-life varying from 7 days (metabolite of fluoxetine) to 10 to 16 hours (paroxetine). Individual SSRIs are thought to have similar efficacy, with a flat dose-response curve, although there may be a selective inter-individual response. Their efficacy is thought to be similar to TCAs, although there is a school of thought that TCAs are more effective in melancholic depression. Whether this is because of the immediate sedative and anxiolytic effects of TCAs, or a real antidepressant effect, is unclear.

SSRIs are generally well tolerated, with a higher compliance than TCAs. Reported adverse effects are usually mild and transitory, and include nausea, diarrhoea, headaches, insomnia, drowsiness and agitation. SSRIs are relatively well tolerated in overdose.

Clinical experience with SSRIs may suggest that the early adverse effect of agitation can worsen the symptom profile (not borne out, however, by research in general depression[32]) and fail to provide early relief of insomnia and anxiety. However, Montgomery and Findberg[33] found SSRIs to be more effective than TCAs in treating depressed patients with co-existing anxiety. Furthermore, Nutt[34] argues that SSRIs have an important role in the treatment of mixed anxiety-depressed states, on the basis of the implication of serotonergic function in the pathogenesis of anxiety. In clinical practice, SSRIs are increasingly being used as first line treatment, and their anxiolytic effect, with less hypnotic effect than TCAs, certainly makes them appropriate for puerperal disorders. The initial agitation can be controlled with short term use of benzodiazepines until the anxiolytic effects become apparent.

One of the major benefits of SSRIs appears to be that a response is observed in the majority of patients to a dose of 1 tablet daily and therefore undertreatment does not usually occur. In contrast, the administration of subtherapeutic doses of TCAs has been common in the past.

Despite the advantages of SSRIs over TCAs, the appropriateness of these newer antidepressants for the management of postpartum depression remains to be evaluated. Furthermore, little is known regarding the excretion of these compounds into breastmilk, although Nulman and Koren[35] found no ill effects in 11 infants who were breastfed while their mothers were receiving fluoxetine. They calculated that less than 10% of the adult dose was delivered to the nursing infants. However, milk : plasma ratios were not provided in this paper, and as fluoxetine has a long elimination half-life, caution should be exercised when administering the drug to breastfeeding mothers. Large studies of the use of fluoxetine in pregnancy suggest that it has no major teratogenic effects.[36] However, Chambers et al.[37] found more minor abnormalities in infants whose mothers were exposed to fluoxetine in the first trimester than in those whose mothers were not, and that third trimester administration of the drug was associated with higher perinatal complications, including prematurity, respiratory difficulties and jitteriness, than were observed in infants of women who were only exposed to the drug in the first and second trimester. Data on sertraline, including a 1-year follow up of breastfed infants, concluded no negative sequelae.[38]

Monoamine Oxidase Inhibitors and Related Compounds

Monoamine oxidase inhibitors (MAOIs) exert their effect by inhibition of the enzyme monoamine oxidase, which is responsible for the metabolism of serotonin and tryptophan, thus enhancing the availability of these compounds.

MAOIs are rapidly absorbed and produce maximum enzyme inhibition in 5 to 10 days; results may be exaggerated in genetically predisposed slow acetylators.

Adverse effects are similar to TCAs. In addition, an interaction between MAOIs and foods containing tyramine can result in a hypertensive crisis, necessitating adherence to a strict tyramine-free diet and avoidance of a number of other medications.

MAOIs are less efficacious than TCAs, but may be the treatment of choice where there has been a previous response to this class of drugs, and may have a particular role when panic and anxiety symptoms exist. However, given the dietary difficulties and the option of new, well tolerated compounds, the role of MAOIs is diminishing.

A newer group of MAOIs, the reversible inhibitors of monamine oxidase (RIMAs), are well tolerated and lack the drawbacks of the original compounds; in particular minimal dietary restrictions and fewer adverse drug interactions are associated with their use. This class includes drugs such as moclobemide, which is characterised by inducing reversible inhibition of predominantly MAO-A and to a lesser extent MAO-B. Moclobemide has been evaluated in breast milk, and was found to have a low milk to plasma ratio; in our study this averaged 0.68 with a range of 0.39 to 1.21. Based on this, infants were exposed to <1% of the maternal dose.[39]

Serotonin–Noradrenaline Reuptake Inhibitors

The most recent development in antidepressants has seen the introduction of serotonin-noradrenaline reuptake inhibitors (SNRIs) such as venlafaxine. As a group, these antidepressants selectively inhibit both serotonin and noradrenaline reuptake, and have a positive dose-response relationship and an earlier onset of action than and a safety profile similar to the SSRIs.[40]

Early work on venlafaxine in breastfeeding women had been reported by Ilett et al.;[41] three mothers and infants studied had a high mean milk to plasma ratio of 4.1, with metabolites found in the infants. These preliminary results suggest that venlafaxine would not be the drug of first choice in breastfeeding women. Another of the newer antidepressants with a differing action, nefazodone, was studied in three women; these data suggested a low diffusion of this medication into breastmilk.[42]

4.2.3 Anxiolytics

Although women with postpartum depression frequently present with anxiety symptoms, anxiolytics have a minimal or no role to play in therapy. Relief of severe symptoms is usually achieved with antidepressants, antipsychotics where there are psychotic symptoms, and anxiety management techniques. This avoids the need for multidrug therapy, as well as the problems of dependence and tolerance, and the impaired learning and concentration that can be a feature of the minor tranquillisers. Short term, low dose sedation while waiting for the effects of the newer antidepressants is probably the main indication for these drugs. Where debilitating panic attacks are occurring, the diagnosis of panic disorder should be considered, and minor tranquillisers may be indicated in this situation.

4.2.4 Lithium

As many researchers view puerperal psychosis as an affective variant of bipolar disorder,[43] lithium as a treatment and in prophylaxis has received some attention.

Primarily a mood stabiliser rather than an antidepressant, lithium is thought to act by altering cell membrane permeability. It alters synthesis and turnover of serotonin and inhibits the release and increases the parasynaptic destruction of noradrenaline. It is readily absorbed, with peak concentrations within 3 to 4 hours, and is primarily excreted via the kidneys.

Adverse effects include many of those of the TCAs. Lithium must be maintained at plasma concentrations between 0.5 and 1.2 mmol/L in order to prevent toxicity, and even at these concentrations may have long term effects on the kidney and thyroid. It may also be teratogenic and should be avoided in the first trimester of pregnancy, and used only with careful monitoring later in pregnancy, given the changes in glomerular filtration rates throughout pregnancy and the postpartum period.

In clinical practice, lithium use is indicated where previous response to it has occurred, where there is evidence of mood swings and when response to antidepressants is slow or results in a manic swing.

Women with a previous history of puerperal or nonpuerperal mania have a 100 times greater risk of recurrence with a subsequent pregnancy.[4] The research of Stewart et al.[44] suggests a role for lithium in prophylaxis, with its use directly following delivery preferred. Further replication is required as numbers in the study were small.

The disadvantage of lithium treatment is the difficulty posed for women who wish to breastfeed, as lithium is excreted into breastmilk.[44,45] In 1 reported case where the mother had been treated with lithium throughout the pregnancy, the baby was hypotonic and cyanotic at birth.[44] The baby improved when breastfeeding was ceased, but deteriorated when it was recommenced. Maternal serum lithium concentration was 1.5 mmol/L, and the breastmilk and infant serum concentration was 0.6 mmol/L. Although the maternal concentration was admittedly high, with the circulation changes that occur in the mother at delivery, toxicity in the infant and mother is a risk. Indeed, toxic symptoms, as in this case, may appear at lower concentrations in the infant than in the mother.

In contrast, Schou and Amdisen[46] reported eight cases of breastfed babies whose mothers were on lithium treatment. The breastmilk : plasma ratio ranged from 0.24 to 0.67, with maternal concentrations being 1.5 to 5.6 times those of the infant. No adverse effect was noted in the infants.

Nevertheless, there has been a reluctance for women being treated with lithium to breastfeed, with concern over the effect of long term administration on the infant's kidney and thyroid, as well as over shorter term toxicity. It is advised that the use of lithium and the merits of breastfeeding versus maternal mental health and bottle feeding be discussed with the woman and her family through, or even prior to, her pregnancy.

4.3 Electroconvulsive Therapy

Electroconvulsive therapy (ECT) has been evaluated as an effective treatment for severe depression. Although its use has declined in the last 20 years, effectively due to stigma, it remains an available treatment throughout Australia, Britain, Canada and some parts of the US.

ECT remains the treatment associated with the most rapid onset of effects, and is considered the treatment of choice in acutely suicidal patients. Reed et al.[47] evaluated its effectiveness in puerperal, compared with non-puerperal, psychoses. Findings suggested postpartum illnesses were particularly responsive.

4.4 Psychotherapies

Little work on treatment has been published that differentiates postpartum depression from depression at other times of life. Cooper and Murray,[48] however, looked at psychological treatments of major depression (using DSM-III-R[49] criteria) in women at 6 weeks postpartum. Women in the study were primiparous, and were randomly assigned to either: (i) nondirective counselling that focused on maternal mood; (ii) cognitive-behavioural therapy with a mother-infant focus; or (iii) brief dynamic counselling, also with a mother-infant focus. There were 40 women in each group and 48 controls who received no treatment, who were followed up at 9- and 18-months postpartum.

The women were asked if they were 'satisfied' with the therapeutic approach and responded positively in 74, 90 and 65% of cases, respectively, amongst the intervention groups. Treatment was noted to significantly advance remission. Cognitive-behavioural therapy showed better short and long term effects in women with no past history of depression, while dynamic counselling produced better results in those who had such a history. With respect to maternal or infant outcome, there were no statistically significant different results between any of the intervention groups. Perception of infant behaviour improved over time for both the study and control group, but there was no improvement in any of the groups in the independent rating of the mother-infant relationship, or infant cognitive development or attachment.

Although these findings may reflect the sample size, taking patient satisfaction into account, cognitive-behavioural therapy may be the psychological treatment of choice. Appleby et al.[50] compared cognitive behavioural therapy with fluoxetine in women with postpartum depression and found both to be efficacious. Meager and Milgrom[51] also report on the use of group therapy for postpartum depression; their results were encouraging, but only 10 women were involved in the study.

An unanswered question is how to improve the outcome for the infant. Research in this area has documented the effects of maternal depression on child development,[52,53] but few investi-

gators have assessed prevention or intervention. This is especially critical given
the high rate of disturbances observed in
the mother-infant interaction where the
mother is depressed. In all cases of depression or psychosis, the safety of the
infant needs to be assessed and re-
assessed. It is also important to look at

Table III. Common faults in the management of postpartum psychiatric disorders

Failure to recognise the disorder
Inadequate dosage (particularly tricyclic antidepressants)
Failure to address precipitating or perpetuating factors (e.g. marital issues)
Failure to address the mother-infant relationship

the quality of the relationship. Individual or group work can help women explore their feelings
of guilt and inadequacy; more focused work may be needed to enable a positive relationship
to form, free of the woman's current and prior psychopathology.

The high rate of paternal psychiatric illness[14] should also be remembered, and therapy
should also be considered for the father where appropriate. This may include short term or
ongoing marital therapy.

4.5 Support

Support services are essential in the management of postpartum psychiatric disorders.
Women with postpartum disorders, whether depressed or recovering from psychosis, may be
anxious and lack concentration and confidence in the care of their child. It is important to
ensure that partners and families understand the difficulties the woman faces, and that their
ongoing support is enlisted. Community services such as maternal child health nurses, home
help, child care and self help groups can also be an important adjunct to management.

5. Conclusion

Postpartum psychiatric disorders have, until now, suffered from not being regarded as entities
separate from other disorders. As a result, treatment trials have overlooked the specific issues
related to these disorders; current work is readdressing this. Common management faults are
summarised in table III.

Principally, the disorders need to be identified early and treated aggressively, with consideration for maternal and infant safety. The choice of medication, preferably a single medication, needs to relieve the psychotic symptoms and agitation quickly. In severe cases, ECT may be
the treatment of choice, with long term consideration of the woman's need to remain alert to
care for her child.

When the woman is breastfeeding, lithium and benzodiazepines (long acting/high dose)
should be avoided. When using other drugs, the apparently low risks to the infant (although
infants should be closely monitored until steady-state is reached) versus the known benefits of
treatment to the mother and so indirectly to the infant need to be considered. At times, high
doses may be required; undertreatment should be avoided.

TCAs have been the agents most extensively studied for the treatment of postpartum psychiatric disorders, in particular with regard to safety in breastfeeding, and there has been recent
work on use of these drugs as prophylaxis. The disadvantages of these drugs, particularly for
postpartum women, are sedation, postural hypotension and bodyweight gain.

The role of the newer antidepressants is yet to be established, with SSRIs potentially having
particular efficacy in view of the high levels of anxiety often apparent in postpartum disorders.

Minor tranquillisers have a minimal role. Lithium has a significant role in puerperal psychosis as a treatment and prophylaxis, but only as a third or fourth line of treatment in postpartum depression.

It is important to emphasis the need for psychotherapy; childbirth may act as a trigger for many psychosocial stresses, with long term implications for all family members.

References

1. Pitt B. Maternity blues. Br J Psychiatry 1973; 22: 431-3
2. Cooper PJ, Campbell E, Day A, et al. Nonpsychotic psychiatric disorder after childbirth. Br J Psychiatry 1988; 152: 799-806
3. American Psychiatric Association. Diagnostic and statistical manual of mental disorders. 4th ed. Washington, DC: American Psychiatric Association, 1994
4. Kendell RE. Epidemiology of puerperal psychosis. Br J Psychiatry 1987; 150: 662-73
5. Brockington IF, Cernik KF, Schofield EM, et al. Puerperal psychosis, phenomena and diagnosis. Arch Gen Psychiatry 1981; 38: 829-33
6. Dennerstein L, Lehert P, Riphagen F. Postpartum depression-risk factors. J Psychosom Obstet Gynaecol Suppl 1989; 10: 53-65
7. Dalton K. Prophylactic progesterone treatment for postnatal depression. Marce Society Annual 1983. London: Marce Society, 1983
8. Sichel D, Lee S, Cohen L, et al. Prophylactic estrogen in recurrent postpartum affective disorder. Biol Psychiatry 1995; 38: 814-8
9. Gregoire A, Kumar R, Everitt B, et al. Transdermal oestrogen for treatment of severe postnatal depression. Lancet 1996; 347: 930-3
10. Harris B, Othman S, Davies JA, et al. Association between postpartum thyroid dysfunction and thyroid antibodies and depression. BMJ 1992; 305: 152-6
11. OHara MW, Reim LP, Campbell SB. Postpartum depression: a role for social network and life stress variables. J Nerv Ment Dis 1983; 171: 336-41
12. Brown GW, Harris T. The social origin of depression. London: Travistock, 1987
13. Uddenberg N, Englesson I. Prognosis of postpartum mental disturbance: a prospective study of postpartum women and their 4 1/2 year old children. Acta Psychiatr Scand 1978; 58: 201-12
14. Harvey I, McGrath G. Psychiatric morbidity in spouses of women admitted to a mother-baby unit. Br J Psychiatry 1988; 152: 506-10
15. Coghill SR, Caplan HL, Alexander H, et al. Impact of maternal depression in cognitive development of young children. BMJ 1986; 292: 1165-7
16. Matheson I, Panele H, Altersen AR. Respiratory depression caused by N-desmethyldoxepin in breastmilk [letter]. Lancet 1985; 2: 1124
17. Buist A, Dennerstein L, Burrows G. Review of a mother and baby unit in a psychiatric hospital. Aust NZ J Psychiatry 1990; 24: 103-8
18. Bowlby J. Attachment and loss. 1. Attachment. London: Hogarth, 1969
19. Oates M. The development of an integrated community orientated service for severe postnatal depressive. In: Brockington IF, Kumar R, editors. Motherhood and mental illness 2. London: Wright, 1984: 223-38
20. Kris EB, Carmichael DM. Chlorpromazine maintenance therapy during pregnancy and confinement. Psychiatr Q 1957; 31: 690-5
21. Leonard BE. Behavioural teratology and toxicology. In: Grahame-Smith DG, Cowen PJ, editors. Psychopharmacology: preclinical psychopharmacology. Amsterdam: Excerpta Medica, 1983: 248-99
22. Hill RC, McIvor R, Wojnar-Horton RE, et al. Risperidone distribution in human milk; a case report and estimated infant exposure during breastfeeding. J Clin Psychopharm. In press
23. Dev V, Krupp P. The side effects and safety of clozapine. Rev Contemp Pharmacother 1995; 6: 197-208
24. Banerjee SP, Kung LS, Riggi SS. Development of beta adrenergic receptor subsensitivity by antidepressants. Nature 1977; 268: 455-6
25. Pollock B, Perel J. Tricyclic antidepressants: contemporary issues for therapeutic practice. Can J Psychiatry 1989 Aug; 34: 609-17
26. Buist A, Norman T, Dennerstein L. Breastfeeding and psychotropic medication. J Affect Disord 1990; 19: 197-206
27. Brown A, Buist A. Childhood sexual abuse – a life cycle hypothetical. Aust Psychiatry 1995 Aug; 3 (4): 273
28. Buist A, Norman T, Dennerstein L. Plasma and breastmilk concentration of dothiepen and northiadin in lactating women. Hum Psychopharmacol 1993; 8: 29-33
29. Buist A, Janson H. The effect of exposure to dothiepin and northiaden in breast milk on child development. Br J Psychiatry 1995; 167: 370-3
30. Appleby L, Turnbull G. Parasuicide in the first postnatal year. Psychol Med 1995 Sep; 25 Suppl.: 1087-90
31. Wisner KL, Wheeler SB. Prevention of recurrent postpartum major depression. Hosp Community Psychiatry 1994; 45: 1191-6
32. Lane R, Baldwin D, Preskorn S. The SSRIs: advantage and disadvantages and differences. J Psychopharmacol 1995; 9 (2 Suppl.): 163-78
33. Montgomery SA, Fineberg N. Is there a relationship between serotonin receptor subtypes and selectivity of response in specific psychiatric illness? Br J Psychiatry 1989; 155 (Suppl. 8): 63-70
34. Nutt D. The anxiety factor in depression. J Psychopharmacol 1995; 9 (2 Suppl.): 185-9
35. Nulman I, Koren G. The safety of fluoxetine during pregnancy and lactation. Teratology 1996; 53: 305-8
36. Isenberg KE. Excretion of fluoxetine in human breastmilk [letter]. J Clin Psychiatry 1990; 51: 169
37. Chambers CD, Johnson KA, Dick LM, et al. Birth outcomes in pregnant women taking fluoxetine. N Engl J Med 1996; 335: 1010-5
38. Nulman I, Rovet J, Stewart DE, et al. Neurodevelopment of children exposed *in utero* to antidepressant drugs. N Engl J Med 1997 Jan 23; 336 (4): 258-62

39. Buist A, Denerstein L, Maguire KP, et al. Plasma and human milk concentrations of moclobemide in nursing mothers. Hum Psychopharmacol Clin Exp 1998; 13: 579-82
40. Preskorn SH, Janicak PE, Davis JM, et al. Advances in the pharmacotherapy of depressive disorders. In: Janicak PG, editor. Principles and practice of psychopharmacology. Vol. 1, no. 2. Maryland: Williams and Wilkins, 1995
41. Ilett K, Hackett LP, Dusci LJ, et al. Distribution and excretion of venlafaxine and O-desmethylvenlafaxine in human milk. Br J Clin Pharmacol 1998; 45: 459-62
42. Dodd S, Buist A, Burrows GD, et al. Determination of nefazodone and its pharmacologically active metabolites in human blood plasma and breast milk by high performance liquid chromatography. J Chromatography B Biomed Sci App 1999; 730 (2): 249-55
43. Brockington IF, Cox-Roper A. Nosology of puerperal mental illness. In: Brockington IF, Kumar R, editors. Motherhood and mental illness. London: Academic Press, 1982: 1-16
44. Stewart DE, Klompenhouwer JL, Kendell RE. Prophylactic lithium in puerperal psychosis. The experience of three centres. Br J Psychiatry 1991; 158: 393-7
45. Tunnessen WW, Hertz CG. Toxic effects of lithium in newborn infants: a commentary. J Paediatr 1972; 81: 804-7
46. Schou M, Amdisen A. Lithium and pregnancy. III. Lithium ingestion by children breastfed by women on lithium treatment. BMJ 1973; 2: 138
47. Reed P, Sermin N, Appleby L, et al. A comparison of clinical response to electroconvulsive therapy in puerperal and non-puerperal psychoses. J Affective Disorders 1999; 54: 255-60
48. Cooper P, Murray L. Three psychological treatments for postnatal depression: a controlled comparison. Marce Society Conference, 1994 Sep 25-28; Cambridge, 54
49. American Psychiatric Association. Diagnostic and statistical manual of mental disorders. 3rd ed., rev. Washington, DC: American Psychiatric Association, 1987
50. Appleby L, Warner R, Whitton A, et al. A controlled study of fluoxetine and cognitive-behavioural counselling in the treatment of postpartum depression. BMJ 1997; 314: 932-6
51. Meager I, Milgrom J. Group treatment for postpartum depression : a pilot study. Aust N Z J Psychiatry 1996; 30 (6): 852-60
52. Coghill SR, Caplan HL, Alexander H, et al. Impact of maternal depression in cognitive development of young children. BMJ 1986; 292: 1165-7
53. Wrate RM, Roony AC, Thomas PF, et al. Postnatal depression and child development. A three-year follow-up study. Br J Psychiatry 1985; 146: 622-7

Correspondence: Dr *Anne Buist*, Austin-Repatriation Hospital, Department of Psychiatry, Repatriation Hospital Site, Banksia Street, Heidelberg, Victoria 3084, Australia.

Advances in the Diagnosis and Treatment of Premenstrual Dysphoria

Meir Steiner[1,2,3] and *Leslie Born*[2,3]

1 Department of Psychiatry and Behavioural Neurosciences, McMaster University, Hamilton, Ontario, Canada
2 Women's Health Concerns Clinic, St Joseph's Hospital, Hamilton, Ontario, Canada
3 Father Sean O'Sullivan Research Centre, St Joseph's Hospital, Hamilton, Ontario, Canada

Perhaps the most startling revelation in the burgeoning research on premenstrual syndromes is the recent agreement among many renowned women's health researchers on the diagnostic entity of the more severe form of premenstrual syndrome (PMS), namely premenstrual dysphoric disorder (PMDD).[1] In addition, a plethora of new research findings on aetiological factors and treatments for PMS and PMDD has become available in the past several years. The purpose of this review, therefore, is to provide health practitioners with current information on premenstrual syndromes, including their epidemiology, aetiology, diagnosis and treatment.

PMS can be defined as a pattern of emotional, behavioural and physical symptoms which occur premenstrually and remit after menses. These symptoms typically include minor mood changes, breast tenderness, bloating and headache.[2] More than 100 physical and psychological symptoms have been attributed to the premenstruum.[3] PMDD, usually comprising extremely distressing emotional and behavioural symptoms (irritability, dysphoria, tension, mood lability), first appeared in the appendix of the DSM-III-R[4] as late luteal phase dysphoric disorder (LLPDD); it was later re-named and incorporated into the appendix of the DSM-IV.[5]

Premenstrual exacerbation denotes women with continuing psychiatric disorders or medical conditions who report intensification of their symptoms premenstrually and sometimes an emergence of new symptoms.[6] Women with premenstrual exacerbation may also meet criteria for PMS or PMDD.

1. Epidemiology

1.1 Prevalence

Epidemiological surveys have estimated that as many as 75% of women with regular menstrual cycles experience some symptoms of PMS.[7] The majority of these women do not require medical or psychiatric interventions. Since the emergence of the term 'premenstrual syndrome' in the 1950s,[8] PMS has become an increasingly discussed topic in popular media sources; thus, the more effective self-management techniques are easily accessed by women through the media or through their peers. Women who feel they are unable to self-manage their PMS are most often seen in primary care settings and by gynaecologists.

PMDD, on the other hand, affects only 3 to 8% of women in this age group.[9-14] These women report premenstrual symptoms, primarily mood symptoms, severe enough to seriously interfere with their lifestyle and relationships.[15,16] Women with PMDD do not usually respond to conservative and conventional interventions.

A high proportion of women presenting with PMDD have a history of, or continuing episodes of, mood or anxiety disorders.[17-19] For example, a lifetime history of major depressive disorder among PMDD patients has been reported in the range of 30 to 70%.[20] In prospective studies, 14 to 16% of women with PMDD had a lifetime history of anxiety disorder, while comorbid anxiety diagnoses have been reported to be as high as 32%.[21] Thus, it is important to exclude the possibility that the presentation is of a different major psychiatric or medical problem with premenstrual onset.

1.2 Age and Parity

Women from menarche to menopause may report clinically significant menstrually related symptoms and, in general, the literature supports this finding.[1] However, age may be associated with the reporting of premenstrual symptoms[7] and the clinical presentation of PMS or PMDD. Onset of distressing symptoms is typically when women are in their late twenties to mid-thirties.[22]

There is some evidence of worsening of premenstrual symptomatology following childbirth,[7] although this association has yet to be confirmed prospectively.

1.3 Menstrual Cycle Characteristics

There are mixed reports on the association of menstrual cycle characteristics with severity of premenstrual symptoms. One study found a higher prevalence of PMS in women whose menses lasted longer than 6 days.[23] Others have found an association between PMS symptoms and longer[24] or shorter (specifically in women with purely depressive symptoms)[25] menstrual cycle length.

1.4 Past or Current Psychiatric Illness

A high proportion of women presenting with PMDD have a history of previous episodes of mood disorders (major depression,[20] minor depression,[26] postpartum depression,[26] seasonal affective disorder,[27] bipolar disorder[26]), and some women with PMDD have a history of suicide attempts,[28] anxiety disorders (panic disorder, generalised anxiety disorder, phobia),[21] personality disorders[26] or substance abuse.[26] Women with an ongoing mood disorder report premenstrual exacerbation of symptoms and an emergence of new symptoms.[28-34]

1.5 Family History

Population-based twin studies of the familial risk factors for premenstrual symptoms have suggested that PMS may be heritable.[35,36]

1.6 Psychosocial Stressors

A substantial body of literature focusing on life stressors involving major life events, relationships with significant others, work, social support[37] or history of sexual abuse[38] suggests that life stress is positively associated with PMS symptoms.

1.7 Sociocultural Considerations

Research on premenstrual syndromes has taken place in the US, Europe, the Mediterranean and the Middle East, Africa and South-East Asia. Specific conclusions, about cultural differences in premenstrual symptomatology however are hampered by differences in study methodology. Notwithstanding, some broad cultural patterns regarding the nature and frequency of reported premenstrual symptoms can be delineated.

Affective symptoms (irritability, mood swings, tension) and bodyweight gain appear more prevalent among women from the US, compared with a higher frequency of somatic symptoms (swelling, breast pain, backache) in Italian and Bahraini groups,[39] as well as in Swiss, Indian and Chinese groups.[13,40,41] One report has suggested that 'menstrual socialisation' may influence symptom(s) expectation and reporting.[42]

In addition, associations between educational level and severity (i.e. women with higher levels of education reporting more severe symptoms),[43] as well as educational level and type (i.e. the more highly educated group reporting a greater prevalence of psychological symptoms) of premenstrual symptoms have been suggested.[39]

Thus, it is important to consider that cultural context, even level of education, may influence womens' premenstrual experiences and therefore the nature of what is relayed to clinicians.

2. Pathophysiology

The aetiology of PMS and PMDD is still largely unknown. That PMS and PMDD are biological phenomena (as opposed to psychological or psychosocial events) is primarily underscored by recent, convincing evidence of the heritability of premenstrual symptoms[36] and the elimination of premenstrual complaints with suppression of ovarian activity[44] or surgical menopause.[45,46] The current consensus seems to be that normal ovarian function rather than simple hormone imbalance is the cyclic trigger for biochemical events within the CNS and other target tissues which unleash premenstrual symptoms in vulnerable women.[44,47,48] This viewpoint is attractive in that it encourages investigation of the neuroendocrine-modulated central neurotransmitters and the role of the hypothalamic-pituitary-gonadal axis in PMDD. Notwithstanding, a surge of recent research has encompassed other aetiological influences including female biological rhythms (sleep, body temperature) and psychosocial factors.

2.1 Ovarian Steroids

The role of the female sex hormones in premenstrual symptomatology has been considered of central importance, yet in women with PMDD the ovarian axis is apparently functioning normally with normal hormone (estrogen and progesterone) levels.[44] Recently, attention has shifted from a focus on estrogen and progesterone to the role of androgens in premenstrual dysphoria.

Early investigations of androgens have suggested that women with PMS or PMDD have elevated levels of serum testosterone in the luteal phase compared with controls (but still within the normal range), which may contribute primarily to the symptom of irritability.[49-51] This hypothesis of increased androgenicity is backed both by animal and human studies of androgens and irritability and/or aggression.[52] Androgens promote sexual drive in humans and have also been tentatively linked with mood (e.g. depression and premenstrual irritability) and impulsive behaviour (e.g. compulsions and binge eating). Enhanced serotonin (5-hydroxytryptamine; 5-HT) availability [e.g. with the use of selective serotonin reuptake inhibitors (SSRIs)], on the other hand, is associated with reduction in irritability, depression and impulsive behaviour, as well as reduced libido. An inverse relationship between serotonin and androgens, and their effects on human behaviour has been proposed; the behavioural effects of androgens may be therefore partly mediated by a reduction in serotonin activity.[52]

Reduction of premenstrual dysphoria with androgen antagonists in women with PMS who showed higher mean levels of total testosterone in the late luteal phase also lends support to the idea of increased androgenicity.[53,54] Others, however, have not observed differences in plasma testosterone levels in comparisons of women with or without PMS,[55-57] and one study has reported significantly lower total and free plasma testosterone levels in a sample of 10 women with PMS.[58] Further comparative studies of women with PMS and PMDD are therefore required.

Several studies have examined the role of allopregnanolone (a metabolite of progesterone) in the manifestation of premenstrual symptomatology. Treatment studies have suggested that progesterone and progestagens may actually provoke, rather than ameliorate, the cyclical symptom changes of PMDD.[59] Allopregnanolone, on the other hand, is thought to modulate γ-aminobutyric acid (GABA) receptor functioning and produce an anxiolytic effect;[60] quantitative differences in progesterone and allopregnanolone levels between patients with PMS and controls have been examined, although the findings thus far are contradictory.[60-63]

The serum levels of ionised magnesium (Mg) and ionised calcium (Ca) have been studied across the menstrual cycle in association with levels of estrogen, progesterone and testosterone; investigators have suggested that changes in levels of Mg or Ca or a dramatic change in the Ca/Mg ratio may underlie the premenstrual syndromes.[64] However, significant fluctuations of total and ionised Ca during the menstrual cycle occur in both women with and without documented PMS.[65]

2.2 Endocrine Abnormalities

An alternative strategy to measuring various plasma hormone levels in an attempt to discern the aetiology of PMDD has been to search for endocrine abnormalities that have been repeatedly associated with various other forms of psychopathology. The main advantage of this approach is its potential to help further our understanding of PMDD as well as its relation to other psychiatric disorders. The current literature suggests that thyroid dysfunction may be found in a small group of women with premenstrual symptoms but that PMDD should not be viewed as a masked form of hypothyroidism.[66-68]

A dysregulation of cardiovascular[69] and neuroendocrine responses[69-71] to stress has been suggested in women with premenstrual symptomatology.

2.3 Neurotransmitters

Of the neurotransmitters studied to date, increasing evidence suggests serotonin may be important in the pathogenesis of PMDD.[72-76] PMDD shares many features of other mood and anxiety disorders linked to serotonergic dysfunction.[31,77,78] In addition, reduction in brain serotonin neurotransmission is thought to lead to poor impulse control, depressed mood, irritability and increased carbohydrate craving; all mood and behavioural symptoms associated with PMDD.

The serotonergic system is in close reciprocal relationship with gonadal hormones.[50,79] In the hypothalamus, estrogen induces a diurnal fluctuation in serotonin,[80] whereas progesterone increases the turnover rate of serotonin.[81]

More recently, several studies concluded that serotonin function may also be altered in women with PMDD. Some studies used models of neuronal function (such as whole blood serotonin levels, platelet uptake of serotonin and platelet tritiated imipramine binding) and found altered serotonin function during all phases of the menstrual cycle.[74,82-85] Other studies that used challenge tests (with tryptophan, fenfluramine, buspirone, chlorophenylpiperazine) suggested abnormal serotonin function in women who were symptomatic, but differed in their findings as to whether the response to serotonin was blunted or heightened.[86-90] Acute tryptophan depletion (suppressing brain serotonin synthesis) was significantly associated with exacerbation of premenstrual symptoms, in particular irritability.[91] Additional evidence suggesting the involvement (although not necessarily aetiological) of the serotonergic system has emerged from treatment studies: drugs facilitating serotonergic transmission, such as SSRIs, are very effective in reducing premenstrual symptoms.[92] These studies imply, at least in part, a possible change in serotonin 5-HT$_{1A}$ receptor sensitivity in women with premenstrual dysphoria.

The current consensus is that women with premenstrual dysphoria may be behaviourally or biochemically sub- or supersensitive to biological challenges of the serotonergic system.[93,94] It is not yet clear whether these women present with a trait or state marker (alternatively, both conditions could be possible) of premenstrual syndromes.[95]

The GABA, adrenergic and opioid neurotransmitter systems have also been implicated in the pathophysiology of PMS and PMDD. Investigators found reduced GABA$_A$ receptor sensitivity in patients with PMS in the late luteal phase,[96] and reduced plasma levels of GABA in the late luteal phase have been noted in women with PMDD.[97]

Abnormal α_2-adrenergic receptor function is implicated in anxiety and depressive disorders; in a recent, controlled study of patients with PMDD, α_2-adrenergic receptor density positively correlated with symptom severity during the luteal phase. Moreover, high follicular phase α_2-adrenergic receptor density predicted luteal phase symptom severity.[98]

The role of endogenous opioids in the pathophysiology of PMDD, i.e. that the sharp drop in levels ('withdrawal') during the late luteal phase may lead to increased irritability, anxiety, tension and aggression, has been the target of some investigation.[99-101] Preliminary investigation revealed that women with PMS have decreased luteinising hormone response to naloxone during the mid-luteal phase, indicating a loss of central opioid tone.[100] A small sample of women with PMS had a significant reduction in symptoms following oral treatment with the opioid receptor antagonist, naltrexone,[101] which supports an aetiological role for the opioidergic system.

2.4 Circadian Rhythms

Desynchronised circadian rhythms can induce mood disorders. Women with PMS frequently experience nocturnal sleep disturbance and daytime sleepiness, suggesting a temporary desynchronisation of circadian rhythms. Patients with PMDD have decreased levels of nocturnal melatonin (serotonin is converted to melatonin in the pineal gland),[102,103] prompting further investigation into plasma melatonin circadian rhythms during the menstrual cycle. The results of preliminary studies in women with PMDD suggested an altered response to bright light therapy in the symptomatic luteal phase.[104] However, a study of sleep pattern changes in women with and without PMS found no significant differences in sleep patterns across the menstrual cycle.[105] In related studies, significant alterations of circadian changes in body temperature during the luteal phase have been documented in individuals with PMS[106] and PMDD.[107] Taken together, these findings suggest that changes in chrono-biological rhythms may be important in the pathophysiology of premenstrual syndromes. However, these hypotheses require further comparative investigations of women with and without premenstrual syndromes.

2.5 Genetic Predisposition

In a recent, longitudinal, population-based twin study of 1312 menstruating female twins, researchers estimated the heritability of premenstrual symptoms at 56%, with negligible influence from family-environmental factors and minimal influence related to genetic and environmental risk factors for lifetime major depression.[36] These data are congruent with the results of previous twins studies of genetic factors.[35,108] A twin study of genetic and environmental variation in the menstrual cycle suggested that the age of menarche and menstrual cycle regularity, as well as propensity for premenstrual symptom reporting, may be inherited.[109]

2.6 Sociocultural Factors

Menstruation and premenstrual symptomatology have been referred to as the 'curse', contributing to a negative perception of a natural cyclical event. The importance of subjective perception in the experience of menstrual events has been underscored in a recent report on the significant reduction of negative symptoms in a sample of women who met criteria for LLPDD following a psychosocially based intervention which emphasised positive reframing (positive connotation).[110] Social beliefs about menstruation, however, vary among different cultures and can influence both expectations about the menstrual cycle and the reporting of symptoms.[42]

PMDD, caution some, may be 'a culturally-bound syndrome', and there may be a risk of 'unnecessary pathologising' of menstrual cycle changes.[111] Cultural context may have a bearing on the frequency of reporting PMS symptomatology as well as the type (e.g. somatic *vs* affective) of symptoms reported.[23] A positive relationship between prior knowledge (negative consequences) about PMS and severity of premenstrual symptoms reported was demonstrated in a study of 86 healthy Mexican women;[112] yet, these results must be interpreted with caution as the level of individuals' education may also influence the nature and severity of symptoms reported (the aforementioned 86 individuals had maximum grade 6 education).[39,43]

In a recent US study of 101 women, investigators found that social support had little aetiological correlation with premenstrual symptoms,[113] although participation in peer support groups may help to reduce symptoms.[114,115]

3. Screening and Diagnosis

Women with premenstrual dysphoria are most often seen in primary care or by their obstetrician/gynaecologist. The results of a recent US study on the experience of women with PMS who sought medical attention suggested a high rate of missed diagnoses.[116]

As there is a lack of objective diagnostic tests for PMS or PMDD (attempts to pinpoint hormonal measures have yielded little success[117]), a complete medical and psychiatric history must be elicited. In addition to a retrospective history of the premenstrual symptoms, this interview also should include a complete review of physical systems (including gynaecological, endocrinological, allergies, and the like) and medical disorders, and a detailed review of family loading for mental illness. Because the symptoms of anaemia and thyroid disease often mirror those of PMS or PMDD, the patient should undergo laboratory investigations if any hints of an underlying medical cause for the symptoms arises. A high prevalence rate of past sexual abuse (40%) has been found among women seeking treatment for premenstrual symptoms,[38] therefore screening for domestic violence is an essential aspect of the assessment. Women presenting with PMDD frequently have a history of previous episodes of mood disorders and those with continuing mood disorders report premenstrual intensification of symptoms and perhaps emergence of new symptoms.

Table I. Assessment of premenstrual dysphoria

Interview
Retrospective history of premenstrual symptoms
Seasonal variation
Complete medical and psychiatric history
History of sexual (or other) abuse
Family loading for mental illness, including substance use

Laboratory
Laboratory testing, especially thyroid, anaemia and gonadal hormones

Daily chart
Prospective daily self-rating of symptoms for 2 menstrual cycles (using e.g. PRISM, COPE)

Within-cycle change

$$\frac{\text{luteal score} - \text{follicular score}}{\text{luteal score}} \times 100$$

Diagnosis of premenstrual dysphoric disorder
Meets DSM-IV[5] criteria
≥50% change in symptoms from the follicular to the luteal phase

COPE = Calendar of Premenstrual Experiences; **PRISM** = Prospective Record of the Impact and Severity of Menstruation.

Prospective daily rating of symptoms is essential in making a diagnosis of PMS or PMDD. To date, there is no consensus amongst investigators as to the best instruments for confirming the diagnosis of PMDD prospectively, nor is there consensus as to the instruments most appropriate to measure treatment effects in clinical trials.

At least two 1-page daily calendars are appropriate for use in a clinical setting and aid in the required prospective measurement of symptoms. The Prospective Record of the Impact and Severity of Menstruation (PRISM)[118] and the Calendar of Premenstrual Experiences (COPE)[119] allow respondents to rate a variety of physical and psychological symptoms, indicate negative and positive life events, record concurrent medications, and track menstrual bleeding and cycle length. These instruments contain the core symptoms and most of the additional symptoms considered for the DSM-IV diagnosis of PMDD.

In a detailed study of 3 prospective symptom rating scales (used to establish severity of premenstrual mood symptoms and measure efficacy during a multicentre, controlled treatment trial for premenstrual dysphoria),[120] researchers found that single-item visual analogue scales (VASs; for irritability, tension, depression, mood swings), and the Premenstrual Tension Syndrome Observer (PMTS-O) and Self-Rating (PMTS-SR)[121] scales were sensitive to premenstrual symptoms worsening and were also sensitive to change (over time). Furthermore, premenstrual mood symptoms as measured by VASs significantly correlated with PMTS-O and

PMTS-SR scale scores, denoting an easy to administer, reliable and valid method of data collection.[122]

Given the sometimes close resemblance between PMDD and rapid-cycling bipolar II disorder,[123] Macmillan and Young[124] have recommended the Bipolar Mood Diary (a daily mood record derived from the COPE) in conjunction with a PMS daily record to facilitate delineation between PMS and a cyclic depressive illness.

A certain familiarity with the multi-axial diagnostic system of the DSM-IV is assumed. In order to apply the DSM-IV criteria, women must chart symptoms daily for 2 cycles, and their chief complaints must include 1 of 4 core symptoms (depression, tension, irritability, lability of mood) and at least 5 of 11 total symptoms. The symptoms should have occurred with most menstrual cycles during the last year and have interfered with social or occupational roles. Some women may report significant seasonal variation in premenstrual symptoms.[125] The charting of troublesome symptoms should demonstrate clear worsening premenstrually and remission within a few days after the onset of menstruation.

The within-cycle percentage change is calculated by subtracting the follicular score from the luteal score, dividing by the luteal score and multiplying by 100.[126]

The assessment of premenstrual dysphoria is summarised in table I. After completion of the 2-cycle prospective diagnostic assessment phase, women may qualify for one of the following diagnostic categories:

1. *PMS*. Women who receive this diagnosis meet International Classification of Diseases (ICD-10)[2] criteria for PMS, which include mild psychological discomfort and mostly feelings of bloating and bodyweight gain, breast tenderness and swelling, swelling of hands and feet, various aches and pains, poor concentration, sleep disturbance and change in appetite. Only one of these symptoms is required for this diagnosis, although the symptoms must be restricted to the luteal phase of the menstrual cycle, reach a peak shortly before menstruation and cease with the menstrual flow or soon after.

2. *PMDD*. Women who receive this diagnosis meet DSM-IV criteria for PMDD. The essential features include the 'on-off' nature of symptoms, the emphasis on core mood symptoms, and the requirement that the symptoms must interfere markedly with lifestyle. A change in symptoms of at least 50% from the follicular to the luteal phase is suggested for this diagnosis.[120]

'Pure-pure' PMDD denotes women who have no other past and/or present psychiatric disorder. 'Pure' PMDD denotes women who have no other current psychiatric disorder, but have a history of a past psychiatric disorder.[6]

3. *Premenstrual exacerbation*. This category denotes the episodic onset of a major psychiatric disorder or of a medical condition premenstrually. This may include women with continuing psychiatric disorder(s) such as depressive (major depression, dysthymia, cyclothymia, bipolar disorder) and anxiety (panic, phobic, obsessive-compulsive, generalised anxiety disorder) disorders, bulimia, substance abuse and psychotic disorders. It should be noted that the cyclical nature of their symptoms may or may not necessarily match the phases of their menstrual cycle. Women who receive this diagnosis may also meet criteria for PMS or PMDD.

4. *Menstrual psychosis*. In some women, transient psychotic symptoms may appear in rhythm with the menstrual cycle (premenstrual, catamenial, paramenstrual or mid-cycle). These relatively rare phenomena have been the focus of much debate, yet the literature is, for the most part, confined to case reports. The features of menstrual psychosis may include: acute

or sudden onset, against a background of normality; brief duration with full recovery; psychotic features, i.e. confusion, delusions, hallucinations, stupor and mutism, manic symptoms; and an approximately monthly periodicity, in a regular relation with the menstrual cycle.[127]

5. *No diagnosis.* None of the symptoms are severe enough to warrant a diagnosis, although the patient may subjectively sense disruptive symptoms.

Applying these diagnostic criteria to women who seek help for premenstrual complaints will facilitate the clinician in planning treatment interventions.

4. Premenstrual Dysphoric Disorder: A Distinct Clinical Entity

PMDD appears in the appendix of the DSM-IV under the heading 'depressive disorder not otherwise specified'. Yet questions regarding its diagnostic entity (likely stemming from the high rates of comorbidity between PMDD and depressive disorders/anxiety disorders) persist in the literature. Researchers have attempted to resolve the former, for the most part, by summing up similarities in features between PMDD and other mood disorders[20,128,129] or between PMDD and anxiety disorders.[21,130] Other researchers have concentrated on the measurement of PMDD, in particular the methods[122,131] and items[132,133] which easily delineate individuals with PMDD.

Recently, a group of experts reached a consensus that PMDD is a distinct clinical entity.[1] The findings are summarised as follows:

- PMDD has a distinct clinical picture with characteristic symptoms of irritability, anger and internal tension
- the onset and offset of its symptoms are closely linked to the menstrual cycle
- the genetic component of PMDD does not seem to be related to depressive disorders
- in PMDD, the hypothalamic-pituitary-adrenal axis functions normally, unlike its functioning in major depression
- PMDD differs in response to treatment in comparison with other mood disorders, i.e. efficacy of intermittent drug administration, rapid onset of response, and maximal response at low doses, as well as rapid recurrence of symptoms with discontinuation of treatment
- eliminating the menstrual cycle will cure women with PMDD but not those with other mood disorders (after pregnancy, symptoms return once cycles have been re-established).

Table II. Nonpharmacological therapies for premenstrual syndromes

Diet	Reduce caffeine (especially coffee), alcohol, chocolate, tobacco, salt, refined sugar
	Frequent meals with high protein content
	Reduce bodyweight to within 20% of ideal
Exercise	Regular, aerobic exercise
Nutritional supplements	Pyridoxine (vitamin B6): 100 mg/day[a] (monitor for adverse effects)
	Elemental calcium: 1200 mg/day[a]
	Magnesium: 200 mg/day (for symptoms associated with fluid retention)[a]
Light therapy	Cool-white fluorescent light
	2500 lux for 2 hours in the morning or evening[a]
	10 000 lux for 30 minutes in the evening[a]
Psychotherapy	Individual cognitive therapy – positive reframing techniques[a]
	Coping skills training[a]
	Peer support group

a   As evidenced with randomised, controlled studies.

Additional evidence regarding the distinctness of PMDD compared with major depression in terms of biochemical markers[134] and circadian variables[135] has also come to light.

5. Treatment

Therapeutic interventions for premenstrual syndromes range from conservative (lifestyle and stress management) techniques to treatment with psychotropic medications and hormonal therapies, to surgical procedures to eliminate ovulation or ovarian function (for the more extreme cases). While all of these treatments are successful in relieving symptoms for some of the women treated, to date no one intervention has proven to be effective for all. Most pharmacological therapies are now being tested in randomised controlled trials. In contrast, the efficacy of many nonpharmacological therapies has yet to be scientifically demonstrated, although there are numerous case reports of women who obtain relief with some of these approaches.

For women who do not meet criteria for PMDD, or other physical and psychological disorders, but still have mild to moderate symptoms of PMS, conservative treatments are appropriate, and management without pharmacological interventions should be encouraged. Stressful life events should be queried and monitored. These patients may best respond to individual or group psychotherapy in combination with diet and lifestyle changes. Patients should also be taught to review their own monthly diaries and identify triggers to symptom exacerbation.

Women who manifest severe physical symptoms or a psychiatric disorder with premenstrual exacerbation should be treated for their primary condition. Premenstrual symptoms usually remit considerably with successful treatment of the primary condition, and residual symptoms can be treated as indicated.

5.1 Nonpharmacological Approaches

Lifestyle and stress management is a necessary adjunct to any therapeutic intervention, and patients should be educated and encouraged to practice these principles. The nonpharmacological approaches should be tried as first-line therapy, especially for milder symptoms (table II).

5.1.1 Diet and Exercise

The elimination or reduction of caffeine (especially coffee), alcohol, chocolate and tobacco, and adopting a diet composed of frequent high protein and low refined sugar meals is strongly recommended. Patients should be encouraged to decrease sodium in the diet when oedema or fluid retention occurs and, if possible, to reduce bodyweight to within 20% of their ideal. Regular exercise (including aerobic exercise) is important and particularly effective when combined with the regular practice of stress management techniques.

5.1.2 Nutritional Supplements

Pyridoxine (Vitamin B6)

There is limited evidence to suggest that daily doses of pyridoxine (vitamin B6) up to 100mg are likely to be beneficial in treating overall premenstrual symptoms, and of some benefit in treating premenstrual depression.[136] No conclusive evidence has been found of neurological adverse effects at this dose range; however, women receiving pyridoxine should be monitored for muscle weakness, numbness, clumsiness and paraesthesia.

Table III. Summary of drugs and administration regimens shown to be effective in the treatment of premenstrual syndromes[a]

Type	Dosage	Comments	Ref.
Antidepressants			
Fluoxetine	20 mg/day	Selective serotonin (5-hydroxytryptamine; 5-HT) reuptake inhibitors are the first-line treatment for premenstrual mood symptoms	120, 146, 147
	20 mg/day 14 days before menses	Effective for psychological and physical symptoms, as well as improving psychosocial functioning	148[b]
	10 mg/day		149
Sertraline	50-150 mg/day		150
	50 mg/day luteal phase only		151
	50 or 100 mg/day luteal phase only	Intermittent use (luteal phase only) offers decreased costs and reduced adverse effect burden	152
	100 mg/day luteal phase only		153
	50-150 mg/day luteal phase only		154
Paroxetine	10-30 mg/day		155
	5-30mg late luteal phase only		156[b]
Citalopram	10-30 mg/day luteal phase only		157
Clomipramine	25-75 mg/day		158
	25-75 mg/day 14 days before menses		159
Tryptophan	6 g/day ovulation → day 3		160
Anxiolytics			
Alprazolam	0.25-4 mg/day	Dependence and tolerance can develop. Withdrawal symptoms can occur during menses. Relieves physical symptoms; mixed reports on improvement of psychological symptoms	161
	0.25-2 mg/day (0.25-0.5mg up to 4 times daily)		149, 162, 163
	0.25-2 mg/day 6-14 days before menses		164, 165
Buspirone	25-60 mg/day 12 days before menses		166, 167
Ovulation suppression			
Danazol	200-400 mg/day during symptomatic days only	Efficacious treatment for premenstrual migraines and mastalgia. At lower dosage (200 mg/day) ovulation is not suppressed (i.e. fewer adverse effects)	168-170
Leuprorelin	3.75-7.5mg intramuscular injection monthly	Potential risk for: osteoporosis, cardiovascular disease with long term use. Several months of use to reach full treatment effect	44, 171, 172
	7.5mg intramuscular injection monthly with 'add-back' conjugated estrogen 0.625 mg/day (Monday to Saturday) and 10mg medroxyprogesterone orally for 10 days during every fourth cycle	'Add-back' reduced physical and psychological symptoms	173
	3.75 mg/month with 'add-back' transdermal estradiol 0.1mg or progesterone vaginal suppository 200mg twice daily	'Add-back' was associated with a significant recurrence of PMS	44
Buserelin	400-900 µg/day intranasal	Lower dose relieved premenstrual depression and irritability, and some physical complaints	174, 175
Goserelin	3.6mg subcutaneous injection monthly	Significant physical but not psychological relief. 'Add-back' reduced the clinical response	176
Estradiol	100g twice weekly patch with 'add-back' dydrogesterone 10mg or medroxyprogesterone 5mg from days 17-26 of each cycle		177

a   Only double-blind, randomised, placebo-controlled studies, assessed prospectively for at least 2 complete cycles, in women with PMS/LLPDD/PMDD are quoted.

b   Recent prospective case studies of PMDD.

LLPDD = late luteal phase dysphoric disorder; **PMDD** = premenstrual dysphoric disorder; **PMS** = premenstrual syndrome.

Calcium

A daily supplementation of Ca carbonate containing 1200mg of elemental Ca effectively reduced overall luteal phase symptoms in a large sample of women with confirmed PMS,[137] suggesting a link between Ca deficiency and PMS. Symptom reduction occurred by the third treatment cycle.

Magnesium

There is some evidence to suggest that a daily supplement of 200mg of Mg for a minimum of 2 months is of benefit in treating premenstrual symptoms of fluid retention (bodyweight gain, swelling of extremities, breast tenderness and abdominal bloating).[138]

5.1.3 Light Therapy

Significant improvement in severe premenstrual symptomatology has been observed in placebo-controlled studies of bright (cool-white fluorescent) light therapy. During symptomatic days, a minimum of 2500 lux for 2 hours in the morning or in the evening,[139,140] or 10 000 lux for 30 minutes in the evening[141] can significantly reduce depression, irritability and physical symptoms. The benefits of bright-light therapy were maintained in patients who completed at least 12 months of treatment.[140]

5.1.4 Psychotherapy

Individual psychotherapy can aid psychological and social functioning, particularly in those who have endured distressing premenstrual symptoms for an extended length of time. There is some evidence from controlled studies that women with PMS may benefit from individual cognitive therapy[142] or coping skills training[143] in the reduction of premenstrual symptoms. There are conflicting reports, however, about the usefulness of cognitive-behavioural techniques such as restructuring, thought-stopping and anger management.[144]

There is also recent case evidence of the benefits of positively reframing perceptions of the menstrual cycle among women with PMS.[110,145] These latter studies also affirm the usefulness of peer support in the management of PMS.

5.2 Pharmacological Approaches

Pharmacological approaches include psychotropic medications and hormonal interventions. The newer antidepressants in particular, including many of the SSRIs, as well as clomipramine (a tricyclic antidepressant with relatively potent serotonin reuptake inhibiting properties), and tryptophan have demonstrated excellent efficacy and minimal adverse effects in women with PMS and PMDD in whom conservative treatment has failed. Two anxiolytics (alprazolam and buspirone) have also been successful in the reduction of psychological symptoms; however, adverse effects and possible dependence inhibit their use. There is also evidence of success with estradiol implants, gonadotropin-releasing hormone analogues, danazol (a synthetic androgen) and oral contraceptives; however, many women are unable to tolerate the adverse effects of these interventions. A summary of suggested pharmacological approaches is displayed in table III.

5.2.1 Selective Serotonin Reuptake Inhibitors

There is consistent, scientific evidence of the efficacy and tolerability of many of the SSRIs in the treatment of PMDD. Therefore, the SSRIs should be considered as the first-line pharmacological treatment for premenstrual mood symptoms.[92,178] Early studies demonstrated the efficacy of SSRIs and clomipramine with daily doses,[120,146,147,149,150,155,158,179] yet more recent intermittent dose administration studies (10 to 17 days per cycle) have shown equal efficacy in the alleviation of PMDD. Intermittent application of fluoxetine,[148] sertraline,[151-154] paroxetine[156] and citalopram,[157] as well as clomipramine[159] and tryptophan,[160] offers a more attractive treatment option with decreased costs and a reduced adverse effect burden (e.g. less effect on libido, less likely to develop tolerance) for a disorder that is itself intermittent.

Severe PMS and PMDD symptoms respond to relatively low doses of SSRIs, for example, 10 to 20 mg/day of fluoxetine[148,149] or 50 to 100 mg/day of sertraline.[151,154] In addition, there is strong evidence that response to treatment with SSRIs or clomipramine will be relatively immediate (i.e. within the first month of treatment). Therefore, if there is no change in symptomatology, even after several dose increases, an alternative therapy should be considered within 2 to 3 menstrual cycles.

5.2.2 Anxiolytics

The efficacy of alprazolam[161-165] and buspirone[166,167] in the treatment of PMS or PMDD has been demonstrated in randomised placebo-controlled trials, although two additional controlled trials utilising alprazolam showed contrary results.[180,181] The effect, however, of alprazolam and buspirone on PMDD symptomatology is much smaller than that with the SSRIs. Intermittent dose administration is also effective with both of these medications.

Dependence and tolerance are concerns with alprazolam, and the possibility of withdrawal symptoms suggests a gradual taper during menses in some women. Increased food cravings (particularly for foods containing fat) and food intake is a possible adverse effect of alprazolam, as is bodyweight gain.[181,182]

5.2.3 Hormonal Interventions

The suppression of ovulation eliminates the symptomatology of PMS and PMDD. The benefits and risks of this approach, however, should be carefully evaluated with the patient.

The gonadotropin-releasing hormone agonists leuprorelin (leuprolide),[44,171-173] buserelin[174,175,183] and goserelin[176,184] are effective in reducing physical and psychological premenstrual symptoms, as are danazol[168-170] and estradiol patches.[177,185] Recipients of gonadotropin-releasing hormone agonists, however, may experience reduction of some, but not all, mood and/or physical symptoms.[171,176,183] A decreased incidence of adverse effects is obtained with transdermal estradiol at a dose of 100μg with 'add-back' progestogen (progestin) [during days 17 to 26].[177] Danazol has demonstrated efficacy in the relief of premenstrual migraine and premenstrual mastalgia; the (usual) troublesome adverse effects are significantly reduced with lower doses.[169,170]

The reduction of estrogens to postmenopausal levels, however, can induce a host of unwelcome and perhaps irreversible adverse effects. In addition to hot flushes, headache, increased emotional lability, vaginal dryness and decreased libido, there may also be loss of bone mineral density, bodyweight change and breast atrophy. The re-establishment of menstruation may be delayed, and infertility up to 18 months or longer can occur. The addition ('add-back') of estrogen plus progestin to depot leuprorelin[173] provided significant relief of premenstrual symptoms, and no significant changes in lipids, endometrium or bone density were observed. Women who received 'add-back' estrogen or progesterone alone with leuprorelin, on the other hand, had a significant recurrence of psychological and physical symptoms.[44] 'Add-back' estrogen and progestogen with goserelin did not significantly improve premenstrual symptomatology when compared with placebo.[184]

To date, only two controlled studies of oral contraceptives in the treatment of PMS have been published;[186,187] the results indicated that a triphasic oral contraceptive effectively reduced physical symptoms (especially breast pain and bloating), but reports on the relief of psychological symptoms with this intervention have been less firm.

5.3 Surgical Approach

A surgical approach (ovariectomy) should be the last resort and line of treatment for women with PMDD who have not found relief with pharmacological intervention. Two studies have demonstrated the effectiveness of ovariectomy in the (complete) relief of severe premenstrual symptomatology.[45,46]

6. Conclusion

The aetiology of premenstrual syndromes has yet to be clarified in a comprehensive fashion. However, there is a consensus that PMDD is a distinct clinical disorder. We are now able to identify and classify those women who present with severe psychological symptoms and determine whether these symptoms are attributable only to the premenstruum or are an exacerbation of a psychiatric or physical disorder. Women who do not have a concurrent disorder and who meet criteria for PMS but not PMDD should be treated conservatively. Women who meet criteria for PMDD can be successfully treated either on an intermittent or daily basis with low dose SSRIs or clomipramine. Suppression of ovulation can reduce premenstrual symptomatology, but it also brings about early menopause with its distressing emotional and physical sequelae. The addition of hormone replacement to a gonadotropin-releasing hormone agonist can decrease the unwanted adverse effects of these treatments; however, only leuprorelin has demonstrated efficacy. A surgical approach (ovariectomy) should be considered only as a last resort.

References

1. Endicott J, Amsterdam J, Eriksson E, et al. Is premenstrual dysphoric disorder a distinct clinical entity? J Women's Health Gender-Based Med 1999; 8: 663-79
2. World Health Organization. Tenth revision of the International Classification of Diseases (ICD-10). Geneva: World Health Organization Publishers, 1996: 717
3. Budeiri DJ, Li Wan Po A, Dornan JC. Clinical trials of treatments of premenstrual syndrome: entry criteria and scales for measuring treatment outcomes. Br J Obstet Gynaecol 1994; 101: 689-95
4. American Psychiatric Association. Diagnostic and statistical manual of mental disorders. 3rd rev. ed. Washington, DC: American Psychiatric Association, 1987: 367-9
5. American Psychiatric Association. Diagnostic and statistical manual of mental disorders. 4th ed. Washington, DC: American Psychiatric Association, 1994: 717-8
6. Steiner M, Wilkins A, Diagnosis and assessment of premenstrual dysphoria. Psychiatr Ann 1996; 26: 571-5
7. Johnson SR. The epidemiology and social impact of premenstrual symptoms. Clin Obstet Gynecol 1987; 30: 367-76
8. Greene R, Dalton K. The premenstrual syndrome. BMJ 1953; 1: 1007-14
9. Haskett RF, DeLongis A, Kessler RC. Premenstrual dysphoria: a community survey. Presented at Annual American Psychiatric Association Meeting: 1987 May; Chicago
10. Johnson SR, McChesney C, Bean JA. Epidemiology of premenstrual symptoms in a nonclinical sample. I. Prevalence, natural history and help-seeking behaviour. J Reprod Med 1988; 33: 340-6
11. Rivera-Tovar AD, Frank E. Late luteal phase dysphoric disorder in young women. Am J Psychiatry 1990; 147: 1634-6
12. Andersch B, Wendestam C, Hahn L, et al. Premenstrual complaints. I. Prevalence of premenstrual symptoms in a Swedish urban population. J Psychosom Obstet Gynaecol 1986; 5: 39-49
13. Merikangas KR, Foeldenyi M, Angst J. The Zurich Study. XIX. Patterns of menstrual disturbances in the community: results of the Zurich Cohort Study. Eur Arch Psychiatry Clin Neurosci 1993; 243: 23-32
14. Ramcharan S, Love EJ, Fick GH, et al. The epidemiology of premenstrual symptoms in a population based sample of 2650 urban women. J Clin Epidemiol 1992; 45: 377-81
15. Freeman EW, Sondheimer K, Weinbaum PH, et al. Evaluating premenstrual symptoms in medical practice. Obstet Gynecol 1985; 65: 500-5
16. O'Brien PMS, Abukhalil IEH, Henshaw C. Premenstrual syndrome. Curr Obstet Gynecol 1995; 5: 30-7
17. Hendrick V, Altshuler LL, Burt VK. Course of psychiatric disorders across the menstrual cycle. Harv Rev Psychiatry 1996; 4: 200-7
18. Bailey JW, Cohen LS. Prevalence of mood and anxiety disorders in women who seek treatment for premenstrual syndrome. J Womens Health Gend Based Med 1999; 8: 1181-4

19. Blehar MC, DePaulo Jr JR, Gershon ES, et al. Women with bipolar disorder: findings from the NIMH Genetics Initiative sample. Psychopharmacol Bull 1998; 34: 239-43
20. Yonkers KA. The association between premenstrual dysphoric disorder and other mood disorders. J Clin Psychiatry 1997; 58 Suppl. 15: 19-25
21. Yonkers KA. Anxiety symptoms and anxiety disorders: how are they related to premenstrual disorders. J Clin Psychiatry 1997; 58 Suppl. 3: 62-7
22. Freeman EW, Rickels K, Schweizer E, et al. Relationships between age and symptom severity among women seeking medical treatment for premenstrual symptoms. Psychol Med 1995; 25: 309-15
23. Deuster PA, Adera T, South-Paul J. Biological, social, and behavioral factors associated with premenstrual syndrome. Arch Fam Med 1999; 8: 122-8
24. Woods NF, Most A, Dery GK. Prevalence of perimenstrual symptoms. Am J Public Health 1982; 72: 1257-64
25. Hargrove JT, Abraham GE. The incidence of premenstrual tension in a gynecologic clinic. J Reprod Med 1982; 27: 721-4
26. Pearlstein TB, Frank E, Rivera-Tovar A, et al. Prevalence of axis I and axis II disorders in women with late luteal phase dysphoric disorder. J Affect Disord 1990; 20: 129-34
27. Parry BL. Mood disorders linked to reproductive cycle in women. In: Bloom FE, Kupfer DJ, editors. Psychopharmacology: the fourth generation of progress. New York (NY): Raven Press, 1995: 1029-42
28. Harrison WM, Endicott J, Nee J, et al. Characteristics of women seeking treatment for premenstrual syndrome. Psychosomatics 1989; 30: 405-11
29. Fava M, Pedrazzi F, Guaraldi GP, et al. Comorbid anxiety and depression among patients with late luteal phase dysphoric disorder. J Anxiety Disord 1992; 6: 325-35
30. McLeod DR, Hoehn-Saric R, Foster GV, et al. The influence of premenstrual syndrome on ratings of anxiety in women with generalized anxiety disorder. Acta Psychiatr Scand 1993; 88: 248-51
31. Endicott J. The menstrual cycle and mood disorders. J Affect Disord 1993; 29: 193-200
32. Bancroft J, Rennie D, Warner P. Vulnerability to perimenstrual mood change: the relevance of a past history of depressive disorder. Psychosom Med 1994; 56: 225-31
33. Kaspi SP, Otto MW, Pollack MH, et al. Premenstrual exacerbation of symptoms in women with panic disorder. J Anxiety Disord 1994; 8: 131-8
34. Graze KK, Nee J, Endicott J. Premenstrual depression predicts future major depressive disorder. Acta Psychiatr Scand 1990; 81: 201-5
35. Condon JT. The premenstrual syndrome: a twin study. Br J Psychiatry 1993; 162: 481-6
36. Kendler KS, Karkowski LM, Corey LA, et al. Longitudinal population-based twin study of retrospectively reported premenstrual symptoms and lifetime major depression. Am J Psychiatry 1998; 155: 1234-40
37. Severino SK, Moline ML. Premenstrual syndrome: a clinician's guide. New York (NY): The Guilford Press, 1989: 132-5
38. Paddison PL, Gise LH, Lebovits A, et al. Sexual abuse and premenstrual syndrome: comparison between a lower and higher socioeconomic group. Psychosomatics 1990; 31: 265-72
39. Dan AJ, Monagle L. Sociocultural influences on women's experiences of perimenstrual symptoms. In: Gold JH, Severino SK, editors. Premenstrual dysphorias: myths and realities. Washington, DC: American Psychiatric Press, Inc., 1994: 201-11
40. Chandra PS, Chaturvedi SK. Cultural variations in premenstrual experience. Int J Soc Psychiatry 1989; 35 (4): 343-9
41. Chang AM, Holroyd E, Chau JP. Premenstrual syndrome in employed Chinese women in Hong Kong. Health Care Women Int 1995; 16: 551-61
42. Sveinsdottir H. Prospective assessment of menstrual and premenstrual experiences of Icelandic women. Health Care Women Int 1998; 19: 71-82
43. Marvan ML, Diaz-Erosa M, Montesinos A. Premenstrual symptoms in Mexican women with different educational levels. J Psychol 1998; 132: 517-26
44. Schmidt PJ, Nieman LK, Danaceau MA, et al. Differential behavioral effects of gonadal steroids in women with and in those without premenstrual syndrome. N Engl J Med 1998; 338: 209-16
45. Casson P, Hahn PM, Van Vugt DA, et al. Lasting response to ovariectomy in severe intractable premenstrual syndrome. Am J Obstet Gynecol 1990; 162: 99-105
46. Casper RF, Hearn MT. The effect of hysterectomy and bilateral oophorectomy in women with severe premenstrual syndrome. Am J Obstet Gynecol 1990; 162: 105-9
47. Roca CA, Schmidt PJ, Bloch M, et al. Implications of endocrine studies of premenstrual syndrome. Psychiatr Ann 1996; 26: 576-80
48. Rubinow DR, Schmidt PJ. The treatment of premenstrual syndrome – forward into the past. N Engl J Med 1995; 332: 1574-5
49. Eriksson E, Sundblad C, Lisjo P, et al. Serum levels of androgens are higher in women with premenstrual irritability and dysphoria than in controls. Psychoneuroendocrinol 1992; 17: 195-204
50. Eriksson E, Alling C, Andersch B, et al. Cerebrospinal fluid levels of monoamine metabolites. A preliminary study of their relation to menstrual cycle phase, sex steroids, and pituitary hormones in healthy women and in women with premenstrual syndrome. Neuropsychopharmacol 1994; 11: 201-13
51. Steiner M, Coote M, Wilkins A, et al. Biological correlates of irritability in women with premenstrual dysphoria [abstract]. Eur Neuropsychopharmacol 1997; 7 Suppl. 2: S172
52. Eriksson E, Sundblad C, Landén M, et al. Behavioural effects of androgens in women. In: Steiner M, Yonkers K, Eriksson E, editors. Mood disorders in women. London: Martin Dunitz Ltd, 2000
53. Rowe T, Sasse V. Androgens and premenstrual symptoms – the response to therapy. In: Deneerstein L, Frazer I, editors. Hormones and behaviour. New York (NY): Elsevier Science Publishers, 1986: 160-5
54. Burnet RB, Radden HS, Easterbrook EG, et al. Premenstrual syndrome and spironolactone. Aust NZ J Obstet Gynaecol 1991; 31: 366-8
55. Dougherty DM, Bjork JM, Moeller FG, et al. The influence of menstrual-cycle phase on the relationship between testosterone and aggression. Physiol Behav 1997; 62: 431-5
56. Bäckström T, Aakvaag A. Plasma prolactin and testosterone during the luteal phase in women with premenstrual tension syndrome. Psychoneuroendocrinol 1981; 6: 245-51
57. Rubinow DR, Hoban MC, Grover GN, et al. Changes in plasma hormones across the menstrual cycle in patients with menstrually related mood disorder and in control subjects. Am J Obstet Gynecol 1988; 158: 5-11
58. Bloch M, Schmidt PJ, Su TP, et al. Pituitary-adrenal hormones and testosterone across the menstrual cycle in women with premenstrual syndrome and controls. Biol Psychiatry 1998; 43: 897-903
59. Hammarback S, Bäckström T, Holst J, et al. Cyclical mood changes as in the premenstrual tension syndrome during sequential estrogen-progestagen postmenopausal replacement therapy. Acta Obstet Gynecol Scand 1985; 64: 393-7
60. Rapkin AJ, Morgan M, Goldman L, et al. Progesterone metabolite allopregnanolone in women with premenstrual syndrome. Obstet Gynecol 1997; 90: 709-14

61. Schmidt PJ, Purdy RH, Moore Jr PH, et al. Circulating levels of anxiolytic steroids in the luteal phase in women with premenstrual syndrome and in control subjects. J Clin Endocrinol Metab 1994; 79: 1256-60
62. Wang M, Seippel L, Purdy RH, et al. Relationship between symptom severity and steroid variation in women with premenstrual syndrome: study on serum pregnenolone, pregnenolone sulfate, 5 α–pregnane-3,20-dione and 3 α–hydroxy-5-alpha-pregnan-20-one. J Clin Endocrinol Metab 1996; 81: 1076-82
63. Bicikova M, Dibbelt L, Hill M, et al. Allopregnanolone in women with premenstrual syndrome. Horm Metab Res 1998; 30: 227-30
64. Muneyvirci-Delale O, Nacharaju VL, Altura BM, et al. Sex steroid hormones modulate serum ionized magnesium and calcium levels throughout the menstrual cycle in women. Fertil Steril 1998; 69: 958-62
65. Thys-Jacobs S, Alvir MJ. Calcium-regulating hormones across the menstrual cycle: evidence of a secondary hyperparathyroidism in women with PMS. J Clin Endocrinol Metab 1995; 80: 2227-32
66. Korzekwa MI, Lamont JA, Steiner M. Late luteal phase dysphoric disorder and the thyroid axis revisited. J Clin Endocrinol Metab 1996; 81: 2280-4
67. Nikolai TF, Mulligan GM, Gribble RK, et al. Thyroid function and treatment inn premenstrual syndrome. J Clin Endocrinol Metab 1990; 70: 1108-12
68. Schmidt PJ, Grover GN, Roy-Byrne PP, et al. Thyroid function in women with premenstrual syndrome. J Clin Endocrinol Metab 1993; 76: 671-4
69. Girdler SS, Pedersen CA, Straneva PA, et al. Dysregulation of cardiovascular and neuroendocrine responses to stress in premenstrual dysphoric disorder. Psychiatry Res 1998; 81: 163-78
70. Woods NF, Lentz MJ, Mitchell ES, et al. Perceived stress, physiologic stress arousal, and premenstrual symptoms: group differences and intra-individual patterns. Res Nurs Health 1998; 21: 511-23
71. Cahill CA. Differences in cortisol, a stress hormone, in women with turmoil-type premenstrual symptoms. Nur Res 1998; 47: 278-84
72. Steiner M, LePage P, Dunn EJ. Serotonin and gender specific psychiatric disorders. Int J Psychiatry Clin Pract 1997; 1: 3-13
73. Rapkin AJ. The role of serotonin in premenstrual syndrome. Clin Obstet Gynecol 1992; 35: 629-36
74. Rojansky N, Halbreich U, Zander K, et al. Imipramine receptor binding and serotonin uptake in platelets of women with premenstrual changes. Gynecol Obstet Invest 1991; 31: 146-52
75. Steiner M. Female-specific mood disorders. Clin Obstet Gynecol 1992; 35: 599-611
76. Yatham LN. Is 5-HT$_{1A}$ receptor subsensitivity a trait marker for late luteal phase dysphoric disorder? A pilot study. Can J Psychiatry 1993; 38: 662-4
77. Wurtman JJ. Depression and weight gain: the serotonin connection. J Affect Disord 1993; 29: 183-92
78. Meltzer HY. Serotonergic dysfunction in depression. Br J Psychiatry 1989; 155 Suppl. 8: 25-31
79. Tuiten A, Panhuysen G, Koppeschaar H, et al. Stress, serotonergic function, and mood in users of oral contraceptives. Psychoneuroendocrinology 1995; 20: 323-34
80. Cohen IR, Wise PM. Effects of estradiol on the diurnal rhythm of serotonin activity in microdissected brain areas of ovariectomized rats. Endocrinology 1988; 122: 2619-25
81. Ladisich W. Influence of progesterone on serotonin metabolism: a possible causal factor for mood changes. Psychoneuroendocrinology 1977; 2: 257-66
82. Ashby Jr CR, Carr LA, Cook CL, et al. Alteration of platelet serotonergic mechanisms and monoamine oxidase activity in premenstrual syndrome. Biol Psychiatry 1988; 24: 225-33
83. Rapkin AJ, Edelmuth E, Chang LC, et al. Whole blood serotonin in premenstrual syndrome. Obstet Gynecol 1987; 70: 533-7
84. Steege JF, Stout AL, Knight DL, et al. Reduced platelet tritium-labeled imipramine binding sites in women with premenstrual syndrome. Am J Obstet Gynecol 1992; 167: 168-72
85. Taylor DL, Mathew RH, Ho BT, et al. Serotonin levels and platelet uptake during premenstrual tension. Neuropsychobiology 1984; 12: 16-8
86. Bancroft J, Cook A, Davidson D, et al. Blunting of neuroendocrine responses to infusion of L-tryptophan in women with perimenstrual mood change. Psychol Med 1991; 21: 305-12
87. Bancroft J, Cook A. The neuroendocrine response to d-fenfluramine in women with premenstrual depression. J Affect Disord 1995; 36: 57-64
88. Fitzgerald M, Malone K, Li S, et al. Blunted serotonin response to fenfluramine challenge in premenstrual dysphoric disorder. Am J Psychiatry 1997; 154: 556-8
89. Steiner M, Yatham LN, Coote M, et al. Serotonergic dysfunction in women with pure premenstrual dysphoric disorder: is the fenfluramine challenge test still relevant? Psychiatry Res 1999; 87: 107-15
90. Su TP, Schmidt PJ, Danaceau M, et al. Effect of menstrual cycle phase on neuroendocrine and behavioral responses to the serotonin agonist m-chlorophenylpiperazine in women with premenstrual syndrome and controls. J Clin Endocrinol Metab 1997; 82: 1220-8
91. Menkes DB, Coates DC, Fawcett JP. Acute tryptophan depletion aggravates premenstrual syndrome. J Affect Disord 1994; 32: 37-44
92. Steiner M, Judge R, Kumar R. Serotonin re-uptake inhibitors in the treatment of premenstrual dysphoria: current state of knowledge. Int J Psychiatry Clin Pract 1997; 1: 241-7
93. Halbreich U, Tworek H. Altered serotonergic activity in women with dysphoric premenstrual syndromes. Int J Psychiatry Med 1993; 23: 1-27
94. Leibenluft E, Fiero PL, Rubinow DR. Effects of the menstrual cycle on dependent variables in mood disorder research. Arch Gen Psychiatry 1994; 51: 761-81
95. Kouri EM, Halbreich U. State and trait abnormalities in women with dysphoric premenstrual syndromes. Psychopharmacol Bull 1997; 33: 767-70
96. Sundstrom I, Andersson A, Nyberg S, et al. Patients with premenstrual syndrome have a different sensitivity to a neuroactive steroid during the menstrual cycle compared to control subjects. Neuroendocrinology 1998; 67: 126-38
97. Halbreich U, Petty F, Yonkers K, et al. Low plasma gamma-aminobutyric acid levels during the late luteal phase of women with premenstrual dysphoric disorder. Am J Psychiatry 1996; 153: 718-20
98. Gurguis GN, Yonkers KA, Phan SP, et al. Adrenergic receptors in premenstrual dysphoric disorder: I. Platelet α$_2$ receptors: G$_i$ protein coupling, phase of menstrual cycle, and prediction of luteal phase symptom severity. Biol Psychiatry 1998; 44: 600-9
99. Mortola JF. Premenstrual syndrome. Trends Endocrinol Metab 1996; 7: 184-9
100. Rapkin AJ, Shoupe D, Reading A, et al. Decreased central opioid activity in premenstrual syndrome: luteinizing hormone response to naloxone. J Soc Gynecol Invest 1996; 3: 93-8

101. Chuong CJ, Coulam CB, Bergstralh EJ, et al. Clinical trial of naltrexone in premenstrual syndrome. Obstet Gynecol 1988; 72: 332
102. Parry BL, Berga SL, Kripke DF, et al. Altered waveform of plasma nocturnal melatonin secretions in premenstrual depression. Arch Gen Psychiatry 1990; 47: 1139-46
103. Parry BL, Berga SL, Mostofi N, et al. Plasma melatonin circadian rhythms during the menstrual cycle and after light therapy in premenstrual dysphoric disorder and normal control subjects. J Biol Rhythms 1997; 12 (1): 47-64
104. Parry BL, Udell C, Elliott JA, et al. Blunted phase-shift responses to morning bright light in premenstrual dysphoric disorder. J Biol Rhythms 1997; 12: 443-56
105. Chuong CJ, Kim SR, Taskin O, et al. Sleep pattern changes in menstrual cycles of women with premenstrual syndrome: a preliminary study. Am J Obstet Gynecol 1997; 177: 554-48
106. Nakayama K, Nakagawa T, Hiyama T, et al. Circadian changes in body temperatures during the menstrual cycle of healthy adult females and patients suffering from premenstrual syndrome. Int J Clin Pharmacol Res 1997; 17: 155-64
107. Parry BL, LeVeau B, Mostofi N, et al. Temperature circadian rhythms during the menstrual cycle and sleep deprivation in premenstrual dysphoric disorder and normal comparison subjects. J Biol Rhythms 1997; 12: 34-46
108. Kendler KS, Silberg JL, Neale MC, et al. Genetic and environmental factors in the aetiology of menstrual, premenstrual and neurotic symptoms: a population-based twin study. Psychol Med 1992; 22: 85-100
109. van den Akker OBA, Stein GS, Neale MC, et al. Genetic and environmental variation in menstrual cycle: histories of two British twin samples. Acta Genet Med Gemellol 1987; 36: 541-8
110. Morse G. Positively reframing perceptions of the menstrual cycle among women with premenstrual syndrome. J Obstet Gynecol Neonatal Nurs 1999; 28: 165-74
111. Stotland NL, Harwood B. Social, political, and legal considerations. In: Gold JH, Severino SK, editors. Premenstrual dysphorias: myths and realities. Washington, DC: American Psychiatric Press, 1994: 185-200
112. Marvan ML, Escobedo C. Premenstrual symptomatology: role of prior knowledge about premenstrual syndrome. Psychosom Med 1999; 61: 163-7
113. Fontaine KR, Seal A. Optimism, social support, and premenstrual dysphoria. J Clin Psychol 1997; 53: 243-7
114. Seideman RY. Effects of a premenstrual syndrome education program on premenstrual symptomatology. Health Care Women Int 1990; 11: 491-501
115. Walton J, Youngkin E. The effect of a support group on self-esteem of women with premenstrual syndrome. J Obstet Gynecol Neonatal Nurs 1987; 16: 174-8
116. Kraemer GR, Kraemer RR. Premenstrual syndrome: diagnosis and treatment experiences. J Women's Health 1998; 7: 893-907
117. Rubinow DR, Schmidt PJ, Roca CA. Hormone measures in reproductive endocrine-related mood disorders: diagnostic issues. Psychopharmacol Bull 1998; 34: 289-90
118. Reid RL. Premenstrual syndrome. Curr Probl Obstet Gynecol Fert 1985; 8: 1-57
119. Mortola JF, Girton L, Beck L, et al. Diagnosis of premenstrual syndrome by a simple, prospective, and reliable instrument: the calendar of premenstrual experiences. Obstet Gynecol 1990; 76: 302-7
120. Steiner M, Steinberg S, Stewart D, et al. Fluoxetine in the treatment of premenstrual dysphoria. N Engl J Med 1995; 332: 1529-34
121. Steiner M, Haskett RF, Carroll BJ. Premenstrual tension syndrome: the development of research diagnostic criteria and new rating scales. Acta Psychiatr Scand 1980; 62: 177-90
122. Steiner M, Streiner DL, Steinberg S, et al. The measurement of premenstrual mood symptoms. J Affect Disord 1999; 53: 269-73
123. Hendrick V, Altshuler LL. Recurrent mood shifts of premenstrual dysphoric disorder can be mistaken for rapid-cycling bipolar II disorder. J Clin Psychiatry 1998; 59: 479-80
124. Macmillan I, Young A. Bipolar II disorder vs. premenstrual dysphoric disorder. J Clin Psychiatry 1999; 60: 409-10
125. Maskall DD, Lam RW, Misri S, et al. Seasonality of symptoms in women with late luteal phase dysphoric disorder. Am J Psychiatry 1997; 154: 1436-41
126. Steiner M, Yonkers K. Depression in women. mood disorders associated with reproductive cyclicity. London: Martin Dunitz Ltd, 1998: 13-20
127. Brockington I. Menstrual psychosis. Arch Women's Ment Health 1998; 1: 3-13
128. Halbreich U. Premenstrual dysphoric disorders: a diversified cluster of vulnerability traits to depression. Acta Psychiatr Scand 1997; 95: 169-76
129. Odber J, Cawood EH, Bancroft J. Salivary cortisol in women with and without perimenstrual mood changes. J Psychosom Res 1998; 45: 557-68
130. Facchinetti F, Tarabusi M, Nappi G. Premenstrual syndrome and anxiety disorders: a psychobiological link. Psychother Psychosom 1998; 67: 57-60
131. Ekholm UB, Ekholm NO, Bäckström T. Premenstrual syndrome: comparison between different methods to diagnose cyclicity using daily symptom ratings. Acta Obstet Gynecol Scand 1998; 77: 551-7
132. Gehlert S, Chang CH, Hartlage S. Establishing the diagnostic validity of premenstrual dysphoric disorder using Rasch analysis. J Outcome Meas 1997; 1: 2-18
133. Gehlert S, Chang CH, Hartlage S. Symptom patterns of premenstrual dysphoric disorder as defined in the DSM-IV. J Womens Health 1999; 8: 75-85
134. Rapkin AJ, Cedars M, Morgan M. Insulin-like growth factor-1 and insulin-like growth factor-binding protein-3 in women with premenstrual syndrome. Fertil Steril 1998; 70: 1077-80
135. Parry BL, Mostofi N, LeVeau B, et al. Sleep EEG studies during early and late partial sleep deprivation in premenstrual dysphoric disorder and normal control subjects. Psychiatry Res 1999; 85: 127-43
136. Wyatt KM, Dimmock PW, Jones PW, et al. Efficacy of vitamin B-6 in the treatment of premenstrual syndrome: systematic review. BMJ 1999; 318: 1375-81
137. Thys-Jacobs S, Starkey P, Bernstein D, et al. Calcium carbonate and the premenstrual syndrome: effects on premenstrual and menstrual symptoms. Am J Obstet Gynecol 1998; 179: 444-52
138. Walker AF, De Souza MC, Vickers MF, et al. Magnesium supplementation alleviates premenstrual symptoms of fluid retention. J Women's Health 1998; 7: 1157-65
139. Parry BL, Mahan AM, Mostofi N, et al. Light therapy of late luteal phasae dysphoric disorder: an extended study. Am J Psychiatry 1993; 150: 1417-9
140. Parry BL. Light therapy of premenstrual depression. In: Lam RW, editor. Seasonal affective disorder and beyond. Washington, DC: American Psychiatric Press, 1998: 173-91
141. Lam RW, Carter D, Misri S, et al. A controlled study of light therapy in women with late luteal phase dysphoric disorder. Psychiatry Res 1999; 86: 185-92
142. Blake F, Salkovskis P, Gath D, et al. Cognitive therapy for premenstrual syndrome. J Pyschosom Res 1998; 45: 307-18

143. Morse CA, Dennerstein L, Farrell E, et al. A comparison of hormone therapy, coping skills training, and relaxation for the relief of premenstrual syndrome. J Behav Med 1991; 14: 469-89
144. Pearlstein TB. Nonpharmacologic treatment of premenstrual syndrome. Psychiatr Ann 1996; 26: 590-4
145. Morse GG. Effect of positive reframing and social support on perception of perimenstrual changes among women with premenstrual syndrome. Health Care Women Int 1997; 18: 175-93
146. Su T-P, Schmidt PJ, Danaceau MA, et al. Fluoxetine in the treatment of premenstrual dysphoria. Neuropsychopharmacology 1997; 16: 346-56
147. Pearlstein TB, Stone AB, Lund SA, et al. Comparison of fluoxetine, bupropion, and placebo in the treatment of premenstrual dysphoric disorder. J Clin Psychopharmacol 1997; 17: 261-6
148. Steiner M, Korzekwa M, Lamont J, et al. Intermittent fluoxetine dosing in the treatment of women with premenstrual dysphoria. Psychopharmacol Bull 1997; 33: 771-4
149. Diegoli MS, da Fonseca AM, Diegoli CA, et al. A double-blind trial of four medications to treat severe premenstrual syndrome. Int J Gynaecol Obstet 1998; 62: 63-7
150. Yonkers KA, Halbreich U, Freeman E, et al. Symptomatic improvement of premenstrual dysphoric disorder with sertraline treatment. JAMA 1997; 278: 983-8
151. Young SA, Hurt PH, Benedek DM, et al. Treatment of premenstrual dysphoric disorder with sertraline during the luteal phase: a randomized, double-blind, placebo-controlled crossover trial. J Clin Psychiatry 1998; 59: 76-80
152. Jermaine DM, Preece CK, Sykes RL, et al. Luteal phase sertraline treatment for premenstrual dysphoric disorder. Results of a double-blind, placebo-controlled, crossover study. Arch Fam Med 1999; 8: 328-32
153. Halbreich U, Smoller JW. Intermittent luteal phase sertraline treatment of dysphoric premenstrual syndrome. J Clin Psychiatry 1997; 58: 399-402
154. Freeman EW, Rickels K, Arredondo F, et al. Full- or half-cycle treatment of severe premenstrual syndrome with a serotonergic antidepressant. J Clin Psychopharmacol 1999; 19: 3-8
155. Eriksson E, Hedberg MA, Andersch B, et al. The serotonin reuptake inhibitor paroxetine is superior to the noradrenaline reuptake inhibitor maprotiline in the treatment of premenstrual syndrome. Neuropsychopharmacol 1995; 12: 167-76
156. Sundblad C, Wikander I, Andersch B, et al. A naturalistic study of paroxetine in premenstrual syndrome: efficacy and side-effects during ten cycles of treatment. Eur Neuropsychopharmacol 1997; 7: 201-6
157. Wikander I, Sundblad C, Andersch B, et al. Citalopram in premenstrual dysphoria: is intermittent treatment during luteal phases more effective than continuous medication throughout the menstrual cycle? J Clin Psychopharmacol 1998; 18: 390-8
158. Sundblad C, Modigh K, Andersch B, et al. Clomipramine effectively reduces premenstrual irritability and dysphoria: a placebo controlled trial. Acta Psychiatr Scand 1992; 85: 39-47
159. Sundblad C, Hedberg MA, Eriksson E. Clomipramine administered during the luteal phase reduces the symptoms of premenstrual syndrome: a placebo controlled trial. Neuropsychopharmacol 1993; 9: 133-45
160. Steinberg S, Annable L, Young SN, et al. A placebo-controlled clinical trial of L-tryptophan in premenstrual dysphoria. Biol Psychiatry 1999; 45: 313-20
161. Harrison WM, Endicott J, Rabkin JG, et al. Treatment of premenstrual dysphoria with alprazolam and placebo. Psychopharmacol Bull 1987; 23: 150-3
162. Smith S, Rinehart JS, Ruddock VE, et al. Treatment of premenstrual syndrome with alprazolam: results of a double-blind, placebo-controlled, randomized crossover trial. Obstet Gynecol 1987; 70: 37-43
163. Harrison WM, Endicott J, Nee J. Treatment of premenstrual dysphoria with alprazolam. Arch Gen Psychiatry 1990; 47: 270-5
164. Berger CP, Presser B. Alprazolam in the treatment of two subsamples of patients with late luteal phase dysphoric disorder: a double-blind, placebo-controlled crossover study. Obstet Gynecol 1994; 84: 379-85
165. Freeman EW, Rickels K, Sondheimer SJ, et al. A double-blind trial of oral progesterone, alprazolam, and placebo in treatment of severe premenstrual syndrome. JAMA 1995; 274: 51-7
166. Rickels K, Freeman E, Sondheimer S. Buspirone in treatment of premenstrual syndrome [letter]. Lancet 1989; I: 777
167. Brown CS, Ling FW, Farmer RG, et al. Buspirone in the treatment of premenstrual syndrome. Drug Ther 1990; 20 Suppl.: 112-21
168. Sarno AP, Miller Jr EJ, Lundblad EG. Premenstrual syndrome: beneficial effects of periodic low-dose danazol. Obstet Gynecol 1987; 70: 33-6
169. Hahn PM, VanVugt DA, Reid RL. A randomized, placebo-controlled crossover trial of danazol for the treatment of premenstrual syndrome. Psychoneuroendocrinology 1995; 20: 193-209
170. O'Brien PM, Abukhalil IE. Randomized controlled trial of the management of premenstrual syndrome and premenstrual mastalgia using luteal phase-only danazol. Am J Obstet Gynecol 1999; 180 (1 Pt 1): 18-23
171. Brown CS, Ling FW, Andersen RN, et al. Efficacy of depot leuprolide in premenstrual syndrome: effect of symptom severity and type in a controlled trial. Obstet Gynecol 1994; 84: 779-86
172. Freeman EW, Sondheimer SJ, Rickels K. Gonadotropin-releasing hormone agonist in the treatment of premenstrual symptoms with and without ongoing dysphoria: a controlled study. Psychopharmacol Bull 1997; 33: 303-9
173. Mezrow G, Shoupe D, Spicer D, et al. Depot leuprolide acetate with estrogen and progestin add-back for long-term treatment of premenstrual syndrome. Fertil Steril 1994; 62: 932-7
174. Hammarback S, Bäckström T. Induced anovulation as treatment of premenstrual tension syndrome. A double-blind crossover study with GnRH-agonist versus placebo. Acta Obstet Gynaecol Scand 1988; 67: 159-66
175. Bancroft J, Boyle H, Warner P, et al. The use of an LHRH agonist, buserelin, in the long-term management of premenstrual syndromes. Clin Endocrinol 1987; 27: 171-82
176. West CP, Hillier H. Ovarian suppression with the gonadotrophin-releasing hormone agonist goserelin (Zoladex) in management of the premenstrual tension syndrome. Hum Reprod 1994; 9: 1058-63
177. Smith RN, Studd JW, Zamblera D, et al. A randomised comparison over 8 months of 100 micrograms and 200 micrograms twice weekly doses of transdermal oestradiol in the treatment of severe premenstrual syndrome. Br J Obstet Gynaecol 1995; 102: 475-84
178. Eriksson E. Serotonin reuptake inhibitors for the treatment of premenstrual dysphoria. Int Clin Psychopharmacol 1999; 14 Suppl. 2: S27-S33
179. Freeman EW, Rickels K, Sondheimer SJ, et al. Differential response to antidepressants in women with premenstrual syndrome/premenstrual dysphoric disorder: a randomized controlled trial. Arch Gen Psychiatry 1999; 56: 932-9
180. Schmidt PJ, Grover GN, Rubinow DR. Alprazolam in the treatment of premenstrual syndrome. A double-blind, placebo-controlled trial. Arch Gen Psychiatry 1993; 50: 467-73
181. Evans SM, Haney M, Levin FR, et al. Mood and performance changes in women with premenstrual dysphoric disorder: acute effects of alprazolam. Neuropsychopharmacology 1998; 19: 499-516
182. Evans SM, Foltin RW, Fischman MW. Food 'cravings' and the acute effects of alprazolam on food intake in women with premenstrual dysphoric disorder. Appetite 1999; 32: 331-49
183. Sundstrom I, Nyberg S, Bixo M, et al. Treatment of premenstrual syndrome with gonadotropin-releasing hormone agonist in a low dose regimen. Acta Obstet Gynecol Scand 1999; 78: 891-9

184. Leather AT, Studd JW, Watson NR, et al. The treatment of severe premenstrual syndrome with goserelin with and without 'add-back' estrogen therapy: a placebo-controlled study. Gynecol Endocrinol 1999; 13: 48-55
185. Watson NR, Studd JW, Savvas M, et al. Treatment of severe premenstrual syndrome with oestradiol patches and cyclical oral norethisterone. Lancet 1989; II: 730-2
186. Bäckström T, Hansson-Malmstrom Y, Lindhe BA, et al. Oral contraceptives in premenstrual syndrome: a randomized comparison of triphasic and monophasic preparations. Contraception 1992; 46: 253-68
187. Graham CA, Sherwin BB. A prospective treatment study of premenstrual symptoms using a triphasic oral contraceptive. J Psychosom Res 1992; 36: 257-66

Correspondence: Prof. *Meir Steiner,* Women's Health Concerns Clinic, Room FB639, St Joseph's Hospital, 50 Charlton Avenue East, Hamilton, Ontario L8N 4A6, Canada.
E-mail: mst@fhs.csu.mcmaster.ca